. . . a realistic and hopeful guide for coping with the blues—with warmth, empathy, personal insights, and good humor.

—Rik Isensee, L.C.S.W., author of *Love Between Men* and *Are You Ready? The Gay Man's Guide to Thriving at Midlife*

Dealing with depression is one of the most serious aspects of my work. Queer Blues *is an incredibly comprehensive look at the issue of depression and queer people. It's a must read for mental health professionals, GLBT people, and their loved-ones.*

—JoAnn Loulan, M.F.T., author of *Lesbian Sex*

QUEER BLUES

THE LESBIAN & GAY GUIDE TO OVERCOMING DEPRESSION

KIMERON HARDIN, PH.D.
MARNY HALL, PH.D.

Foreword by Betty Berzon, Ph.D.

New Harbinger Publications, Inc.

Publisher's Note

Chart on page 159 is from *You Can Beat Depression: A Guide to Prevention and Recovery,* *2nd Ed.,* ©2000 by John Preston, and is reproduced for Kimeron Hardin by permission of Impact Publishers, Inc., P.O. Box 6016, Atascadero, CA 93423-6016. Further repro-duction is prohibited.

Distributed in the U.S.A. by Publishers Group West; in Canada by Raincoast Books; in Great Britain by Airlift Book Company, Ltd.; in South Africa by Real Books, Ltd.; in Australia by Boobook; and in New Zealand by Tandem Press.

Cover design by Blue Design
Cover photos by (from left to right): Special Photographer's Library/Photonica; Issague
Fujita/Photonica; Steve/Mary Skjold/Index Stock Imagery
Edited by Erin Corrigan
Text design by Michele Waters

ISBN 1-57224-244-2 Paperback

New Harbinger Publications' Web site address: www.newharbinger.com

03   02   01

10   9   8   7   6   5   4   3   2   1

First printing

This book is dedicated to two queer American heroes who grappled with the blues: Kelli Peterson, a founder of the first Gay-Straight Alliance organization in Utah, and Bayard Rustin, the backbone of the civil rights movement in the 1960s. Although separated by generations, skin color, and gender, they share the same orientation and inimitable spirit.

Contents

Foreword

By Betty Berzon, Ph.D.

Somewhere around the middle of the twentieth century I lost myself. It was more than just depression, it was a spiraling down into an airless vacuum, an enveloping silence, an affirmation of non-existence. I was twenty-two years old. My first lover had left me, finally pushed out by my disconnection from her, and my agony at the state of my life. I didn't want to live anymore. I didn't want to be a homosexual. I would rather be dead.

I woke up in hospital rooms that had bars on the windows. My wrists were tethered to the bed rails. Once again I had tried to kill myself and failed. I could not seem to prevail over the life force inside me, the force that kept me coming back to try again to cope with this terrible thing, this homosexual person that I didn't want to be.

I asked for help and got it, a young psychiatrist who assured me over and over that I was not really gay, that I could recover. He was a kind and wonderful man. I loved him. He was going to make me normal. He was doing what he believed to be the right thing, at the time. Homosexuality was a disease and he was going to cure me. I was very grateful.

I got out of the hospital for the last time. I reorganized my life, returned to school, and studied psychology. Eventually, I even went to work as an aide in the hospital where I had been a patient. That was a big step. In my white coat, the keys to the buildings jangling in my pocket, I felt as if I had climbed a mountain. I was there. I knew I would never be a patient again.

My social life, the little I had time for, completely turned around. With the doctor's help I was being cured. I dated men, talked

about it in therapy, and got the old reinforcing smile and nod whenever I did. I thought about marriage and family, auditioned candidates, and developed a social network of heterosexual friends whose
lives matched my own. I was like everybody else, at last.

The depression didn't disappear entirely. As a matter of fact it
was disconcerting that periodically, over the next eighteen years, I
would become depressed for what seemed like no reason at all. These
bouts lasted days, sometimes weeks. Once it was so bad some of the
staff of the Western Behavioral Sciences Institute, in La Jolla, California, where I was a research associate, came to my house and sat with
me, in shifts. I was embarrassed but grateful.

I recovered from these bouts, didn't do myself any harm, and
went right on working in therapy to build my normal, healthy
straight life.

And then, on my fortieth birthday, it all came to an end. I spent
the weekend alone. I didn't know why I had arranged that, not yet.
On Saturday night I had a disturbing dream. In the dream I am looking for somewhere to be. I wander the streets, going from house to
house, going into houses that look familiar, but they are all inhabited
by strangers who look at me but don't see me. I move faster and
faster until I am running but I don't know if I am running to something or away from something. I want so much to be somewhere, but
I am only wandering, crying, anguished. I wake up. I am disoriented,
not sure where I am.

The rest of the weekend I just think. I know what has happened
but I don't want to know. Then, I can't push it away anymore. The
unconscious has triumphed. Within an instant I understand the dream
and what it means. I know what I have to do. The charade is over.

With great difficulty, I reorganize my life. I move to Los
Angeles and begin the slow process of reinventing myself. I have a
gay male friend. He goes with me to lesbian bars. I cling to him. I am
not doing well learning to be a lesbian. Then something magical happens. There is a gay rights movement just beginning to stretch and
yawn and wake up to its own existence. I am introduced to a group
of activists who have an idea about starting a community center for
gay people. Because of my experience in the 1960s conducting workshops at growth centers around the country, I am enlisted to help
them. It is 1971. There has never been anything like a community
center for gays. It seems like a wild idea to me. These activists have
no money. Who will come to such a place? Most gays are closeted,
and only have contact with one another in their tight-knit social
groups. I had no idea how wrong I was.

In the process of helping launch the first-ever Gay and Lesbian Connunity Services Center, I become a part of the nascent gay rights movement. The activists open my mind to the possibilities for gay and lesbian people fighting back against injustice, being acknowledged as first class citizens, receiving equal treatment. I am fascinated by what I hear. I want to believe it. They keep up a steady drumbeat of consciousness-raising rhetoric. Gradually, it seeps in. For the first time in my life I begin to feel not just okay about being gay, but kind of excited about it, about being part of a revolution that is meant to change the world.

Now, thirty years later, much of it all seems like a dream, a really good dream. We have changed the world. Those young activists are now the elders of the movement. I have been very much a part of it all, starting organizations, training counselors, working with gay and lesbian individuals and couples in therapy, writing books. Gay now defines my life, my normal, healthy gay life.

Coming to grips with, and overcoming, the internalized homophobia that spoiled so many of my early years has brought me balance. Fighting my true nature for so long had left me without the emotional energy to also fight the depression that fight caused. I now occasionally have a down day or two, but who doesn't? It does not interfere with my functioning. It is just part of the landscape of my psychic being. I have "befriended" my depression.

How helpful it would have been to have a book like *Queer Blues* to give me information and perspective on what was happening to me during my twenties and thirties. These authors have demystified depression, made it understandable, so that it is not just an incomprehensible black cloud that descends unexpectedly to darken one's life. Depression has a cause, though the cause may not be immediately discernable. It may be triggered by physical illness, aging, or loss. It may have biological components, genetic origins, environmental influences, or be the product of internal conflict, as I believe mine was.

Much is known now about all aspects of depression, the underlying causes, the biological and chemical factors, and the process by which it develops. The authors here have taken the risky tack of explaining how the brain works, and how it interacts with the complex functioning of the body during depression. It is an intriguing tale, not only informative but also fascinating.

Much is also known, and spelled out here, about the great variety of treatments now available for the "blues." In the era when I suffered my worst depression, there were not yet antidepressants, just a funny little pill called Dexamyl that was a combination of dexadrine (an upper) and sodium amytal (a downer), somebody's idea of how to bring balance to a day.

Later, when I worked as an aide in the hospital where I'd been a patient, there were still no antidepressants, just a procedure that involved sending jolts of electricity through a person's brain to induce convulsions and who knows what else. No one quite understood why that helped to alleviate depression, but it seemed to. As a member of the electro-shock team, my job in the hospital was to gently hold the ankles while the patient convulsed, the idea being to prevent broken bones. Others, taller and stronger than I, restrained other parts of the patient's body. While electro-shock is still used today, we are light-years ahead of those times when it was the treatment of choice for depression.

Queer Blues offers an excellent inventory of the wide range of choices in remedies (prescribed and otherwise) available now to deal with depression, including useful information about the pros and cons of many of them. The authors don't stop with just the ingestibles but go on to write about treatment approaches that involve formal psychotherapy and less formal forms of talking one's way out of depression, making use of the resources and people already present in one's life.

Queer Blues in a sense is a community resource, as it deals with what it calls "gay angst," the condition underlying depression caused by living gay or lesbian in a homophobic society. Negative stereotypes, religious condemnation, and gay-bashing in all its forms can easily become internalized homophobia, wearing away at self-esteem and spoiling identity.

There have always been the "cultural blues" running like a fault under our community, but as we have learned to build our own identities, we have gained the strength and resilience to combat homophobia and resist its negative effects. We have learned not to internalize the condemnation. They can still dish it out. We just don't have to swallow it.

As Kimeron and Marny deconstruct the cultural blues, there are clues to how we can fight against the depression that too often accompanies internalized homophobia. We can support one another and draw power from our sense of community. One feature of the blues is the isolation it causes people to feel. There is a lot we can do about that, together.

Queer Blues is a useful guide to the terrain of depression, how to navigate through it, and how to escape its boundaries. More than anything it sends the message that you are not alone, one of the many gifts this book provides its readers.

I would like to thank the following people for their help and encouragement in producing this work: my partner, William Watson; my best friend, Robert Allen, M.D.; my brilliant co-author, Marny Hall, Ph.D.; and of course, my wonderful clients and friends.
—K.H.

I am very grateful for Kimeron's unflagging enthusiasm and good humor.

Eric Brandt, Dr. Francisco Gonzalez, Amanda Kovattana, Helena Lipstadt, Karlyn Lotney, Dr. Dee Mosbacher, Dr. Esther Rothblum, Dr. Judith Stelboum, Dr. Martha Stephens, and Dr. Jackie Wilson made significant contributions to the project. My gratitude to each of you. Thanks also to the intimates who supported and, when necessary, diverted me: O'pelia, Iphigenia, Scout, Scamp, Kamela, the twins—Perse and Demmie—Leander, my precious Irini-Bird, and the land shark who shall remain nameless.
—M.H.

We both would like to give a big thanks to Todd Cornett, M.D., and Nanette Gartrell, M.D., both of whom were gracious with their time and advice.

We are also grateful for the support and assistance we received from the people at New Harbinger, including Heather Garnos, Erin Corrigan, Catharine Sutker, Amy Shoup, Matthew McKay, and the rest of the crew.

Introduction

On December 31, 1999, many of us sat glued to our TV sets. We were waiting for that momentous sunrise—the dawning of 2000—to be broadcast directly from the most easterly point of the globe. When the sun finally crept up over the Pacific rim, it cast a gorgeous pink glow over a bottle-green, glassy sea. It was a pulse-stopping moment. The next hour it happened again. Then again. And again. During the last day of 1999 and the first day of 2000, CNN replayed that magical millennial moment scores of times. Surely, out of all those hundreds of new dawns, one—just one—belonged to us.

The omens look favorable. At the beginning of the twenty-first century, gays have come farther politically, socially, and spiritually than ever. We are beginning to win the struggle for legal recognition of our partnerships. Legal adoptions of children are possible in some states. Local ordinances in a number of cities prohibit employers and landlords from discriminating against us. We are appearing in positive roles—with increasing frequency—in movies and on TV. More of us are coming out—to our friends, our families, our coworkers. Pride celebrations here and abroad are gathering momentum. In short, the long struggle for full membership in the human community seems to be paying off. Even the most ardent opponents are beginning to tone down the antigay rhetoric.

Why then do we need a book about gay and lesbian depression? There are several reasons. The first concerns the democratic nature of depression. It can affect anyone—rich or poor, old or young, white or black, and of course gay or straight. Depression is so ubiquitous in our culture that one out of nine Americans will experience at least one episode of depression this year. According to the same research projections, one person in twenty will be so depressed that he or she will require medical treatment. What do these figures mean for gays and lesbians? It's easy to make the calculations. Say we use the standard guesstimate—that ten percent of the population is gay. If the surveys are correct, and 17.6 million Americans currently suffer from depression, then 1.7 million of those sufferers are gay. That is a staggering number. And because of the particular risks facing gay and lesbians, it may even be greater. Some research studies suggest that over half of all lesbians and gays will experience depression at some time during their lives. A book that treats depression from a gay—rather than a heterocentrist—perspective is clearly long overdue.

A second reason becomes apparent when we review our gains in the political arena. These successes are dramatic, but perhaps they stand out because they are hard won victories in battles that are far from over. Many overt and covert forms of discrimination continue. In fact, our increased visibility has meant, in many instances, an increased backlash. Gay-bashing is up. In nine of thirteen regions reporting to the National Coalition of Anti-Violence Programs, there was a forty percent increase in antigay violence. One of the classic responses to fear of violence and to social ostracism, harassment, and discrimination is depression. In other words, as gays and lesbians we are very likely to oppress ourselves, to internalize the negative feelings that are directed at us. We may internalize the guilt foisted upon us by the religious institutions that have declared homosexuals "immoral" or "sinful." Perhaps we grew up as sissies or tomboys and have internalized the disapproval that our families of origin showered on us for our gender-bending ways. If our self-esteem has been eroded by disapproval or rejection, and if our gay socialization has taken place primarily in bars, we are likely to add another element to a surefire recipe for depression: substance abuse. Any of the foregoing elements—rejection, internalized homophobia, low self-esteem—can lead to self-destructive feelings and behaviors, e.g., helplessness, suicidal thoughts, alcohol and drug abuse, and unsafe sexual behaviors. These, in turn, can cause more depression. Because gays and lesbians are at risk on so many fronts, we get into a negative spiral: misguided attempts to cure depression lead to more depression which, in turn, lead to more problematic remedies, and so on. It is very hard to get off such an unmerry-go-round.

AIDS is another risk factor. Despite effective new treatment protocols, AIDS continues to factor into our high rate of depression. We may be HIV-positive ourselves and face an uncertain future. Perhaps we have lost a mate to AIDS or our friendship networks have been decimated.

Finally, anxiety may be a factor. Negotiating everyday interactions can be difficult enough for people who don't have to also deal with social acceptance concerns. Add the pressure of deciding when it is safe and appropriate to disclose your personal life, and you may tilt into despair.

A final reason for the book is purely practical. The phenomenal growth of managed care has meant the tight rationing of mental health services. Those of us who are most informed and most able to advocate for our needs are most likely to get access to such benefits. Consequently, it is very important for gays and lesbians to be conversant with the most effective treatment modalities both psychotherapeutic and chemical for depression.

The news isn't all bad. All those years spent marching under the banners demanding equality served us well. We appear to be fierce advocates for our own interests. We get help when we need it. We aren't embarrassed about seeking psychotherapy, and in fact, use therapy at a higher rate than the non-gay population. This book is simply an addition to the resources that gays and lesbians use so well: It is a tool specifically calibrated to deal with depression.

The book is divided into two sections. The first chapters identify the various forms of depression and the social, psychological, cultural, and biological causes of it. The second part of the book offers practical methods for managing your depression.

This book is designed as a do-it-yourself, self-paced guide. Take whatever time you need to absorb and apply our ideas and suggestions to your specific situation. Many chapters will present concepts or questions for you to consider and use as "homework." We recommend that you take what seems useful or helpful and bypass the parts that seem irrelevant to your situation. In other words, in order to get the most out of the book, it is almost necessary for you to rewrite it—to make it *your* story of depression. If you like, you can read the book from cover to cover initially and then come back for a second, more in-depth read (and rewriting). The second time around, you might want to tackle the exercises, perhaps even discuss some of them with a partner or a friend. The book is not intended as a cure-all or quick fix, but we *will* suggest some practical ways to manage what may seem at times like an intractable case of the blues.

If you are currently seeing a psychotherapist, this book may be a helpful adjunct to your therapy. It isn't intended, however, as a substitute for psychotherapy, particularly if you find that problems come up that cause you (or have caused you) immediate harm or distress, such as depression that interferes with everyday function-ing, feelings of hopelessness, suicidal or homicidal thoughts, or sig-nificant alcohol or other drug use. If you are working through this book alone and you find that you begin to have uncomfortable or uneasy feelings that frighten you, you may want to consider finding a psychotherapist to help you manage these troubling feelings. Chap-ter 7 was designed to help you find an effective psychotherapist that is lesbian or gay, or gay-affirmative.

An introduction wouldn't be complete without leaving you with a sense of who we are and how we came to write this book. We are both licensed psychotherapists, originally from different parts of the country, but ultimately landing in the "Mecca" of the San Fran-cisco Gay (oops, we mean "Bay") Area. Between us, we have over thirty-five years of clinical experience in both private practice and university or hospital settings and both have seen lesbian and gay people over the years as individuals and in couples. We both also have separately authored several books prior to this one, specifically for the lesbian and gay community. After Kimeron began pondering the idea for a book on depression for lesbians and gays, a mutual acquaintance actually suggested that we team up to add some depth and variety of perspective. Our first meeting went well. Perhaps the fact that we had unwittingly arranged to meet at—of all places—a very cruisy, straight yuppie bar helped us bond instantly. Not so ironically perhaps, we have also both suffered from depression in our pasts, lending what some might consider a certain we've-been-there credibility to our suggestions.

About Us

Kimeron grew up in a southern fundamentalist Christian family with a family member who suffered from depression. He admits that his first courses in psychology as an undergraduate were attempts to understand himself and his family from a more objective perspective. These courses were also useful for him in exploring his own sexual identity, as was his membership for the first time in a sociopolitical group, the Carolina Gay Association on the campus of the University of North Carolina. By his third year there, he began to formulate a plan for his professional career involved doing clinical psychotherapy with individuals and actively disseminating scientifically and psy-chologically accurate information about lesbians and gays. He went on to obtain both a master's degree and a Ph.D. degree in Clinical Psychology. During his graduate education years and in subsequent professional practice, Kimeron has been continually active with lesbian and gay clients and political groups. He was a charter member of the first gay and lesbian group officially recognized at Western Carolina University, Lavender Bridges, and provided the first in-service, or in-house training, on AIDS to the faculty and students of the University of Southern Mississippi, where he did his doctoral work. Professionally, he has provided workshops on building gay and lesbian self-esteem and led the first workshop in Louisiana for lesbian and gay couples on building relationships. His last book, *The Gay and Lesbian Self-Esteem Book: A Guide to Loving Ourselves*, released in 1999, was a gay bestseller.

It was not until two years after the breakup of a six-and-a-half year relationship in 1991 that Kimeron began exhibiting signs of depression. After about two months of trying to go it alone, he got into psychotherapy and finally decided, with his therapist, to try an antidepressant. Through this combination of interventions, he was able to successfully manage his symptoms and has since learned to monitor himself more regularly and to use preventative measures to avoid a repeat.

Marny grew up in tomboy country—the rolling hills and woods of upstate New York. After her baby butch indiscretions came to light, she was packed off to a school for wayward adolescents. There she learned very quickly to mask her inclinations. It was, after all, a decade before Stonewall. She came out a second time, in college, and thereafter remained resolutely queer. After college, she traveled for two years, exploring the lesbian byways of Europe, the Middle East, and North Africa. Back in New York, she acquired a master's degree in Social Work, got the nomadic itch again, and in 1969, ended up in San Francisco. It was a thrilling time. Women's Liberation and Gay Liberation were in full flower. At the intersection of these two movements, radical lesbian politics was taking shape. It had a galvanizing effect on Marny's work. Along with theorizing and writing, Marny began a lesbian-only private psychotherapy practice. In the mid-'80 she got her Ph.D. in Social Psychology, made a video for gays in the workplace, and published *The Lavender Couch: A Consumer's Guide To Psychotherapy for Lesbians and Gay Men*. In the nineties, she wrote a lot more, edited a book on sex, and published *The Lesbian Love Companion: How to Survive Everything from Heartthrob to Heartbreak*.

After a bruiser break-up in the mid-'80s, Marny became despondent. For six months, she could barely get up in the morning. She cried on the shoulders of her pals, went to therapy religiously, considered taking antidepressants. Eventually she recovered. Good companions, satisfying work, and plenty of exercise, have prevented a relapse and have, over time, been her antidepressants of choice.

We have attempted to blend our voices into a seamless and continuous narrative, but we recognize that at times our individual personalities have sneaked into the forefront—which may provide an amusing, if unintentional, subplot. We have attempted to balance our language so that we do not favor one gender over the other. Consequently, you will therefore see the phrase "lesbian and gay" in some sections and "gay men and lesbians" in others. We also may occasionally use the term "queer," which we consider inclusive of both groups and any other sexual minority that wishes to be included. Some people will ask about why we have not used the more inclusive term GLBT (meaning "gay/lesbian/bisexual/transgender"). Despite the fact that we have worked with clients who are bisexual and transgender, we do not wish to stray beyond our expertise as gay and lesbian authors and clinicians. We feel strongly that bi- and transsexuals, our sisters and brothers in the struggle for human rights, have been exposed to the emotional risks that are part of such struggles. Consequently, they will probably benefit from much of the material in the book. Nevertheless, we are cautious about generalizing from the lesbian and gay clients we have seen to bisexual and transgender people. It is our hope that both groups see our choice as one of respect for the potential and important differences between us and as an attempt to recognize our own limitations.

It is our mutual hope that when you have finished this book, you will have found something meaningful, practical, and ultimately useful in either managing or preventing depression. As you have reached the end of this first passage, we want to take this moment to congratulate you on taking the first steps toward overcoming the blues.

CHAPTER 1

Shades of Blue

What Depression Is and Isn't

BRNNNNNG! The alarm jerks you out of your endlessly recurring nightmare. You drag yourself out of bed and slouch down the hall to the bathroom, sighing and leaving the light off while you sneak a peek at the troll scowling back at you from the bathroom mirror. You are flooded with despair at the human condition . . . No, not the human condition . . . the inhuman condition: your own pathetic state. You wonder if you can afford to use another vacation day to skip the rat race. Your gut tells you that things will not go well at work, and sure enough, your prophesy comes true. You can't focus. Along with your ability to concentrate, your energy has deserted you. You are sure your watch has stopped, and you study the second hand. No . . . five seconds pass, then ten, then twenty. It is still ticking, barely creeping along. The afternoon seems interminable. The dull ache in the pit of your stomach draws your attention away from your tasks and makes the mailroom guy's jokes even LESS funny than usual (if that's possible). Every five minutes, you seem to sigh or yawn, inviting wisecracks from Julie who sits across from you in her own dungeon-like cubicle. Life is uniformly gray, emptied of all pleasure, of all meaning. Even your escape from your cubicle at the end of the day doesn't improve your spirits. Going to the gym is impossible when you feel so exhausted. You bolt straight home to a frozen pizza and bad TV. You wish that tomorrow could be different, but you know it won't be. You're quite certain that nothing will ever change.

What about this free fall into despair? Will it ever end? You try to convince yourself that everybody feels a bit down at least once in a while. Have you just endured one of those occasional miserable days or are you seriously depressed? The not-so-simple answer is that the day you have just suffered through could have been either.

We hear the word depression used very frequently in our day-to-day lives. It has come to describe a whole range of emotional events—everything from brief moments of sadness to nonstop crying jags, from the absence of any discernable feeling, a certain flatness, to despair profound enough to provoke serious suicide attempts. Despite the myriad ways we use the word, there seems to be a division—albeit fuzzy—between two levels of depression. There are the minor dips and major plunges, the lower-case blues and the capital-D Depressions. A big-D psychotherapy client of Marny's was using this two-tiered system when she remarked, "You know my girlfriend is really different from me. She gets depressed the way that non-depressed people get depressed." In this chapter we will focus on the opposite side of the coin—on the way depressed people get depressed. By providing a specific checklist of behaviors and feelings, we will help you distinguish clinical depression from its cousins—other sorts of mood disorders or emotional problems—as well as from the normal episodes of sadness that punctuate most of our lives. Clear definitions, composed of specific criteria, may help you figure out whether you should find a comforting shoulder to cry on or start to consider some other, more aggressive, treatment options.

Many of you may need no such definitional assistance. You are convinced that your bouts of bleakness fit the criteria for clinical depression, but you could use more information. Perhaps you want to know what type of depression you are suffering from. Perhaps you want some way to gauge its severity. We hope this chapter will provide the help you need—in the form of self-assessment tools—to answer those questions.

A Word about Our Framework

Where did our framework come from? The definitional criteria we are using to identify and measure depression come from the accumulated wisdom of mental health specialists—psychologists and psychiatrists—who are typically consulted for help with mood problems. Their lore has been collected and classified in a guidebook entitled the *Diagnostic and Statistical Manual of Mental Disorders* (2000). This manual, generally referred to as the DSM, is updated every few years—therefore the most current version is called the DSM-IV-TR.

Before we proceed, we want to mention the limitations of the DSM. While many clinicians regard this classification system as gospel in terms of diagnostic categories, it should be noted that it is really a highly dynamic system—a work in progress. When new research provides new insights about a traditional diagnosis, that diagnosis may be revised or discarded. A case in point: The original DSM, published in 1952, listed homosexuality as a disease, as it was commonly believed to be in that era. Later versions, DSM-II and DSM-III, continued to refer to homosexuality as aberrant, specifically as "Ego-Dystonic Homosexuality" (meaning you were gay but you didn't like it). Eventually, in 1987, when the clinical and scientific data no longer supported the concept of homosexuality as an illness, it was removed altogether as a diagnosable clinical disorder from the revised DSM-III. There is no mention of it in the current edition, DSM-IV-TR. This deletion of any pathologizing mention of homosexuality from the DSM is good news. The bad news is that the DSM has missed the chance to replace its formerly negative version with a gay-sensitive update.

At the same time that certain mental disorders were decreed obsolete and removed from the DSM, its authors were becoming more sensitive to the cultural contexts of mental illness. The current volume discusses a number of cultures, and the ways that the members of these cultures manifest emotional or mental disturbances. For example, one of the terms listed in this section is *nervios*. Commonly used by Latinos, *nervios* refers to "both a general state of vulnerability to stressful life experiences and to a syndrome brought on by difficult life circumstances." The DSM authors mention several symptoms—tearfulness, vertigo, and insomnia, for example—that characterize *nervios*. But although the DSM authors cite a number of other culturally specific syndromes, they drop the ball when it comes to gays and lesbians. In this section of the DSM, there is no mention of the cultural dimension of gay and lesbian depression. We feel strongly that lesbian and gay depression, typically characterized by feelings of worthlessness and powerlessness, has a distinctive shape. We also feel that homophobia, internalized over time, gives gay depression its unique profile. As a distinctly cultural aspect of depression, internalized homophobia should have been included in the DSM. As you read the following definitions, therefore, it is important to remember that they only tell part of the story. We will fill in the missing parts in the following chapters.

An Overview of Depression

The topography of human emotions is complex. It includes mountain peaks of exuberance, rolling tranquil hills, and chasms of despair.

The feelings we described on the first page occupy a legitimate place on the map. We are guessing that everyone reading this book has felt, at times, that life is not worth living. Chances are, we do not experience these occasional bad days, or even longer sorrowful reactions to troublesome events, as unusual or problematic. Problems begin when such low or bad moods last so long that they begin to disrupt our lives. Our relationships and our jobs may suffer. Some of us may even lose the ability to take care of our basic needs. Emotions that are both persistent and disruptive have been given the official title of *mood disorders* by mental health practitioners. According to the DSM IV, there are two main types of mood disorders: *depressive disorders* and *bipolar disorders*. Depressive disorders include a condition referred to as m*ajor depressive disorder*. A cluster of symptoms characterize major depressive disorders; among them are a depressed mood lasting over two weeks and loss of interest in socializing, eating, and sleeping. A second type of depressive disorder is known as *dysthymia*. It may include milder versions of some of the same symptoms as a major depressive disorder, When someone has been depressed for two years, they may be diagnosed as dysthymic.

Bipolar disorders (formerly known as "manic-depression") are more complicated than simple depressive disorders. The term bipolar refers to the opposite ends of an emotional continuum. One end of the spectrum is characterized by very low moods, the other end by high or manic moods. In other words, depression—for some people—can be punctuated by periods of exaggerated cheerfulness, excitement, or irritability. It is not unusual to see a person with bipolar disorder shift from a manic state to a depressed state and then back again to mania. To qualify as mania, these fluctuations must last at least a week, and the depressed person must show several other unusual or "speeded up" symptoms. Such symptoms may include an inability to sleep, a conviction that he can engage in risky behaviors without any dangerous consequences, and an inflated notion of his power—commonly known as delusions of grandeur. Depressed people who are experiencing a manic swing also may complain that their words cannot keep pace with their torrent of thoughts.

The shift from the depressive phase to the manic state is called *cycling*, and each cycle can last from minutes or hours to days or weeks. It is common to see one cycle last longer than another cycle (e.g. more manic episodes than depressed ones or visa versa), and women generally tend to have more depressive episodes and men tend to have more manic episodes. When a person shows some evidence of mood cycling that lasts for at least two years, but they do not meet all the criteria for the diagnosis of bipolar disorder, they may be diagnosed with a cyclothymic disorder. For a more detailed description of all these depressive disorders, you may want to leaf through the DSM-IV the next time you find yourself browsing in a bookstore or library.

It is estimated that approximately one percent of the population suffers from bipolar disorders. In recent years, some studies have concluded that bipolar disorders and creativity go hand in hand. Perhaps bipolar artists—in manic phases—simply produce more art and, therefore, stand a better chance of mastering their craft and being recognized. Or perhaps there really is a correlation between the brain chemicals that produce mania and those that account for creativity. In any case, historical accounts of the lives of several preeminent gay painters and writers suggest that, had they been alive today, they would been diagnosed as bipolar. One can only speculate whether Virginia Woolf or Tennessee Williams, to name two of the most famous bipolar queer authors, would still have produced such brilliant oeuvres if they had been given Prozac or Lithium for their mood swings.

Symptoms of Major Depression

If you were to visit a mental health provider with symptoms of a depressive disorder, they would make their diagnosis based on the number and types of symptoms you report, their duration, severity, and their impact on your life. Major depression is diagnosed when an individual, who has not experienced the loss of a loved one, and who is not ill or on any particular medication, exhibits at least five of the following nine symptoms for at least two weeks:

1. Sad, irritable, or depressed mood most of the day, almost every day

2. Loss of interest or pleasure in most activities during the day, almost every day

3. A change of more than 5 percent of your body weight in a month, either up or down, when not dieting, or a significant change in your appetite, up or down

4. Difficulty falling asleep or sleeping too much almost every day

5. Unusual restlessness or sluggishness almost every day

6. Feeling excessively tired, fatigued, or low-energy almost every day

7. Anhedonia, or loss of interest or pleasure

8. Feeling worthless, or unreasonable or excessive guilt almost every day

9. Difficulty concentrating, thinking, or making decisions almost every day

10. Thoughts of death or dying or suicide, with or without a specific plan to carry it out

People who exhibit the clinical signs of depression also tend to avoid social encounters. Solitude seems preferable to the overwhelming stress of social contact. When they do interact with others, depressed people may find themselves becoming impatient and lashing out unexpectedly. Commonly, the remorse that follows such exchanges only increases feelings of guilt and shame, and therefore depression. Loss of interest in sex is also a common complaint. Negative thinking produces a "half-empty-glass" perspective: perceived slights and invalidating exchanges are magnified, affirming or positive events downplayed. People who are depressed may cry frequently and effortlessly, or, despite an intense desire to weep, may be unable to shed a tear. Physical symptoms, such as headaches, backaches, stomachaches, and nausea, may also be by-products of depression.

Although most clinicians agree that all depressions share most or all of these common symptoms, there are subtypes of depression aside from the four basic disorders mentioned above (major depressive disorder, dysthymia, bipolar disorder, and cyclothymia) that are worth mentioning briefly here.

Other Varieties of Depression

Single Episode vs. Recurrent. While most people tend to experience at least one significant bout with depression at some point in their lives, others have been found to suffer two or more major depressive episodes throughout their lives. It is possible to suffer episodes of major depression with periods of relatively normal functioning or low level depression (dysthymia) in between.

Endogenous vs. Reactive. Endogenous is simply a fancy word for "internal." When depression develops over a longer period of time, seemingly without any external cause and it is accompanied by physical symptoms like sleep interruption, changes in weight or decreased energy, it is referred to as endogenous. The alteration in mood may be so subtle, so gradual, that the depressed person is unaware of any change. Some clinicians believe that people with endogenous depressions are particularly good candidates for antidepressant medications in addition to other forms of treatment (see chapters 8 and 9 for more details).

In contrast, reactive depressions may occur in response to loss or disappointment in our lives. Losing a close relationship or a beloved job will evoke feelings of sadness. If the sadness becomes prolonged, intensifies, or interferes with daily living, however, it is described as a reactive depression. People suffering from reactive depressions exhibit the symptoms of major depression mentioned earlier.

Hidden or Masked. People who mask their depression may not be aware of any despondency. Their depression may be effectively disguised as physical problems: joint aches, headaches, or indigestion, for example. Other masks for depression may include workaholism or other excessive behaviors, such as non-stop shopping, for example, or various kinds of thrill-seeking.

With Psychotic Features. Some depressions can become so intense that they disrupt normal thinking processes and result in visual or auditory hallucinations or delusions. These psychotic symptoms tend to occur only during severe depressions. They disappear once treatment has been initiated and the depression improves.

Seasonal Affective Disorder (SAD). Some people experience intense bouts of depression during autumn and winter. Research suggests that this disorder is related to both the low intensity and number of hours of sunlight, which in most of North America, begins to diminish noticeably in September. Special light therapies to assist the person during the low light months have been developed specifically for this form of depression. See chapter 8 for more on this condition and treatments.

Postpartum Depression (aka Postnatal Depression). Recent estimates suggest that almost 50 percent of women experience some form of the "baby blues," a state of tearful agitation in the days following delivery. Although a number of factors may be responsible for these feelings, some researchers have suggested that women may be reacting to the dramatic change in hormonal balance that occurs before and after birth. Most women pass through these feelings within a few days; however, unusual stress during or after delivery or a history of depression may set the stage for postpartum depression. The baby blues don't always dissipate, and in some cases, they may get worse. According to Barbara Parry, M.D., an associate professor of psychiatry at the University of California, San Diego, School of Medicine, postpartum depression afflicts ten to fifteen percent of new mothers.. Symptoms, which typically appear shortly after delivery, include deep sadness, frequent crying, insomnia, lethargy, and irritability. The stress of caring for a newborn, including sleep deprivation as well as insufficient support, may contribute to the development of a major depression in new mothers.

Associated with a Medical Condition. AIDS, chronic pain, chronic fatigue syndrome, and fibromyalgia are all mood-affecting conditions. Consequently, depression may be a sign of physical illness. Rather than assuming that down moods are purely psychological events that must be treated as such, it is important to get a standard medical checkup. In addition, the medications prescribed for certain medical conditions are notorious depressants. The steroids sometimes used to treat asthma, for example, have mood-altering side effects. Consequently, before starting any new meds, it is important to investigate the drug's characteristic effect on emotions. There is one other type of depression related to medical conditions. Getting bad news about one's health—a positive HIV test, for example, or a biopsy report that confirms the presence of a malignancy—can be a life-altering event. It is also a mood-altering event. In other words, the mere knowledge that one has a life-threatening illness can be profoundly depressing.

Related to Aging. People over sixty face several difficult, and often depressing, passages. Suicidal statistics reveal this vulnerability. Older white men have the highest rate of suicide in the U.S. Loss, either of partners or peers, or of physical vigor, seems to trigger depressions in the elderly.

Depression experienced by older people may be masked by a certain brand of stoicism. Instead of mentioning their moods, they may complain about various physical problems (e.g., muscle or joint pains, chronic headaches, etc.). In these cases, physical complaints often decrease or completely go away following treatment for depression.

Related to Substance Abuse or Dependency. People who abuse central nervous system depressants such as alcohol, barbiturates, or other drugs are likely to exhibit symptoms of depression. Because of the similarities between the effects of a substance-induced depression and the symptoms of a major depressive disorder, it can be difficult to figure out what is going on. Is the depressed person abusing drugs or alcohol in an attempt to deal with the depression or is the substance abuse itself causing the depression? Perhaps both are happening simultaneously. It is quite common for someone with a chemical dependency problem to have a concurrent mood disorder. In other words, depression can occur before, during, or after substance abuse. Whatever the sequence, addicted and depressed people face dual interventions: Recovery from depression must be paired with recovery from chemical dependency.

Overview of the Causes of Depression

There is some controversy among experts about the exact cause or the major contributing factors to the experience of depression. Generally, however, most agree that depression is the result of a combination of three factors: biological, psychological, and environmental. Definitions of each of these factors may help you start to assess the relative contribution of each to your own level of depression:

Biological contributors to depression include genetic factors such as a family history of depression, brain or bodily chemical imbalances that result from sustained depressed mood, or other metabolic/physiological changes (e.g., not sleeping or eating properly over time). A variety of substances—alcohol, barbiturates, and marijuana, for example—act as central nervous system depressants and, therefore, fall into the category of biological contributors. We will discuss the biological and biochemical aspects of depression in more detail in chapter 3 and in the last section of the book which focuses on ways of overcoming depression.

Psychological contributors include self-defeating thought patterns and chronic feelings of inadequacy, despair, sadness, frustration, and/or emptiness. A tendency to withdraw from friends and family during hard times may also be a personality factor that contributes to depression. Certain self-destructive behaviors may compound the "I'm-a-loser" downward spiral. We will discuss these factors more in chapter 6.

Environmental contributors include external stressors such as work or financial difficulties, or the loss of supportive relationships. The wider historical shifts that affect us all also fall into this category. In the last half century, for example, as life in America has become more complex and unpredictable, overall depression rates in the general population have increased dramatically. This correlation between external events and interior moods strongly implicates environmental factors in depression. For gays and lesbians, this correlation is particularly relevant. It suggests that heterosexism plays a major role in gay depression. It also suggests that recovery from the queer blues must entail some ways of coping with homophobia—both in its external and even more toxic internalized forms. We will discuss this more in chapter 6.

Each of the three contributing factors to depression has its fan club. Certain researchers, for example, are adamant about the biological underpinnings of depression. If a chemical imbalance wasn't to blame, they argue, anti-depressant medications wouldn't be so effective. Other experts insist that the chemical imbalances associated with altered moods are the result, rather than the cause, of depressed moods. These researchers and clinicians are convinced that psychological or environmental factors play the primary role in most depressions, and that our bodies simply follow suit. In actuality, there may be no single formula that describes every person's depression. It is probable that, in a particular individual, one element triggers the depression, and one or more of the other factors keeps it going, or makes it worse—turns it into what is called a *downward spiral* or cycle. Say, for example, you hear you did not get a sought-after promotion. You speculate that your gayness disqualified you. You come home and fight with your partner. Both of you say things that you regret. You begin to question the relationship itself. This initiating event is the environmental stressor that triggers the depression. Anxiety about the argument keeps you awake several nights in a row, leaving you feeling exhausted and frustrated. Flooded by successive waves of regret, anger, love, and hurt, you find yourself unable to eat. Instead of seeing friends, you obsess about your choice: Should you stay or break up? The longer you neglect yourself, skimping on sleep, food, supportive contact from friends, the more you create biochemical changes which reinforce the depression. If you comfort yourself by doubling your alcohol intake, you add another biological factor that contributes to the environmental and psychological processes that have already deepened your despair.

Drawing Your Own Self-Portrait

It may be useful to depict the role of each of the three factors—the biological, psychological, and environmental—in your own depression. While all three can be important, you may find that one or two play heavier roles in your own depression than the other(s). Take a moment to draw your own pie chart as you believe dictates your own situation. Use the blank circle on the next page.

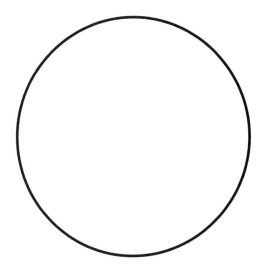

Such pie charts are momentary snapshots. In order to see if the proportions have changed over time, pick another period in your life, say, six months or a year ago. How would the pie chart have looked at that time? Would the proportions be the same? Different? How?

Another way of getting a snapshot of your mood is to rate yourself on the following quiz. The questionnaire, developed by Dr. John Preston, isn't designed to take the place of an evaluation by a clinician. It can, however, give you some way to measure your moods. You might also reproduce it and use it to track your moods over time.

The items below refer to how you have felt and behaved DURING THE PAST WEEK. For each item, indicate your sense of how you experience that issue, by circling the appropriate number next to the item.

I. Biological Functioning

A. Sleep Problems   **Scores**

    1. No sleep problems   0

    2. Occasional sleep problems   1

    3. Frequent awakenings during the night or early morning awakening

          a. 1–3 times during the last week   2

          b. 4 or more times during the last week   3

B. Appetite Problems

    1. No changes in appetite   0

2. Some appetite change (up or down) but no weight gain or loss	1
3. Significant appetite change (up or down) with weight gain or loss (5 lbs. plus or minus during the past month)	3

C. Fatigue

1. Little or no noticeable daytime fatigue	0
2. Fatigued or exhausted during the day	
a. occasionally	1
b. 1–3 days during the last week	2
c. 4 or more days during the last week	3

D. Desire for sex or affection

1. No change in desire	0
2. Decrease in desire	
a. slight	1
b. moderate	2
c. no sexual desire	3

E. Anhedonia

1. Despite times of sadness, I am able to have times of enjoyment or pleasure	0
2. Decreased ability to enjoy life	
a. slight	1
b. moderate	2
c. absolutely no joy in life	3

Total Score: Biological Functioning _____

II. Emotional/Psychological Symptoms

A. Sadness and Despair   Scores

1. No pronounced sadness	0
2. Occasional sadness	1
3. Times of intense sadness	2
4. Intense sadness almost every day	3

B. Self-Esteem

1. I feel confident and good about myself	0
2. I sometimes doubt myself	1

3. I often feel inadequate, inferior, or lacking in   2
self-confidence

4. I feel completely worthless most of the time   3

C. Apathy and Motivation

1. It is easy to feel motivated and enthusiastic   0
about things

2. I occasionally find it hard to "get started" on   1
projects, work, etc.

3. I often feel unmotivated or apathetic   2

4. It is almost impossible to "get started" on projects,   3
work, etc.

D. Negative Thinking/Pessimism

1. I think in relatively positive ways about my life and   0
my future

2. I occasionally feel pessimistic   1

3. I often feel pessimistic   2

4. The world seems extremely negative to me; the   3
future looks hopeless

E. Emotional Control

1. When I feel unpleasant feelings, such emotions may   1
hurt but I do not feel totally overwhelmed

2. I occasionally feel overwhelmed by inner emotions   2

3. I often feel extremely overwhelmed by inner feelings   3
or I feel absolutely no inner feelings

F. Irritability and Frustration

1. I do not experience undue irritability and frustration   0

2. I occasionally feel quite irritable and frustrated   1

3. I often feel irritable and become easily frustrated

    a. 1–3 days during the last week   2

    b. 4 or more days during the last week   3

Total Score: Emotional/Psychological Symptoms   _____

Computing Your Score and Interpreting the Results

A total score can be computed for both the "Biological Functioning" and "Emotional/Psychological Symptoms" sections of the quiz. To compute your score, add up the numbers that you circled and calculate your total for each symptom or section, putting the total score on the line at the end of each of the two sections.

Biological Functioning: Scores of 2 or 3 on any of the items A through E may suggest that your biological functioning has been affected by depression and that antidepressant medication treatment may be indicated, according to Dr. Preston (especially if any scores of 3 are present). If this is the case, it will be important to consult with a psychiatrist, your family physician, or a mental health therapist regarding medical treatment. Chapter 9 discusses medical treatments in detail. If all scores are 0 or 1, antidepressant medications may not be indicated.

Interpretation of the Total Score: _____
0–5 Mild
6–10 Moderate
11–15 Severe Biological Symptoms

Emotional/Psychological Symptoms: Responses of 2 or 3 on any items suggest a more psychologically-based depression.

Interpretation of the Total Score: _____
0–5 Mild
6–10 Moderate
11–18 Severe Psychological Symptoms

High scores on both Biological and Emotional/Psychological sections suggest a mixed type of depression.

Again, this tool is not meant to take the place of a skilled clinician and is not meant to make a formal diagnosis. If you are suffering from feelings that are causing you concern and interfere with your daily functioning or if you are having thoughts of killing yourself or someone else, you should seek immediate treatment from a trained mental health professional within your community. Chapter 7 can help you find a qualified, queer-positive clinician.

Just as each of has a special way of demonstrating pleasure and joy, we also have a sadness signature—a particular way of being or acting when we are down. Our temperaments, our circumstances, even our DNA contribute to the shape and form of our emotional signatures. These elements determine if these signatures are tightly contained, if and when they spike outside the lines, or even spill off the page. In the following chapter, we will look at unique patterns of queer blues, and examine the particular ways in which homophobia shapes the emotional imprints of gays and lesbians.

CHAPTER 2

Blue Passages

How Society Contributes to Depression for Lesbians and Gays

Cultures and subcultures develop unique modes of expressing feelings, both good and bad. Africans, abducted, enslaved and transported to America, managed to convert some of their despair into the blues—and a new musical form was born. There is a surprising footnote to this chapter of American cultural history. Many of the blues artists composing and performing during the Harlem heyday of the '20s and '30s were also gay. Bessie Jackson is a good example. Her song, "BD [bulldyke] Blues" ranks as a pre-pride anthem: "coming a time, BD women, they ain't goin' to need no men. /Oh, the way they treat us is a low down and dirty thing." Ma Rainey was perhaps the most famous (or infamous) of this group of blues singers. A cross-dresser, her song, "Prove It On Me Blues," is a closet classic: "They say I do it, ain't nobody caught me. They sure got to prove it on me . . ." (Faderman, 1991, 77)

Within our tribe, coping with the blues is part of everyday life. If you haven't had your share of mournful times, you probably won't get the blues (the music or the mood). Nor will you understand half the jokes of queer comedians, or grasp the poignancy of most gay movies or books. In fact, if you can't swap tales about your sojourns in hell (and your resurrection in your therapist's office), you may not even be a satisfactory latte companion or dinner date. Much of gay and lesbian culture—art, music, and even personal interactions—is a response to gay angst. But our blues-saturated subculture isn't the only mirror of our lives. In a recent survey of 1700 gays and lesbians by gayhealth.com, a gay health organization, depression topped the list, beating out such concerns as HIV or breast cancer. According to other surveys, lesbians are almost three times as likely to visit a therapist as heterosexual women (Morgan, 1992). Though no comparable therapy data is available for gay men, high drug and alcohol abuse seems to suggest that some of these substances may be popular, if ineffective, forms of do-it-yourself therapy.

How are we to account for the high incidence of queer blues? Some observers—the less sympathetic—would say that the same personality problems that account for gayness also account for other mental problems: higher rates of depression, alcoholism, suicide, etc. Such global assessments probably correlate highly with the homophobia of the person doing the assessing. But they do not tell us much about the mental health of the gay population. For more accurate assessments, we have to consult less biased researchers. In fact, dozens of studies conducted over the last few decades show that the mental health scores of gays and straights are indistinguishable. In a now-classic study, a battery of psychological tests was administered to comparable groups of heterosexual and homosexual volunteers. Before the test scores were shown to a panel of psychologists, the sexual orientation of the test-takers was concealed. The psychologists were never able to distinguish simply on the basis of the scores alone which test-takers were gay and which were straight (Hooker, 1958). In other words, no significant differences between gays and straights show up on standard psychological tests. Gays, as a group, are not more depressed than straights. They may, however, be *differently* depressed. To find out the source of the gay blues, it is important to shift our focus away from the purely psychological and direct it toward social or environmental causes.

The Bad News Blues

We grow up in a culture that teaches us that homosexuality is wrong: a sign of moral failing, emotional disturbance, hormonal disorders, or bad genes. Constant immersion in such negative cultural beliefs is bound to have a corrosive effect on self-esteem, even if we began life with an abundant supply. Though there is no way to prove that negative cultural messages are directly linked with dwindling self-esteem and depression, we can measure it indirectly. Let's look, for example, at a recent study of 157 lesbians conducted by three psychologists. The women who scored highest for depression also showed the most signs of internalized homophobia. They also reported less social support (Szymanski, 2000). It is impossible to say which came first, the internalized homophobia, the depression, or the social isolation, but we can speculate about a couple of probable cause–effect sequences. Perhaps internalized homophobia (from those negative cultural messages) caused the lesbians to avoid contact with other lesbians. As a consequence, these women might begin to feel isolated and depressed. Or perhaps internalized homophobia caused such despair that social contact began to seem more and more daunting—as challenging as climbing a mountain or skimming across a monster wave: easier to just stay home and channel surf. There is a bright side to this study. If depression and absence of social contact are correlated, then perhaps the reverse is also true. In other words, an effective antidepressant may be social contact. Perhaps the best time to pick up the phone, and make a date, is exactly the time when you feel least inclined to do so. The foregoing data, combined with our clinical experience and our membership in the GLBT communities leads to one conclusion: The more virulent-strains of depression that afflict gays and lesbians are, in large part, a predictable consequence of living in a homophobic and heterosexist world.

Cultural oppression comes in many forms. The most obvious sources are, of course, institutional: our schools, our churches, and our families all reinforce the gay-is-wrong message. But antigay messages are built into our everyday lives in other ways: when we turn on the radio and hear gay-bashing rap lyrics, or go to movies where gays or lesbians are commonly caricatured as lonely sex addicts, mincing queens, or repressed psychopaths. After a while, one begins to wonder how Hollywood would survive without its stable of queer freaks. But perhaps the most painful forms of oppression consist of private, personal exchanges: interactions between co-workers, family members, or even encounters with strangers at bus stops or pay phones. Such exchanges can consist of anything from an arched eyebrow to a thrown punch, from subtle avoidance to overt rejection. And somehow, just when you think you've gotten over the pain of these dismissals, another episode provokes another round of despair.

Kimeron remembers how exultant a client of his was, when, after years of ostracism from his large, tightly knit Hispanic family, he managed to establish a bond with one of his sisters. The next week he came back to therapy, anxious and despondent, after finding "cocksucker" spray-painted over the rainbow flag on his car. He couldn't help wondering if another family member had done it.

A client of Marny's, finally persuaded that she needed to get out and meet people, had joined the campaign staff of a progressive candidate who seemed to have a pro-gay platform. The following week, the client tearfully produced the text of the candidate's recent newspaper interview. After stating that no one should be denied the right to love whomever they choose, she had gone on to say that "rats exhibited homosexual behavior in certain circumstances, particularly during overpopulation." The candidate, who was an environmentalist, remarked that she found that interesting because "we are animals and we have a population problem." The client dropped out of the campaign, and retreated to her previous state of social isolation.

These are episodes in the lives of our clients we happen to be privy to. But an infinite number of such events go unrecorded, unregistered by any except the gay or lesbian who experiences them. To get a sense of their cumulative effect over time, it is helpful to divide up gay lives into different stages.

Queer Passages

A standard way of understanding and analyzing our lives is to divide them into stages or developmental passages. Beginning with infancy, and ending with old age, such a schema charts the normal stages that the Homo sapiens who happen to reside in North America in the twenty-first century progress through during the course of their lifetimes. A number of writers and psychologists—perhaps most notably Eric Erikson and Gail Sheehy—have come up with their own version of life passages. For gays and lesbians, getting through such passages is particularly perilous—so dangerous, in fact, that getting from childhood to adolescence, or adolescence to adulthood, can feel like running a gauntlet. To get some an idea of the sometimes psychological, and often times real-world, hazards lying in wait for developing gays and lesbians, it seems important to revisit these traditional passages. But in our version, we turn the passages inside out: That is, we look at them through the eyes of the gay or about-to-become gay person. From this vantage point, heterosexist assumptions that shape the critical juncture of most gay and lesbian lives are painfully apparent.

Preconception and Pregnancy

Preconception has two meanings. It can refer to the state preceding conception of the yet-to-be infant. It can also mean an assumption, a supposition about the ways that things are. In this first phase of our queer developmental schema, the two meanings dovetail. Before the to-be-gay person has even been conceived, certain assumptions about gender are firmly in place. Even if one or both parents will do little more than contribute genetic material, or even if they are gay or bi and have little invested in being normal themselves, chances are both will be well-versed in differences between males and females. It doesn't matter if the egg and sperm donors are fifteen or fifty, if they have grown up in Butte or Brooklyn: They have been repeatedly exposed to gender norms. They know how males and females are supposed to act and dress, and what they are supposed to say and think. And they are equally savvy about any violations of these codes— what is "unmanly" or "unwomanly."

Wanted or unwanted, the pregnancy reconfirms the heterosexist narrative. Whether papa is a vial from the sperm bank or a doting househusband, he is still a papa. And whether mom-to-be is a homeless addict or a dotcom maven, she is still Mother. The pregnancy and her impending role as mom certify her femaleness. And now the gendered world begins to percolate inward. At this stage fantasies abound. The child is going to be an emissary who will correct any gender wobble in either of the parents' lives. Eavesdrop on the naming negotiations of most het couples and such gender issues will become apparent:

Ma-to-be: I kind of like Sidney.

Pa-to-be: What do you mean Sidney! Nobody will know if it is a boy or a girl.

By now, ma-to-be is looking uneasily at pa-to-be as he starts jabbing the air and banging the table for emphasis.

Pa-to-be: Why would you ever want to saddle a boy with such a pansy name! And if it is a girl, everyone will tease her. How about something straightforward: If it's a boy, Jake. If it's a girl, Lucinda.

Parents' gender reparations don't stop with such naming rituals. Say mom felt her gender interfered with her career. Perhaps she'll picture her daughter as a leader, a girl who is popular, smart, athletic, equally comfortable in jeans and frilly frocks. After all, Ma-to-be tells herself: You can never underestimate the power of positive thinking. If Pa-to-be has never lived up to his father's expectations—and what son ever has?—he will picture a winner, a hero on the playing field, and a scholar who aces every test.

But what if little Lucinda *only* likes jeans, and what if little Jake shrivels at the sight of soccer cleats and prefers to totter around on mama's stilettos? What then?

Infancy

We don't care if it's a boy or a girl . . . as long as it's a healthy baby. Perhaps we've said it ourselves, or heard our friends uttering this standard disclaimer. It is the same sentence echoed later on by the progressive parents of gays. *We don't care who you're with, as long as you're happy.* Happy and healthy. That's all that counts, right? Picture the following scenario: A baby is born in a progressive household. Let's even make it a lesbian household. (Ironically enough, gay parents, more than anyone else, reveal the power of the heterosexist narrative.) Say the new arrival gets a unisex name: Kobe or Manzia or Scooter. The couple's friends all come over to celebrate the new arrival. The baby is apple-cheeked and cooing, resplendent in a canary yellow sweater and teensy-weensy Osh-koshes. And no one is gauche enough to ask the question, the question that burns in the air like summer lightning. Say, by chance, everybody continues to pursue, from political correctness, a don't-ask-don't-tell policy. Think for a minute how the presence of a gender-free human in the middle of a social circle—even a gay circle—would operate, how it would disconcert friends and undermine easy social interaction. Picture how no one would ever know what pronoun to use or what questions to ask. (Does this remind you of any other situation?) Imagine how, one day, during a diaper change, someone finally gets a peek at those very private privates. Imagine how fast the news would spread. The FYI velocity would exceed the speed of light, would travel faster even than news of a breakup! Imagine the universal sigh of relief that would waft through the social circle. At last! The child can fit into our preconceptions—even our progressive ones—and we can relax. And this is a gay family, where gender is supposed to be de-emphasized and incidental. (Remember the "we-only-care-if-it's-healthy" line.) Such is the power of the dominant culture norms.

Now think of Mr. and Mrs. John Q. Public who live in a shady suburb of Duluth. Visualize a little fellow decked out in the Minnesota Vikings jersey, who, in keeping with the football motif, is tossed into the air regularly. And picture a baby girl, whose ability to attract attention and praise is directly proportional to her B.Q. (Barbie Quotient). Think of all this, and weep for our little queer-to-be.

Childhood

Our clients often bring family snapshots to therapy. Is it our imagination, or is little Jake hiding behind mom, trying to avoid the camera dad is aiming at him? And look at Lucinda, striking that bandy-legged sailor pose. She's a dead ringer for the older and much adored brother Bobbie, standing right next to her. These are teasers, hints of what is to come. Therapy clients often say they knew they were different way back then—knew at three or four or five that they didn't fit in. Jake, who was afraid of dad, begged mom to let him make pies with her in the kitchen. On the other end of the spectrum, Lucinda, whose idea of heaven was to hang out in the tree house with that older bro, was told it was too dangerous and shooed away. Probably when the photos were taken, thirty or forty years ago, these children may have been considered a little odd. But then, eccentricity wasn't cause for alarm. Everyone assumed that they would grow out of it. Jake would stop trying to play dress up and Lucinda would grow to love her dolls.

Ironically enough it has been the success of the gay movement that has "outed" these children. Thanks to TV series that feature gay characters, and regular news coverage of gay pride, everyone now knows the possible implications of gender deviant behavior. Nowadays such behavior is likely to be regarded with anxiety if not outright foreboding. Today the gay-to-be child is much more likely to be subjected to "corrective" experiences comparable to the retraining left-handed children received a few decades ago. Perhaps they will be hustled off to a therapist. Perhaps Jake will be enrolled in a junior martial arts class or spirited away on fishing excursions with dad. For Lucinda, the corrections may be even slyer, more seductive. Perhaps she will be given not just one doll, but two dolls: Ken *and* Barbie. Or perhaps she will be given a cuddly puppy that will be her responsibility to raise.

But what if Lucinda and Jake are growing up in single gender households? What if there is no dad to take him fishing, to "model" manliness? For one answer, we should revisit some progressive lesbian couples. Talk to them, and you are likely to find that a gay-friendly male who will spend time with their toddler tops their wish list. This desire for a male "model" is particularly urgent if it is a boy. In fact, uncles, cousins, gay male friends are regularly recruited for the task. The children may have no affinity with these recruits, may dread the Sunday trips with these hairy aliens to the beach or zoo. But regardless of the impact of these big-brother interludes, the heterocentrist message is hammered home yet again.

The carefree childhood years aren't so carefree if you happen to be queer. Studies show that children's understanding of gender stereotypes begins at two or three. By age five, children are well-versed in appropriate sex roles. They know what and whom they are supposed to play with. They also know who they are supposed to be attracted to when they get a little older. There may have been occasions—a wedding for example—when they were dressed up in mini tuxedos and gowns. Paired with an opposite-sexed child, the miniature bride and groom were to walk down the aisle together, and present the rings to their grown-up doppelgangers. Later, for the benefit of photographers and videographers, they were urged to snuggle and kiss, and if possible, to lisp "when we get big, WE gonna get married, too." Just in case Jake or Lucinda didn't get the point the first time around, these family portraits will be displayed, shared with other relatives and guests.

Cross-dressing, even if it was tolerated before five, may now be actively discouraged. If a parent defends a child's preference for activities that seem dissonant with his or her apparent gender, the parent, herself, will be punished, either by the other parent, grandparents, or neighbors who happen to get a glimpse of the miniature drag princess or prince. Witnessing a beloved parent, the one who has championed them, taking the heat will be experienced as more painful than direct punishment.

Queer pre-adolescent children are in a terrible bind. If their parents are anxious about their budding gayness, same-sex friendships may be vigilantly supervised or actively discouraged. Opposite sexed friendships may be equally problematic. By now other children have started to enforce heterocentrist norms. Girls who want to play with boys are often rejected and ridiculed. Because males are not permitted to toss their mandarin status aside, the plight of boys who want to hang out with girls may be even more dire. (To get an idea of how powerfully sexism operates in the lives of children, think of the best-selling Harry Potter series, and imagine how the series might have fared if the hero had been Harriet instead of Harry.) Who, then, will befriend the young queer?

Adolescence

By adolescence, young gays and lesbians are experiencing negative reaction and disapproval, even violence, on a regular basis. Because of our cross-gender identification, we may also try very hard to be accepted by the very group that, because of heterosexism, has been trained to despise us. In an anthology entitled *Tomboys* (1995),

Hillary Mullins describes her adolescent brutalization at the hands of males she hung out with. Playing football with a bunch of chums, she was accosted by an older boy. He told her to get lost. When she ignored him, he beat her up. Before he left her "'tear-streaked in the dust,' he hissed, 'That'll teach you to try to be a boy.'" Later, a bunch of older boys molested her. She writes, "This was something I had not been prepared for, a kind of sexism neither my mother nor anyone else had told me anything about . . . From this, my tomboy spunk could not save me. I surrendered to the invasion and degradation, to the treatment that persuaded me that I could not say no, that my needs and feelings weren't as important as my abusers'. Indeed, that is the primary lesson of oppression, the message scored into you over and over: that you are not entirely human, that you are a lesser-than being."

"Lesser-than being" is probably an accurate description of how many young gays feel. Surveys, taken at different times, in different places, are remarkably consistent. In one typical survey, 80 percent of the lesbian, gay, and bisexual adolescents reported verbal abuse based on their sexual orientation. Forty-four percent had been threatened with physical violence, and seventeen percent had been beaten, kicked, or punched (Pilkington, 1995). On the flip side, 23.5 percent of the men polled in a study of community college students reported verbally harassing gay men (Franklin, 1998). Ten percent of the male students had hit, kicked, or beaten gay men. In a heterosexist culture, where gay-baiting and -bashing can almost rate as a national blood sport, it isn't surprising that gay suicide rates are triple those of straight youths. In a 1991 survey, 30 percent of the gay youth had attempted suicide. In a 1994 survey sent out to gay and lesbian youth groups, 40 percent reported suicide attempts (Due, 1995). Certain circumstances up the self-destructive ante for gay youths. Discovering same sex preference early in adolescence, experiencing violence due to gay or lesbian identity, using drugs or alcohol in an effort to cope, and being rejected by family members as a result of being gay are the four factors which put teens at particular risk (Ramafedi, 1991). In addition, there is a high correlation between sexual abuse and gay identity. One conventional and perhaps homophobic interpretation is that there is a cause–effect relationship between abuse and queerness. In other words, abuse causes us to veer off a "normal" developmental track. We would like to propose another interpretation, an explanation based on culturally ingrained heterocentrism rather than individual pathology. As outsiders, young gays may be lonely, and grateful for the attentions of someone, anyone who seems to accept us as we are. In some cases these interested neighbors or relatives happen to be pedophiles.

Being a gay teenager wasn't a picnic before Stonewall, but the increased visibility of gays may have hurt more than helped their cause. In *Joining the Tribe* (1995), an in-depth book about gay youth, author Linnea Due discusses her own secret longing to kiss a raven-haired beauty when she was in college in 1960. Thirty-five years later she crisscrosses the country, interviewing gay kids—kids from barrios and kids from affluent families, gay kids who are out, in, and straddling the fence. These kids' stories are much more complicated than they were in Due's own closeted youth. Take the story of Caroline Anchors. In high school in Philadelphia, she was out and proud. She belonged to a gay youth group that insisted upon being taken seriously. Then Caroline decided she wanted to explore the African-American side of her identity and chose to go to a black college. As soon as came out to her college friends, she became a pariah. But for other kids Due interviewed, the opposite was true. Vic Edminster told her mother at eight years old that "she liked girls." Despite her unwavering and lifelong lesbian identity, she had felt alienated coming of age in gay San Francisco, and hadn't found a lesbian community she could call her own until she went off to college. But there are plenty of other tales as well—stories about kids for whom college isn't an option. Some gay kids who drop out of school get stuck at home in the Bronx or the L.A. barrio, perhaps in low-paying jobs. They can't afford to risk any contact with a gay community. Race, class, as well as gender, complicate the circumstances of gay kids' lives. But one thing is sure, even if one wanted to pass, to keep one's head down, and to avoid being targeted, it is much harder in today's climate of heightened gay awareness.

Gay kids are under siege on many fronts. Perhaps their bodies have betrayed them. They swear they are not the gender they appear to be. They may feel confused about their allegiances. Where do they belong? To their loving but homophobic family? To school chums who scream "faggot" as easily as they breathe? To the anti-gay ethnic group into which they were born? To a gay subculture that seems chilly, remote, and much older? Youth spent under siege takes a heavy toll. If they survive at all, they will carry scars into adulthood.

Adulthood

According to Sheehy, the author of *Passages* (1974), adulthood is a particularly exhilarating interlude. One faces the challenges of preparing for lifework, of finding a mentor and a mate, and of keeping the sense of self one has developed so far. For a gay person, such tasks are daunting. By adulthood, his or her sense of self may be uncertain. Perhaps the most tentative experimentation has been so punished that the gay person has retreated back into the closet. Perhaps he or she has elected to stay confined there until times change, perhaps nurturing the possibility of escape into the anonymity of adulthood and a faraway city. Perhaps the need for disguise even prompted the gay person to acquire the requisite opposite-sexed mate; now, skidding into adulthood, he or she must cope with a wrenching ending and an uncertain future.

Say, by some miracle, the gay person has escaped the typical forms of psychic and physical brutalization: The tasks he or she faces are still formidable. There is the matter of relationships (Gays and lesbians have never had the chance to safely rehearse the courtship rituals that most heterosexuals had ample opportunity to practice in their teen years.) Greedy for long delayed intimacy, or drunk with the new freedom that adulthood has afforded, gays may act like kids in candy stores. Such desperate eagerness may account for that infamous riddle: What, the joke goes, do lesbians bring on their second date? The answer: a U-Haul. Gratification—too long delayed—may also account for the gay male version of the lesbian joke: What do gay men bring on their second date? The only partially tongue-in-cheek answer: What second date? In other words, lesbians may handle long delayed gratification by pairing up too quickly, too intensely. A few years later, the partners may realize that what would have been a torrid six-month affair has turned into an endless nightmare. Gay men, on the other hand, may find the availability of multiple partners makes long-term intimacy unlikely and/or undesirable. Consequently, for very different reasons, gay men and lesbians may both consider themselves "failures" in the relationship department. Such a perception may further erode gay self esteem and fuel depression.

Despite the relative freedom that comes with adulthood, gays may still seek refuge in the closet. Consider work, for example. Stroll through any office and you'll see traces of home life: Photos of the kids and husband or wife, drawings, and mementos compete for space on most desks and walls. The more time we spend working— and forecasters predict that American workaholism will increase— the more we find ways of bringing our office to our home and our home life to the office. This means that e-mails, and, in the near future, video visits with our loved ones during twelve- and fourteen-hour workdays, are going to become as ubiquitous as coffee breaks. It also means that socializing with colleagues at office parties or company picnics is much more likely to include spouses or other family members. The implications for gays are clear: The more closeted we are, the more we cling to the increasingly outmoded strategy of dividing private and work lives, the more we will be outed in spite of our best efforts. Our silence will be a more eloquent declaration of our private lives than photos of a boyfriend or girlfriend propped up on our desk. But nowadays deciding what photos to leave out and which pronouns to use only scratches the surface of the gay employee's quandaries. Say this queer employee is a human resources manager. He is called in to settle a time management dispute between a supervisor he suspects is homophobic and his supervisee, a gay activist who has been taking off extra time to protest HIV drug-company gouging. How could anyone hope to safely negotiate such landmined interpersonal terrain? Compared with such highwire balancing acts, decisions about whether to be closeted or open seem hopelessly naïve. Instead of deciding to reveal or not to reveal, the gay employee must figure out when to be out, to whom, and to what degree. Such decisions must be made in a nanosecond, calibrated as delicately as retinal adjustments to light changes. Imagine the stress such vigilance requires. Now throw in a couple of extra potential demerits. Say, for instance, the gay human resource manager in the scenario mentioned above happens to be an African-American lesbian determined to break through the glass ceiling. Being black and gay and female is a triple whammy. Two psychologists who polled 1500 lesbian and gay male African-Americans about their fears, physical problems, frequency of suicidal thoughts, and a number of other depressive symptoms found that the population suffered from substantially higher levels of chronic strain than their white counterparts. But here's the capper: Homosexual or bisexual black women suffered more depression, including suicidal thoughts, than HIV positive black men! (Cochran, 2000).

These stresses are not confined to the psychological realm. According to a 1997 survey, just 13 percent of U.S. businesses provide health benefits to same sex partners. That number increases to 25 percent for companies that employ over 5000 (Boschert, 1998). Encouraging as the figures may be, they still indicate that the majority of highly productive lesbian and gay employees must find alternate ways to make sure that their unemployed partner, or the children of their partner, is covered. Add to that potential housing discrimination and you've got a lot on your plate. Sheehy says adulthood is the right time to acquire a mentor. If you're gay, make that a fairy godmother and make sure she comes equipped with a homophobe-zapping powerwand.

Midlife, Whew!

Made it. In the clear. If we're lucky, we have a mate, kids, plenty of supportive friends, financial stability, and a career. At the prime of life, we have risen above all the Sturm und Drang of the terrible teens and twenties. We can gaze forward and backward simultaneously. From the pinnacle, the wraparound view is awesome. Lessons of youth combined with the wisdom of age give us an unrivaled perspective. We are transformed. In any case, that is what the pundits say is supposed to happen at midlife. For gays and lesbians the picture is more complex. True, we may have good friends and a stable career. Perhaps we've even sobered up, figured out the riddle of who we are. But in the process of resolving some identity struggles, we may have created others. Say we've been busily engaged in the same sex dating rituals we were never permitted during our actual adolescence. By midlife, we have finally finished playing catch-up. We finally know what we want in a partner. But, in spite of our best attempts, Mr. or Ms. right seems elusive. The stats about longevity of lesbian and gay relationships are discouraging. Studies consistently show that relationships of lesbians or gay men are significantly shorter than those of heterosexual couples. For example, two-year follow-ups of several studies show that 22 percent of those lesbian couples who had considered themselves permanent partners had split. The same was true of 16 percent of gay men. In the same period, only 4 percent of married heterosexual couples divorced (Blumstein, 1983). Echoing such statistics is another study that shows that middle-aged lesbians are nearly twice as likely to live alone as their heterosexual counterparts (27 percent versus 17 percent) (Bradford, 1991). Substitute isolation for integration, transience for transformation, and you have midlife story of a substantial portion of gays and lesbians.

But say you've been one of the lucky ones. You've found a soul mate. Try telling it to your aging parent. As far as she's concerned, you're still her only "single" child. It is up to you to take care of her. Your siblings are off the hook. After all, they have their hands full with their families. In such situations, internalized homophobia may compound the problem. After many years of quasi-exile, a formerly disapproving parent finally accepts you ... more than accepts you. You have become indispensable! Such parental seductions may make it impossible for you to speak up for your own needs or that of your partnership. You spend every spare moment, and plenty you can't spare, shopping for your parent, laundering her clothes, or chauffeuring her to doctor appointments. But just to make things more interesting, let's say that our midlife queer is also dealing with the issue of kids.

Wedged between offspring and parents, caretakers of both, midlifers have been dubbed the "sandwich" generation. But, again, being gay really complicates already complex situations. Perhaps the gay family's kids are products of a previous straight marriage. In such situations, the enculturated homophobia of children, antagonism that's expressed toward their dad or mom's gay mate, must be added to the already combustible mix. Or maybe you don't have kids but have always wanted them. A couple of decades ago—when the midlife gay man or lesbian was twenty herself—such an idea would have been preposterous. Now, it is finally feasible, but the aspiring parents are a grandparently forty or fifty. If the bio clock hasn't stopped ticking altogether, it is certainly slowing down. How shall the gay couple acquire a child? Adoption? For gay parents, the options are limited: Take problem kids deemed unadoptable by "normal" parents or endure the expense and uncertainly of a foreign adoption. If a lesbian mom wants to give birth herself, her options are also limited: the sperm bank or a donor she knows. Both choices have many problems associated with them. Say the gay or lesbian couple has negotiated all these difficulties. There are more to come. Parenting is likely to create another where-do-I-belong quandary. In her research, anthropologist Ellen Lewin has found that lesbian mothers are much more likely to spend time with their own mothers than their gay and lesbian "families of choice." They are more likely to identify with other mothers, who are statistically much more likely to be heterosexual, than they are with their kid-free lesbian chums (Lewin, 1993). It is the ultimate irony. Gays finally feel empowered enough to demand the parenting prerogatives that straights take for granted. And yet, in the process of raising the very children that represent this new entitlement, the straight world reasserts itself again. This intrusion of the dominant culture at midlife is particularly evident during the bitter custody battles that divorcing lesbian moms sometimes engage in. Despite their initial commitment to equal co-parenting, birth moms sometimes resort to the courts to get full-time custody traditionally granted to "real moms." Midlife, then, can be a time when lesbians may find themselves coping with the extra burdens of caring for an aging parent, at the same time they are losing a beloved partner and child.

Midlifers have one thing in common. Gay or straight, most never achieve all of their youthful dreams. Instead of producing the great American queer novel, we will write competent technical manuals. Instead of eradicating racism, poverty, or war, we may spend our best years just trying to keep the peace in an inner city school-room. It is at this inventory-taking juncture that internalized homo-phobia can be particularly virulent. Our dreams were, in part, a compensation for stigma. By doing great things, we were going to make up for feeling like a lesser-than being. But if our goals were superhuman, then quite respectable achievements may seem like fail-ures. This meltdown of dreams in the crucible of homophobia can put gay midlifers at high risk for depression.

Aging

In her book, *For Love and for Life* (1995), Susan Johnson profiles an old lesbian couple. Elsie and Norma have been together for almost forty years. When Johnson first interviews them, both are in their seventies. Their combined social security income is $10,000 a year. Most of their gay friends have drifted away. They remain carefully closeted with their few remaining straight friends. In addition to the usual age-related health problems, Norma is diabetic and needs oxy-gen for her emphysema. Even though relatives in another state have begged them to move closer, they dare not leave the HMO Norma is so reliant upon. It is not exactly a Hallmark version of the sunset years and yet the picture isn't as grim as it might be. Elsie and Norma have a modest house. They still have each other. Think of what would happen if one them died.

For many older gays, the death of a partner is emotionally dev-astating and economically ruinous. Because the widow or widower is not entitled to the deceased partner's social security benefits, survi-vor's incomes can plunge below poverty levels. In addition, partners may be naïve about financial matters or too secretive about the nature of the relationship to have prepared wills naming each other as heir. Consequently, assets may pass to blood relatives who the deceased partner barely knew. (In contrast, even if there is no exist-ing will, heterosexual partners automatically receive their spouse's assets.) The relationship's invisibility may have another, more devas-tating impact. Unlike the heterosexual mate, the gay widow receives none of the sympathy and support that his or her heterosexual coun-terpart can expect. In fact, gay widowers, whose attachments may be evident for the first time, may become objects of ridicule. When a relationship cannot be recognized, or the loss of the survivor vali-dated, the grief becomes "disenfranchised"—detached from the sur-vivor. This detachment, in combination with homophobia, may cause the widows and widowers to devalue the lost partnership (Shernoff, 1988). In other cases, he or she may feel that they have somehow brought on the pain they are feeling: "If I were not gay," they may conclude, " I would not be suffering like this." Consequently, grief following the death of a partner, which activates external and internal homophobia, is a sure recipe for gay depression. Typically, old gays are much less likely to identify the grief/homophobia combo as depression. They are also less likely to disclose intimate details of their lives to health-care providers, and consequently, less likely to get help.

Widowhood is not the only critical juncture for aging gays. At some point, old gays may no longer be able to care for themselves. How much should they reveal about their orientations to their caretakers? It is hard to conceive of coming out as a luxury, but it is just that—a privilege reserved for those gays who can walk away if their disclosure provokes an adverse reaction. But what if you are infirm? Under such circumstances, there is no escape from a homophobic and hostile caretaker you depend upon to clothe and feed you. And so old gays and lesbians, removed from the places and people upon whom they relied, must now remain silent. Add this final indignity to the other age-related issues like sudden loneliness and poverty, and you have an almost certain prescription for depression.

But what about the new breed of old gays: out and proud, self-sufficient, activists—the gays who lobby for elder rights, write newsletters, start organizations? They may have to contend with erasure from an entirely unexpected source. In a recent article in *Curve* magazine called "Age, the Last Closet (2000)," author and activist Victoria Brownworth laments the gay community's denigration of the old. Why, she asks, should so many gay male ads read no fats, no femmes, no over-30s? Such ageism is bound to rekindle internalized homophobia. Gay men over fifty, stigmatized in their youth by heterosexual acquaintances, become pariahs all over again. This time the pain is worse: They are exiled from their own tribe. At such junctures, it is hard to stifle that ever-present internal critic: "See, if you'd been straight, this never would have happened. You'd have a partner, kids, maybe even grandkids doting on you. Instead . . . this . . . a silly old fag no one wants." Or perhaps the distaste goes both ways. After all, what can someone who was fifty at the time of Stonewall have in common with a gender-bending, tattooed gay boy? Imagine how such differences between an old school closeted homosexual and a gen-x queer could aggravate internalized homophobia. Staring across the generational chasm, each might feel horrified that he or she belongs to the same tribe. Better, each might think, not to be gay at all.

According to the stage theorists, seniors have their own set of developmental tasks. Basically, they boil down to a paradox. At the same time they remain engaged in this world, old people must come to terms with their impending departure from it. Homophobia, both internal and external, constitutes a formidable barrier to the successful negotiation of these final tasks. It is hard to stay connected to a world that has always rejected you, and it is hard to leave a world that has never really been yours.

Telling Your Own Story

As we see from the foregoing, homophobia is inextricably entwined with the developmental passages of gays and lesbians. Consequently, the life paths of many queers head straight into the blue zone. In the following outline, you might jot down a few the pivotal events that shaped your sense of your self as a gay person. Note where these events had a positive outcome, and when they contributed to your own depression.

Infancy

Childhood

Adolescence

Adulthood

Midlife

Old age

CHAPTER 3

Blue Genes

Internal Contributions to Depression

There are many catalysts for depression. A breakup may seem to start the downward spiral. In some instances a single incident—overhearing an antigay remark, for example—may trigger the blues. Pessimistic or self-deprecating thoughts are highly correlated with depression; so are alcohol abuse and sleep disruption. Regardless of the immediate triggers, however, depression seems to have a trickle-down—or rather, trickle-up—effect. That is, it leaves biochemical traces in the brain. Or perhaps it is the other way around: Maybe excesses or deficiencies of particular brain chemicals predispose us to be hypersensitive to external events. The brain/mood link is only one of several psychobiological puzzles currently occupying researchers. Another focus of ongoing research is the connection between depression and hormones; still another is blue genes. In this chapter, we'll discuss the ways in which these biological factors contribute to depression.

The "Nervous" System

It is unfortunate that the term "nervous" has evolved into two meanings, one describing the system of the body made up of nerves and the other describing a condition which we'd all like to avoid ("Jeb, them hens is looking mighty *nervous* since Sarah Lou added the fox mural to the henhouse wall."). While we hope to keep our discussions of this nervous system simple, we understand that a few of you might feel a bit like the hens as we progress.

The place to start our discussion of the biological aspects of depression is with the control center of our body, the brain. In addition to sorting and processing information, this formidable organ has the capacity to restructure its own internal architecture.

The Brain

The brain weighs approximately three pounds and contains over 100 billion nerve cells, called *neurons*. The neurons operate much like a competent switchboard operator who, without missing a beat, routes multiple calls to their appropriate destinations. The neurons communicate through two basic processes, one chemical and the other electrical. It appears that changes in these two processes within and between neurons ultimately cause depression, but more about that after we describe the brain's structure.

The brain's tasks are divided and distributed—more or less—among its different components. For example, the outer layer of the brain, or *cortex*, handles our most brainy functions. Our ability to think abstractly, our senses of taste, hearing, vision, and smell all reside in the cortex. In the center of the brain, underneath the cortex, is the *limbic system*. The limbic system consists of several parts, including the amygdala, pituitary, and hippocampus. This system presides over our emotions, replays our memories, and regulates some key body functions, namely sleep, sex, and hunger. Because these are some of the functions that are disrupted during depression, researchers believe that the limbic system, and specifically a part of this system called the hypothalamus, has something to do with bad moods. Other research seems to implicate other parts of the brain in depression, but since much of these data are inconclusive and ongoing, we'll focus on what scientists seem more certain about.

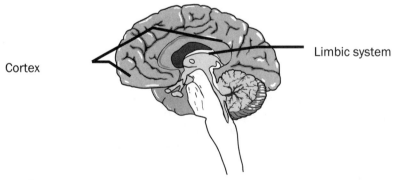

Cortex

Limbic system

The Brain

Nerves and Neurons

Nerves run throughout the body. They are composed of the same neurons, or nerve cells, that make up the brain. They are typically classified as belonging to two overlapping but separate systems. The first, the *peripheral nervous system,* transmits information about pain, pressure, heat and cold from your body to the brain. This system extends from the tips of your toes and fingers to the internal organs in the body, from your muscles, bones, and skin to your brain. The second system, referred to as the *central nervous system* (CNS), consists of the brain and the spinal cord. The major work of the CNS is to receive information from the peripheral nervous system, interpret it, and send back operating instructions. Basically, the CNS is the thought/feeling headquarters. The peripheral nervous system has its own equally important functions, including the relay of important information to and from the brain and spinal cord, but it also is involved in complex decision making in the form of reflexes and interpretation of stimulation.

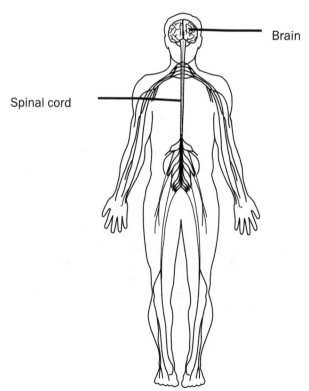

Brain

Spinal cord

The Central Nervous System

One division of the peripheral nervous system is the *autonomic nervous system* (ANS), which is responsible for the body's homeostasis, as well as any bodily changes that may occur with depression or stress (i.e., constipation, diarrhea, changes in blood pressure, breathing, and cardiac functioning). It controls the automatic (or nonconscious) functions and its nerves originate in the CNS and travel along with the peripheral nerves. It is mostly an efferent system (meaning that it controls motor functions rather than sensory functions) that has nerves extending to the various organs, including the heart, gastrointestinal/genitourinary systems, and oil and sweat glands, as well as to the smooth muscle inside of blood vessels.

The ANS is divided into two parts, the parasympathetic and sympathetic systems. Specific nerve cells dwell within the central nervous system and give rise to fibers that end in the *ganglia* (a collection of nerve cells), which then send out fibers to specific organs. The sympathetic fibers run through the *vasomotor* muscles (within the walls of blood vessels), *pilomotor* muscles (in the skin, which cause goosebumps) and other areas of the entire body including the *cardiac muscles* of the heart, the *bronchi* in the lungs, and abdominal/pelvic tissues known as *viscera*. Parasympathetic fibers extend into the *thoracic area*, or midsection, the abdominal and pelvic viscera, the *lacrimal glands* (tear ducts), and other parts of the eye. Both systems are involved in sexual functioning and orgasm. Other sympathetic, postganglionic nerve cells that end in the *adrenal medulla* above the kidneys, secrete adrenaline directly into the blood stream.

Okay. Back to those billions of neurons that make up the nervous system, brain, spinal cord, and peripheral nerves. In recent years, researchers interested in the causes of depression have zeroed in on the communication function of the neurons. Before we discuss the specifics of inter-neuron networks, however, let's take a look at a single one of these specialized cells.

A typical nerve cell is made up of three main parts: the *cell body*, which is the control center of the cell and includes genetic information, the *axon*, which gives the cell its length; and the *terminal button* (sometimes called the *axon terminal*), which is where the cell ends.

Dendrites, the cell's Medusa-like projections, stretch out toward the other neurons they will gather information from. The axon sends information to other neurons and the terminal button secretes chemicals (known as *neurotransmitters*). About half of the neurons in adults are covered with a white, fatty material called *myelin*. Myelin acts as an insulator and protector and allows neurons to send signals more quickly. Despite the incredible density of neurons in the nervous system, they are not directly hooked up. Instead, they communicate by secreting the neurotransmitters from the terminal buttons on the axon into a tiny space between neurons called a *synaptic cleft.* These chemical messages are then received by the dendrites on another nerve cell. When a neuron cell body is stimulated, it causes the electrical charge on the inside of the cell body (remember that communication occurs both chemically and electrically in the nervous system) to go from negative to positive. The positive charge then travels down the axon and signals the terminal button to release other neurotransmitters which then stimulate the dendrites on the next neuron cell body (or bodies). Pictured below is a highly enlarged picture of the terminal button, the synaptic cleft, and the dendrite on the other side of the cleft (altogether called a *synapse)* and some of the processes that occur between cells.

In the picture, Neuron A has been stimulated and is sending a signal to the terminal button to release neurotransmitters into the synapse. Because it is the sending nerve, it is commonly referred to as the *presynaptic neuron.* The neurotransmitter then migrates across the synapse and arrives at Neuron B, called the *postsynaptic neuron.* Some of the neurotransmitter is received by *receptors,* specialized proteins

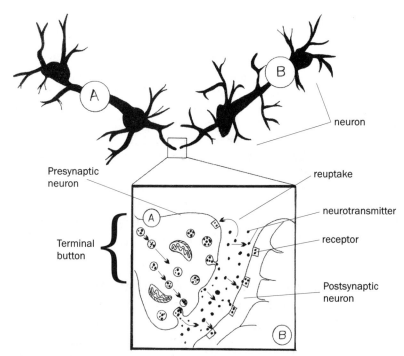

The Synaptic Cleft

on the neuron that serve as access points. Once the neurotransmitter has attached to the receptors, Neuron B becomes excited and repeats the process with other nerves. After Neuron B has been stimulated, some of the neurotransmitter is released back into the original synaptic space and makes its way back to Neuron A. There, reabsorbed through a process called *reuptake*, it awaits the next stimulation signal. Scientists are in the process of identifying as many as a hundred or more variations of a given receptor protein, which means that each subtype of a receptor is responsible for different kinds of reactions to an increase or decrease in a neurotransmitter. More about this later when we discuss the specific neurotransmitters.

Although we have primarily described nerve to nerve communications, a cell body is sometimes triggered by information from outside the body. For example, light can stimulate the neurons in your eyes; touch or pain can stimulate neurons in your skin. Your various senses are equipped with highly specialized receptors that are triggered by specific kinds of stimulation. Neurons can be switched on or off. In their "on" state—referred to as *excitation*—they are stimulated to send a positive charge, or to "fire." In their "off" mode—referred to as *inhibition*—such firing is blocked by electrochemical processes. The balance within the nervous system is a delicate one, shifting continuously between varying states of excitation and inhibition.

At times, these processes can go awry. For example, nerves can produce too little or too much of a neurotransmitter; neurons can be too sensitive or not sensitive enough to the chemicals in the synapse. Sometimes, Neuron A releases a neurotransmitter into the synaptic cleft and then it sucks it back in so quickly that it doesn't have time to travel to Neuron B, another form of reuptake. Occasionally, other substances in the brain may inhibit the neurotransmitter, or destroy it or interfere with the reuptake process, allowing the neurotransmitter to linger in the synaptic space longer than usual. Receptors, and receptor subtypes, can also become less sensitive to the neurotransmitter they are supposed to receive, even when there should be enough chemical in the synaptic cleft.

Chemical Pathways: The Neurotransmitters

Because these changes happen at a sub-microscopic level, much of what we know comes from what we can infer from other data. The first neurotransmitters implicated in depression were discovered by accident in the 1950s. In a study of patients with high blood pressure taking the drug reserpine, almost fifteen percent of them developed symptoms of depression. As it turned out, reserpine was reducing the amount and effectiveness of *monoamines* (chemical neurotransmitters) in the brain. In other words, reserpine was a mood-altering drug. Around the same time, physicians noticed that a drug used to treat tuberculosis also seemed to improve mood in some patients who were depressed. Later studies found that the anti-tuberculin drug was slowing the breakdown of monoamines in the brain, prolonging their normal functioning. These two discoveries together suggested that low levels of monoamines were linked to depression. This discovery led to the development of drugs known as *monoamine oxidase inhibitors* (MAOIs), which prevent the depletion of monoamines in the brain by stopping monoamine oxidase, the enzyme that destroys them.

Since the discovery of the monoamine process, researchers have identified and tracked the neural pathways of three other mood-regulating neurotransmitters. These neurotransmitters are *norepinephrine*, *serotonin*, and *dopamine*; each is associated with its own unique neural pathway. The connection between neurotransmitters and antidepressant medications is discussed in detail in chapter 8.

Norepinephrine

Another early neurotransmitter that was implicated in depression was norepinephrine (also called *noradrenaline*). Norepinephrine is found throughout the brain and the body. In the 1960s, Dr. Joseph Schildkraut, a researcher at Harvard, felt that a deficiency of norepinephrine in specific neural pathways (particularly in the limbic system) was responsible for depression. Too much of the chemical, he concluded, led to mania. Subsequent studies have not always confirmed his hypotheses, and in fact, it appears that having excess norepinephrine simply mimics mania, rather than actually triggering it.

Some studies have shown that the chemicals that show up in the urine or spinal fluid as a result of the normal breakdown of norepinephrine are generally low in people who are depressed. Another interesting discovery is that the cortexes of people who have committed suicide have unusually high numbers of receptors for norepinephrine. From this finding, researchers have concluded that the brains of desperately depressed people, in an effort to get more of the scarce neurotransmitter, appear to produce extra receptors. Recent studies of the brains of patients who died from suicide confirmed that they had more specific types of receptor subtypes than people who had depression but were not suicidal (Meyer, 1999). The study also found that people who were depressed but not suicidal had similar numbers of the same receptor subtypes to people who were not depressed.

Although the exact meaning of these findings is still unknown, it does suggest that perhaps something unique happens in the brain when a depressed person becomes suicidal, and that these receptor subtypes might be important information for drug developers. Studies like these have led to major advances in drug therapy for depression in recent years. At this writing, six different types of norepinephrine receptors have been found. Early antidepressant medications tended to have effects of many different kinds of receptors, some of which improved mood, while other caused significant negative side effects, making the medications difficult to tolerate.

Serotonin

As you may recall, serotonin is another one of the neurotransmitters produced within a neuron. The release of the neurotransmitter into the synapse activates the receptors on the neighbor neuron, and the first "firing" neuron absorbs the neurotransmitter back into itself, described earlier as reuptake. If, for some reason, too little serotonin has been produced or too much has been reabsorbed, communication is impaired between the cells.

Shortages of serotonin are correlated with depression. Perhaps, researchers speculated, low serotonin levels actually caused a decrease in norepinephrine levels, which, in turn, caused depression. Or perhaps the cause–effect link between serotonin depletion and depression was more direct. After all, serotonin-producing neurons extended into the limbic system. Consequently, a shortage of the neurotransmitter would affect emotions, thoughts, appetite, sleep, sex, and other body/mind functions.

As with norepinephrine, there are ways of determining if one's serotonin levels are in fact depleted or low. By measuring the traces of metabolized serotonin that eventually wind up in urine and spinal fluid, researchers can estimate the amount of neurotransmitter originally produced in the limbic system. While some researchers have found low levels of residual serotonin in the body fluids of depressed people, as with much of this early research, this has not been duplicated consistently by other scientists.

If a depressive reaction is theoretically caused by low levels of serotonin, blocking reuptake is one way of allowing more serotonin to get from the presynaptic nerve to the postsynaptic nerve. The success of the second generation of antidepressants (those that followed the MAOIs) provided some of the evidence that the theory was on the right track, but we now know they didn't quite go far enough in terms of sophistication. These drugs, dubbed *tricyclics*, did block the reuptake of both serotonin and norepinephrine. And they relieved depression. Unfortunately, the tricyclics also affected serotonin and norepinephrine receptor subtypes that were unrelated to depression. As a result, people for whom these drugs were prescribed complained of a variety of unpleasant side effects. Years later, other drugs were developed that blocked serotonin reuptake without affecting as many other brain processes. These drugs provided relief from depression without as many of the negative side effects of the tricyclics. Known as *selective serotonin reuptake inhibitors,* or more familiarly as SSRIs, these drugs have significantly changed the way depression is treated, although even they are not without problems. Fifteen different receptor subtypes have been found for serotonin so far, which as we described for norepinephrine receptor subtypes, can lead to problems with other uncomfortable side effects, such as anxiety, sexual problems, and nausea if they are stimulated.

Dopamine

Dopamine has been linked to the centers of the brain that experience pleasure and pain and the connection between the neurotransmitter dopamine and depression is becoming more intriguing to mood researchers. These areas of the brain are also associated with the production of *endorphins,* our body's natural pain relievers. The dopamine link to the experience of both pleasure and pain may explain why some people experience an increase in bodily discomfort, as well as a decrease in ability to feel pleasure, during depression. As with norepinephrine and serotonin, low levels of dopamine have been found in individuals who are depressed, although again, this finding has not been consistently duplicated. There may be dozens of receptor subtypes for dopamine, with evidence for others growing every day.

New Thinking about Neurotransmitters

Though some studies support the notion that depression is caused by a shortage of one of the three main neurotransmitters, the wide range of responses to antidepressants suggests that such explanations are far too simple. For example, it could not be consistently demonstrated that all depressives had too little serotonin and norepinephrine. It was also puzzling that there is a several week lag time between the time these neurotransmitters were increased by antidepressant medications and the first signs of symptom improvement. This had led many clinicians to shift focus from the synapse to the interior of the nerve cells themselves. Now researchers are formulating more complex hypotheses about the links between neurotransmitters and depression. One theory, for example, suggests that some people who are depressed may not have too little of a neurotransmitter, but too much. The theory goes on to suggest that sometimes when there is too much transmitter, it may overwhelm the receiving nerve which, in turn, *downregulates* (or decreases) the number of receptors it has for that transmitter. Such a cause–effect sequence might be comparable to the reaction of tenants unlucky enough to live underneath a twenty-four-hour tap dance studio. After a few sleepless weeks, the studio's neighbors would begin to tune out the sounds. Eventually, they would stop listening altogether. Although this theory is still in the preliminary stages, the implications are clear: each depressed person may come with her own unique electrochemical recipe for the blues. One source of support for this particular theory is the antidepressant drug Tianeptine, only available in France, which appears to *lower* the serotonin in the synapse.

Another more recent theory suggests that a complex interplay between serotonin, norepinephrine, and dopamine is going on in *mood centers* of the brain. These mood centers are essentially groups of different neurons spread throughout the brain, and when they are working well, the neurotransmitters are communicating smoothly and in a timely manner between brain cells involved in controlling mood. When the mood centers are malfunctioning, however, depression sets in. If depression was only a matter of insufficient levels of neurotransmitters, depression could be completely eliminated with medications, but we know that this is not the case. There is a significant time lag between beginning an antidepressant and more normalized neurotransmitter activity. It appears that antidepressants either slow down (downregulate) or speed up (upregulate) the brain cells in the mood centers, which seem to either be firing too fast or too slowly, thus causing depression.

One rapidly developing hypothesis has attempted to incorporate the entire series of changes that occur in chains of neurons. This hypothesis, called the *downstream effects theory*, recognizes a sequence of events that occurs (much like a domino effect) within and between cells that could explain why it typically takes antidepressants several weeks to take effect.

Other Biological Influences on Depression

Because there is some evidence to suggest that excess sodium moves into neurons during mood disorder episodes and that sodium balance returns during recovery, some scientists have suggested that abnormal metabolism of electrolytes in neurons contributes to depression. This theory may help to explain why lithium, a naturally occurring salt, has mood stabilizing effects. Abnormal biorhythms, particularly in the normal phases of sleep, are also being investigated as biological contributors to depression.

Another interesting, but yet unproven, theory about depression comes from evolutionary psychologists who study societal changes and mental health. They suggest that our genetics program us to thrive in a hunter–gatherer society and that these types of cultures are intensely social. Hunter–gatherers grouped themselves into large "clans," with members looking out for each other and each other's children for basic survival. Our lifestyles today however, with their emphasis on independence and mobility, have left us with 25 percent of our population living alone. The Internet, personal computers, and television have contributed to our isolation from others, even within our own homes. Some evolutionary theorists believe, therefore, that there is a mismatch between our genetic predisposition as social beings and our increasing isolation and that this could be a source of depression. As proof, they point to the hunter-gathering Kaluli tribe of New Guinea and the !Kung tribe of Africa, where major depressive disorder does not appear to exist. This theory also adds support to our notion of a depression that is unique to queer people, since many of us experience social rejection and, at times, isolation.

The Chicken or the Egg

So far in this chapter, we have been sketching a biological theory of depression. According to this perspective, the brain is a sophisticated engine that must have all systems in balance to operate efficiently. Mood disorders signal an electrochemical imbalance—a disequilibrium that can be chemically corrected. Consequently, many clinicians are likely to feel that antidepressants are among the best tools to treat people with depression.

Other theories of depression—those that emphasize psychological rather than biological causes—suggest that non-chemical events trigger our funks. We see or hear or think about stressful events, apply our own specific meanings to these events, and then, in response to these perceptions, our moods dip. To relieve depression, the sufferer must change the external stressors or the internal meanings he is attributing to them. According this theory, the most effective interventions are stress-management or self-help strategies that modify unpleasant circumstances or reduce troublesome thinking.

According to this version of events, brain chemistry will return to normal once these stressors are eliminated. This is the perspective favored by behavioral or cognitively oriented psychotherapists, and we discuss this approach in detail in chapter 6.

It is likely that a number of internal and external processes, of chemical and non-chemical events, play a role in depression. Consequently, some combination of interventions that takes into account *all* or *most* of the possible causes probably has the best chance for success. We will discuss treatments in greater detail later in the book.

Depression and Stress: The Hormone Connection

Neurotransmitters are just one type of mood-altering chemical produced by the body. We also produce *hormones*, those chemicals which make their most dramatic appearance at puberty. The changes that women experience during menstruation, pregnancy, and childbirth are also highly influenced by hormones, as is the infamous *premenstrual syndrome* (PMS). For men, hormones (or lack of them) can directly affect sexual functioning and are partially responsible for hair loss as we age. On the more positive side, hormones are also responsible for normal human growth, and for the regulation of our thyroid and adrenal glands.

A significant body of research links depression and hormones. For example, thyroid disease may cause some depressions. Consequently, a lingering depression is a good reason—as good as a broken leg or a nonstop headache—to get a medical exam.

In his wonderful book, *Why Zebras Don't Get Ulcers* (1998), Dr. Robert Sapolsky notes that people undergoing multiple life stressors are highly likely to develop a major depression. The connection is born out by the presence of high levels of adrenal hormones, typically secreted during stress, in the body fluids of depressed people. Researchers have concluded that the hormone–depression sequence begins with a stressful event. When we perceive a physical or psychological threat to our well-being, the hypothalamus increases production of *corticotropin-releasing factor* (CRF), which tells the pituitary to release *adrenocorticoid hormone* (ACTH). It also tells the adrenal glands to release *cortisol*, which evokes the body's normal "fight or flight" response. Among other things, cortisol helps muscles get the fuel they need to function more efficiently. This process, which regulates the body's response to stress, follows what is known as the *hypothalamic-pituitary-adrenal* (HPA) *axis*. As well as suppressing the appetite and sex drive, CRF acts like a stimulant, producing a state of hyperalertness. Activation of this system for brief periods of time during an actual threat is perfectly normal, yet remaining in such a state for a prolonged period is hard on the body. Eventually chronic stress suppresses the immune system, and leads to illness and depression.

The hypothalamic-pituitary-thyroid (HPT) axis has also been studied in people with affective disorders. Like the HPA axis, the HPT axis is a complex and highly integrated network that when disrupted (due to illness, for example) often results in emotional symptoms. Hypothyroidism (caused by an underactive thyroid) has long been known to cause depression. Recently, some researchers have suggested that subclinical forms of hypothyroidism, meaning that it doesn't reach a full-blown level, may be more common in depressed people than has been generally understood previously. More studies are underway to examine the relationship between thyroid function and depression.

Stress also affects the neurotransmitters. When a perceived threat speeds up the normal processes in the brain, the limbic system's supply of norepinephrine is quickly depleted. In short-term stressful situations, our brains soon recover. But when prolonged stress reduces such resilience, we are likely to slide into despair. Let's look, for example, at the profile of a chronically depressed person. During the first three or four episodes, the stress hormones and neurotransmitters seem to respond normally to external stress. After several depressions, however, the person's nervous and endocrine systems seem to have "learned" a depressive pattern. After this threshold is crossed, outside stressors are no longer necessary to trigger a bout of the blues. They seem to have a life of their own. Fortunately, even nervous systems inscribed with depression memories can benefit from effective treatment.

Depression in Women

Women experience higher rates of depression than men. Or perhaps men just don't report or experience depression the same way as women do. If women do indeed experience it more often, perhaps social inequities are to blame. After all, women make less money, have less access to good jobs and housing, and are more likely to be the victims of sexual assault and domestic violence. In addition women are socialized to turn their anger inward; in other words, to become depressed instead of enraged. All these factors contribute to women's depression rates. But the fact that women are more at risk for depression during menstruation, menopause, and immediately after birth (termed postpartum depression) suggests that fluctuating *estrogen* and *progesterone* levels are also playing a significant role in women's moods. Lending support to the hormone–depression link are the reports of women who claim that birth control pills have a negative effect on their moods. Perhaps the ingesting of certain manufactured hormones, in combination with the body's normal supply, triggers a mood alteration; or perhaps the absolute levels of these hormones affects the production of serotonin and norepinephrine levels. As with many hormone questions, the research jury is still out.

Aside from just hormones, women differ from men in many ways that may affect mood, including chromosomes, anatomy, social expectations, gender roles, life experiences, and personal psychology. Research into the complex interactions between these factors and how they affect mood is ongoing and holds great promise in carving out future treatments based on an individual's specific needs.

Genetics

Bipolar disorder seems to cluster in families. Other forms of depression also seem to be passed on from generation to generation. Rather than blaming one gene, researchers believe that a group of interactive genes are linked to depression. But purely genetic culprits are hard to pinpoint. After all, there are other inter-generational conduits for depression. Just growing up with depressed parents is likely to affect children's moods. Children in such households would learn maladaptive ways of coping as unconsciously as they learned to ride their bicycles. Or perhaps, aside from the inevitable role-modeling, depressed parents are more likely to discourage their children directly—assuring them that they will never be able to make the grade. Because the depression-contagion factor is so high among families, researchers can't be certain how much of the depression in a given family stems from nature, and how much from nurture (or lack thereof). To solve the controversy, they studied siblings who had been raised in different families. This study, though it did implicate genetic factors, was inconclusive. After all, while sisters and brothers from the same two parents would have similar DNA, each would have slightly different combinations of mom and dad's genes.

In theory, a study of identical twins, raised apart, could resolve the issue. Indeed such a study was conducted. The findings were startling. If one twin developed a major depression, there was almost a sixty percent chance that the other twin, raised by a separate family, would become depressed. In similar studies of fraternal twins (who come from two different eggs and don't share as many genes), the chance of both becoming depressed was only fifteen percent. The data from the identical twins study have since been discredited for a number of reasons. In the first place, the number of twins placed in different families was small. Secondly, the twins were often raised by families close enough to know of each other; consequently, the twins sometimes had contact. Finally, other research suggests that identical twins may have certain unique susceptibilities to mental illness. The resolution of the nature versus nurture question may have to be postponed until experimental methodologies are more sophisticated. Meanwhile, plenty of research has focused on the "gay" gene.

Genetics and Gayness

Flawed as they are, researchers nonetheless remain very fond of twin studies. According to one study, there is a fifty percent chance that, if one twin is gay, the other will also be queer. In fraternal pairs, there is only a twenty-two percent chance that both twins will be gay. Many gay men feel intuitively that they do have a strong biological predisposition to same sex attraction. Most lesbians seem less convinced. As with most other human traits, however, a specific gene has not been isolated that can fully explain sexual orientation, queer or straight.

National Cancer Institute researcher Dr. Dean Hamer is currently trying to isolate the "gay" gene or genes. He has found one gene on the X chromosome (called Xq28) that does appear to influence, but not fully determine, men's sexual orientation. Dr. Hamer is also quick to point out that he believes that social and psychological factors still play an important role in determining sexual orientation. According to Drs. Letitia Peplau and Linda Garnets, psychology professors at UCLA, such psychosocial factors do determine women's sexual orientation. Peplau and Garnets dismiss biological determinants, and emphasize the interpersonal and sociocultural contexts which, they maintain, shape and reshape women's fluid sexual orientation. An extensive twin study conducted in Australia in the early 1990s suggests that there is a difference between male and female homosexuality. The women surveyed were more likely to report slightly-to-moderate degrees of homosexual attraction while the men who claimed homosexual attraction were more likely to report high degrees (Bailey, 2000).

Dr. Simon LeVay, a neurobiologist at the Salk Institute in San Diego, believes firmly in the genetic predisposition theory of sexual orientation. In 1991, he studied the brains of sixteen heterosexual male cadavers and nineteen gay men who had died of AIDS. He discovered that a part of the hypothalamus in gay men was smaller on average than that of the straight men. Of course, now that we understand that the brain can physically change based on how we think and behave, we come back again to the old chicken/egg riddle: which comes first—the sexual behavior or the brain changes.

In addition to the fact that the study raised more questions than it answered, it was controversial. The study design was flawed. How, for example, could LeVay conclude that AIDS hadn't changed these men's brain structure? This was particularly important since the comparison group was heterosexual men who had not died of AIDS. Other researchers also pointed out that his sample was too small to be meaningful. Some wonder if this particular result was purely coincidental, comparable to the finding that queers have extra-long fourth fingers. Still others feel that Dr. LeVay, a gay man himself, was so determined to prove that sexual orientation is biological that his bias affected his interpretation of his findings. What everyone agrees upon, however, was his influence in shifting the debate about gayness into the biological arena.

In the very next year, researchers at UCLA did find evidence that gay men may have a larger cluster of nerve fibers connecting the left and right sides of the brain than heterosexual men. Again, it was not clear if behavior had caused the brain change, or visa versa.

We do know from animal studies that early experiences—particularly traumatic ones—alter the brain and body in measurable ways. As we noted in chapter 2, young gays and lesbians are particularly likely to be exposed to such stressors. Consequently, the cascade of external and internal factors is likely to kick off queer depression.

If a genetic basis for sexual orientation is ever discovered, it is unlikely to be associated directly with genes that are linked to mood disorders. We believe that the genetic factors that contribute to depression in queer people are the same as those that contribute to depression in non-queer people. What is different are the chronic external stressors gay and lesbians face.

Links between Brain Chemistry, Hormones, and Genetics

No one knows how exactly the neurotransmitter, hormonal, and genetic factors work together to produce depression, but Dr. Charles Nemeroff, a professor of psychiatry and behavioral sciences at Emory University School of Medicine, has proposed a plausible theory that links the three factors. It also explains why people who were traumatized as children go on to develop depression later in life.

Dr. Nemeroff believes that genes may either directly or indirectly lower the monoamines in the synapses or cause individual HPA axes to be more highly reactive to stress. In other words, the genes themselves don't necessarily cause depression; rather, they cause certain individuals to be more vulnerable to life's stressors. Nemeroff theorizes that if such vulnerable individuals experience stress in chidhood, their natural defenses are further suppressed and they are more likely to experience depression later in life. Dr. Nemeroff and his colleagues at Emory proposed that early abuse or neglect not only activate stress responses, but cause permanent increased activity in CRF-producing neurons. These neurons, as we discussed before, appear to be overactive in people who are depressed and seem to become supersensitive to stress, reacting strongly even to mild stressors. This response in people who have inherited a tendency toward depression could then trigger the biochemical and emotional/behavioral aspects of depression.

Imbibed Chemicals: The Ergo Factor

Hormones, brain chemicals, genetics, stress . . . whew! They make an imposing bio-cocktail. But other kinds of cocktails—the kind you order at your favorite bar—have the same mood-altering potential. Alcohol and depression have what we call an ergo relationship: I am depressed, ergo I drink; I drink, ergo I am depressed.

Alcohol is a central nervous system depressant. It alters the functioning of the brain and spinal cord. It impairs reasoning and coordination, as well as lowering inhibitions. After a drink or two, people who suffer from shyness may be able to socialize. Anxious people relax. Unassertive people may become assertive or aggressive. Such is the self-medicating power of alcohol. Some of the genies that emerge from booze bottles aren't so positive. As more alcohol is ingested, social impulses can turn into anti-social ones; and as alcohol blood levels fall, people typically feel tired and depressed. Long-term, heavy use produces an effect called *tolerance*. Tolerance simply means that your body gets so accustomed to regular amounts of alcohol that it takes more and more alcohol to experience the same positive effect you felt when you first started drinking. Tolerance is often the first step toward developing a dependence on alcohol. Over time, alcohol seems to change brain chemistry and make us more depression-prone.

Some medications produce the same short-term benefits are associated with alcohol. For example, Valium, Xanax, and Ativan reduce anxiety. They are also highly addictive and their prolonged use may trigger depression. Conversely, certain antidepressnts can reduce depression but increase anxiety in the long run. Complicating the picture further is the fact that all drugs have side effects. These unanticipated consequences range from negligible to noticeable, from negative to positive. For example, one potentially beneficial side effect of the antidepressant Elavil is drowsiness, which some physicians select to help their patients get to sleep. An antidepressant that is also an inadvertent sleeping pill can be very useful if insomnia has been an irksome symptom of the depression. The FDA (Food and Drug Administration) requires pharmaceutical companies to list the incidence of particular side effects on marketed drugs. If you are taking a prescribed medication, you may want to ask your doctor or pharmacist if depression is a potential side effect.

Mood Foods

More and more research reinforces what many of us know intuitively: What we eat can affect our moods. While a thorough exploration of the full relationship between nutrition and food is beyond our expertise and the scope of this book, we do know that diet affects depression. The mood-food link has been established by several studies.

Elizabeth Somer, M.A., R.D., author of the book *Food & Mood: The Complete Guide to Eating Well and Feeling Your Best* (1995), links fluctuations in our brain's level of serotonin directly to our diet. Serotonin is made in the brain from an amino acid called *tryptophan*. This particular amino acid is abundant in protein-rich foods. As tryptophan levels in the brain fall, so do the levels of serotonin. Paradoxically, that extra helping of roast beef tends to lower both tryptophan and serotonin. Lowered levels of these two chemicals can lead, in turn, to the blues and cravings for foods high in carbohydrates in some, but not all, people with depression. Why do the ones who feel this effect start carbo-loading when feeling down? Drs. Richard and Judith Wurtman at M.I.T. found that carbohydrates elevate brain levels of serotonin. More of this neurotransmitter makes most people feel better. Several specific conditions associated with depression, including seasonal affective disorder and PMS, have been linked with cravings for carbohydrates. These findings are very preliminary and deserve further study, but they do make sense for some people who are depressed.

Both simple sugars and complex sugars (starches) trigger release of insulin after they are digested and enter the blood stream. Starches take longer to digest so they enter the bloodstream over a longer period of time than simple sugars, which have molecules that can enter the bloodstream directly and more quickly. Insulin's role is to aid in the metabolism of sugar and to ensure that blood levels stay within normal, acceptable ranges. Too much sugar in the blood ultimately leads to coma but hypoglycemia (too little sugar) also can make the person feel sluggish, fatigued, and to the outside observer, "depressed." Hypoglycemia has been linked to irritability, hyperactivity, and depressed moods.

There also appear to be links between vitamins and moods. Deficiencies in vitamins A, B1, B2, B6, B12, C, niacin, and folic acid are all associated with depression. Low intake of the minerals calcium, iron, magnesium, selenium, or zinc has been reported to be associated with depression, mood swings, and irritability as well. Unless you are going to consult with someone who specializes in the nutritional alteration of mood, we suggest you stick to conventional wisdom about diet and eat plenty of fruits, vegetables, and grains. You may also find nutritionist Elizabeth Somer's book, *Food & Mood*, helpful. Keep in mind that while these findings are promising and interesting, the simple links we've made here are vast understatements of the complexity of the effect of diet on mood. Perhaps in the future sophisticated depression treatment plans will incorporate nutritional strategies as well as the other techniques we will discuss.

What I Wouldn't Give for a Good Night's Sleep

As mentioned several times earlier in the book, sleep disturbance, whether too much or too little, is a common symptom of depression. As you also remember from the earlier section on brain chemistry, the same areas of the brain that are involved in the experience of mood are also involved in regulating sleep, appetite, and sexual arousal. Depressed people often sleep less, and non-depressed people, when sleep-deprived, often become depressed. In other words, in another of those chicken-and-egg tableaus, depression (with and without mania) can cause insomnia and insomnia can lead to depression and/or mania. It is important to pay attention to the connection, particularly if your life circumstances—a new night shift at work, for example—scramble your sleep patterns. Alcohol and drugs can also interfere with sleep. The benzodiazepines (Valium, Xanax, Ativan), for example, induce lighter first stage sleep. But they also prevent deeper later stage sleep.

Other problems can get in the way of a good night's sleep. A disorder called sleep apnea prevents normal breathing. Sleepers afflicted with the condition may struggle—noisily, according to their partners—to clear the obstruction. Over time, the resulting shortage of oxygen may cause poor rest which in turn may cause depression. Decreased oxygen intake can cause constant headache, which certainly can cause one to have a hard time sleeping. Sleep apnea is serious enough to be deemed an official medical condition. It is usually treated with a breathing regulating device which improves sleep quality, and, consequently, daytime mood.

The connection between sleep and depression is also not always direct. Although in many cases the lack of sleep may be one of multiple contributors to depression, in a specific subgroup of depressed people, sleep deprivation may actually have an antidepressant effect. Of the thirty-six depressed people who participated in a recent study by Dr. Joseph Wu and his colleagues, fully one-third of them reported improvement in mood following a twenty-four-hour period of being deprived of sleep. The authors of the study found that the group of twelve that did respond to sleep deprivation in a positive way had different, specific patterns of brain activity from those who did not respond to being kept awake. Dr. Wu and his team believe that based on their findings, the dopamine system in the brain may be involved and that dopamine is increased during sleep deprivation for specific types of depression (Wu, 1999). Much research is needed into how best to use these interesting findings as a potential intervention, but each advance represents another step in understanding this disorder.

Putting It All Together

If you think about it for a minute, the implications of the foregoing chapters are awesome. You can zero in on depression and view it on a molecular level; or, if a sub-atomic perspective isn't your cup of tea, you can zoom out, and focus a wide-angled social lens on the subject. Both these perspectives, as well as everything in between, are valid. They are also useful. If the method of intervention generated by a particular perspective doesn't seem to help, don't lose heart. Just shift to another viewing magnitude, and another approach. Or try a combination. The angles of vision are infinite, the possibilities for intervention, just as myriad.

In the following chapter we will look at depression from yet another angle. This time, instead of changing the power of magnification, we're simply going to shift to the blues-sufferers themselves and let them tell their own stories.

CHAPTER 4

Blue Portraits

Queer Stories

The blues come in all shapes and sizes. There are small sorrows, midrange depressions, and monster slumps. Funks also come in different rhythms. Some are as inexorable, as routine as a heartbeat. Other blues sufferers may not even be aware that they are sliding into despair ... or mania. Some depressions are characterized by physical symptoms; others by moodiness. Some depressions are reactions to external events; others have deeply buried, internal roots.

Features that distinguish one depression from another are not simply the duration and intensity of symptoms; sociocultural factors like homophobia, ethnicity, and class background also shape the blues. They determine how we will express our sorrows and who will witness them. Some funks, for example, are certified as "real" by licensed professionals. Other depressions remain invisible. Perhaps these blues-sufferers find it more difficult to articulate their symptoms, or perhaps they do not have access to clinicians. Such "unofficial" depressions may still be acknowledged by friends and family; or perhaps they remain well-kept secrets, evident to no one besides the sufferer.

Age, ethnicity, and class background also limit the access blues-sufferers have to remedies. Those depressions diagnosed by professionals are more likely to be treated with psychotherapy and antidepressants. Less mainstream blues-sufferers may turn to friends and family, or try to medicate themselves with non-prescription drugs or alcohol.

Outcome is yet another differential dimension of the blues. Some blues-sufferers recover. Some learn to cope with chronic depression. And some decide life simply isn't worth living. Perhaps the best way to grasp the interplay of so many variables is to explore the lives of a few blues-sufferers. We hope the following profiles provide a glimpse of the myriad hues in the queer blues spectrum.

The Winter Blues

Ruth is fifty-three. She has been depressed since 1982. At first, her despair seemed to have a seasonal rhythm. As the days grew shorter, Ruth's symptoms grew more severe. First came the bad dreams; next the paralyzing apathy. More and more sluggish, Ruth would be unable to go to work. Eventually, she would cease all her usual activities. In the worst times, she couldn't leave home.

Ruth refers to the deepest periods of despair as The Time. *"There is," she says, "language for what happens before and after it. But there is no language for what happens during it." After a few years, the anticipation of* The Time *became a special form of torture. If she is trying a new remedy, hope becomes part of that torment. "The hope always has despair sewn to it," she says. "What if the remedy doesn't work?"*

Over the years she has tried everything: individual psychotherapy, special diets, even homeopathy. For a long period, she was also a regular member of a depression support group. Though it didn't relieve her despondency, it was an eye-opening experience. "I was amazed to learn about the range of depressions. Everyone in the group was different. Some people were moody, some sad, some irritable, but they all identified themselves as depressed. And it was where I first heard the term winter depression. It fit. The label itself was a relief."

Ruth has also gone through the gamut of antidepressants: Tricyclics, SSRIs, and MAOIs have all been prescribed at different times. "The Welbutrin were a nice red," she says. "But they didn't work either." What the antidepressants did do, however, was change the seasonal pattern of her depression. Instead of going downhill in the winter, she could become depressed at any time.

Ruth says her lover did her best to help. But her "pull-yourself-up-by-the-bootstraps" pep talks only made Ruth feel more out of step with the world. After nine years, the partner could no longer cope with Ruth's chronic depression. She left. Ruth relates this without bitterness. "I understand," she says, "the awful tension of wanting to make a depressed person feel better and being unable to."

Over the years, Ruth has used a number of frameworks to explain her depression: Her family were holocaust survivors, and Ruth says that she grew up with family who needed their children to be witnesses to their immense losses. She also believes she has a biological predisposition for depression. Perhaps because Ruth is a poet and a writer, the framework that is most appealing is a fictional one. It is the myth of Demeter and Persephone.

According to the story, Pluto spirited Demeter's daughter, Persephone, away to his underworld kingdom. When she discovered the abduction, Demeter was so grief-stricken that she laid waste to the earth. Nothing would grow again, she vowed, until her daughter was returned to her. A nervous Zeus ordered Pluto to return Persephone. Pluto obeyed Zeus, but because the abductee had already partaken of the underworld fare—munched on a few pomegranate seeds—Persephone had disqualified herself from full-time upper-world residency. Every year, when Persephone returns to the underworld for her obligatory stint, an inconsolable Demeter causes the world to become barren and wintry. Ruth says the myth has more resonance for her than other psychological and biological theories.

Several years ago, Ruth heard about Norman Rosenthal, a Washington, D.C. physician, who used a special lightbox to cure depression. After she had tried his regimen for over a year with no tangible results, he recommended that she move to a more southern latitude. At first she was reluctant to relocate. A radical dyke, she was afraid that she might not be able to find a community as compatible as the one she had lived in for the last eleven years. But she was lucky. Through her network, she was able to make new friends in St. Petersburg. She moved there a few months ago.

It is too soon to say if the climate change will make a difference. She does say that it feels good to be awakened by the sunshine streaming through her window. And, with obvious pleasure, she spots a gamboling shape in the waterway beyond her house. "Amazing," she says. "I think it's a manatee!"

Survivor Blues

Darrell, twenty-seven, heads the Men of Color program at an Atlanta AIDS organization. The director position is the culmination of a long, hard climb. Once a client at the agency himself, Darrell first "graduated" to the status of volunteer outreach worker. Eventually he was hired as a full-time staff member. A year ago, he was promoted to his current post. Darrell credits the other staff at the agency with getting him sane and keeping him grounded.

According to his mother, Darrell has inherited his father's moodiness. She says he was sensitive and withdrawn from the time he was born. Darrell has another story. He has a distinct memory of his first funk, and the event that triggered it. It happened when, as an eight-year-old, he was playing ball on the street with a bunch of neighbor kids. A gang of boys came careening around the corner on their bikes. At the time, Darrell says, they looked both big and bad. But thinking back now, he realizes that they couldn't have been more than ten or twelve. As they whizzed by, they looked him over and, apparently pegging him as one of them, shouted, "Hey, nigga, whatcha playin' with honkies for?" Darrell says he remembers yelling something back. He also remembers "falling into a bottomless tunnel." He felt so bad that he had to go home.

After that, Darrell says, it was easy for him to get into funks. Anything might set him off: getting dissed in school or taunted on the streets. But the worst spell happened when he found out he was HIV-negative.

All his friends had tested positive. He had always figured they were in the same boat. Whatever happened, they'd help each other out. He hadn't bothered to get himself checked out until protease inhibitors came on the scene. As soon as he got his results, he fell into the old familiar tunnel again. It was crazy, he knew, but he felt as though he had already lost everyone he cared about. He was going to be left behind.

After he got his results, he unplugged his phone and stopped going out. Except for work, he dropped out of sight. On weekends, he drank beer and watched TV. In his head, his life was over.

Darrell says he might still be hibernating if his sister hadn't gotten worried about him. Early one Sunday morning she started banging on his front door. She found him in bad shape, funky and hung over.

For all her concern, Darrell says she wasn't at all sympathetic. She surveyed the overflowing ashtrays and empty beer cans littering his apartment. Then, he says, she got on his case. "She told me to get off the pity pot or I was going to end up like our dad. She said that I had always been spoiled rotten. She said she wasn't going to leave until I got my butt off the couch."

Darrell tried to shoo her away, but she kept up the harangue. Eventually he gave up and agreed to go out with her. She took him to her church.

Darrell says she turned up the volume on her hymn-singing so high that she almost broke his eardrum. When he seemed a little slow to get down on his knees, she gave him a good yank. "That was the day," he says, "I got deprogrammed and reprogrammed all at once. Who did it? I don't know. It was either the holy spirit or my sister. You tell me." He shrugs and grins.

"After that," Darrell says, "one thing led to another and somehow I got to a conference for HIV-negative gay men. It was real good for me. Everyone was talking about what it meant to be HIV-negative . . . questioning it. "

A small caucus of African-American HIV-negative men got together at the conference and continued meeting afterward. They got him linked up with the AIDS agency. When he feels a funk coming on, he tells his friends and coworkers. They talk him through it.

Depression that has been the aftermath of the AIDS crisis defies easy classification. It is part old hurts, part fresh grief, part survivor guilt. "I am in sorrow because over 280 friends have died of AIDS," activist David Mixner says. For Mixner, the blues started way before the epidemic. "High school and college were an especially difficult time for me. I was blackmailed, contemplated suicide, made up identities in order to avoid being discovered. I was not allowed to mourn the death of my college lover" (Mixner, 1999).

This sort of multi-layered depression that both Mixner and Darrell have experienced is reflected by some curious statistics. In study after study, there is no difference in depression rates of gays who are HIV-positive and those who are HIV-negative. Both are at high risk for the blues. The depression that has engulfed our communities in the wake of the epidemic is a collective form of blues not mentioned in any of the standard texts on depression.

The Blues Times Two

Harry says he has not always managed his bipolar disorder effectively. Back when his problems began, a half century ago, treatment of serious psychiatric disorders seemed much less scientific. Sometimes they also seemed more punishing than helpful.

"It took years of me struggling with myself and the system before things started to get better," he remembers. Growing up gay in the 1930s was another part of the struggle. He has vivid, painful recollections. "Back then, there wasn't really even a word for what we were," he mused, "and we sure as hell didn't talk about it with our families."

Harry prefers not to chronicle his struggles in detail. "Let's just say that it wasn't all that much fun." He does admit that early on, he spent a good deal of time in psychiatric facilities, trying the "treatment du jour"—everything from cold water baths to insulin injections and major tranquilizers. It wasn't until 1975 that he was even finally diagnosed with bipolar disorder. Before that, he says, he had collected diagnoses that ranged from schizophrenia to psychotic depression. These labels were "semi-educated guesses" that, he believes, prevented him from getting effective treatment. Though his episodes of mania only occurred once or twice a year, they were severe enough to disrupt his life. He would be hospitalized for weeks, even months. Finally the mania would subside and he would start picking up the pieces of his life.

His doctors subscribed to the theory, prevalent at the time, that his mood swings were caused by "homosexual desires."

"Not all of my life was horrible," he says. The "smooth sailing" times included peaceful intervals with "the love of my life." Harry met Alan, an

actor, at a party in 1953. Alan was both "worldly and charming." And when he called Harry "sweet and handsome . . . well that was it. My heart just melted."

Over the course of their forty-three years together, they had almost as many "ups and downs" as Harry had mood swings. But the up times were enough to carry them through the bad ones. Harry credits Alan's unwavering support with getting him through the hospitalizations and the bouts of despair, guilt, and suicidal thinking. They were both relieved when a combination of new medications, individual psychotherapy, and a support group for people living with bipolar disorder kept Harry out of the hospital for longer periods. He eventually managed his condition so successfully that he has now gone over fifteen years without a single inpatient psychiatric stay.

Worse than the most horrible treatment back in the "old days," Harry says, was the day that he lost Alan to emphysema in 1996. The heartache is completely different from the depression he has experienced for so long. Losing Alan was like losing his lover, his father, and his soul mate all at once, he says somberly. Tears well up in his eyes. He clears his throat and turns his head. "The last few years have been especially hard."

About a year after Alan's death, Harry fell and broke his hip. After surgery to correct the fracture, Harry spent a few weeks in a skilled nursing facility. While he was there, learning to walk again, his friends suggested that he consider more supportive living arrangements.

At the continued urging of his friends, Harry sold the home that he and Alan had shared and moved into an assisted living facility. While he finds the center clean and the staff nice, he bemoans the fact that "they don't know squat about gay people." He misses his friends and thinks about Alan every day. When he feels particularly isolated and alone, he questions whether "life is worth it."

Gender Blues

In fifth grade, Kris's Catholic school changed their policy. They split the playground into two parts. Thereafter, the nun who supervised recess announced that the boys would play on the right side and the girls would play on the left. The boys' new space was twice as big as that of the girls. It was also level. The newly designated female zone, as well as sloping, was pitted at its lowest end with mud puddles. Kris knew where she belonged, and she refused to budge. She was sent to the principal's office.

Word of the episode spread like wild fire among her classmates. Soon they began to taunt her. "You think you're a boy. Eeuuuw, gross. You are so ugly. You are just like a boy. You must be a boy." When the taunts became unbearable, Kris would grab or punch whichever tormentor was close at hand. Back to the office she would go, for a time-out and another *lecture and a warning. The worst incident occurred right before summer break. Egged on by his pals, a sixth-grader grabbed her breast and crowed, "Hey, she's a girl! She's got titties." Then in a singsong voice: "I felt your titties. I felt your titties." Before he could dodge her, she got him in a hammerlock. She half-choked, half-dragged him to a giant puddle on the girls' side of the playground, and heaved him in. By then a crowd of other kids had gathered. When she saw the supervising nun striding in her direction, Kris fled into the principal's office. There, defiant and ashamed simultaneously, she blurted out her "crime."*

The nuns called her parents in and told them it would be better if she stayed home for the few weeks remaining in the school year. They also told them that she would not be welcomed back the following year. During the summer, Kris didn't go outside very often. Her brain felt fuzzy. She had trouble sitting in one place for very long. Whenever she ate, she felt sick. Often, after meals, she would lock herself in the bathroom, and stick her finger down her throat until she threw up. When she was sure she would be alone in the house, she used her Swiss Army knife to scratch her chest and her thighs. Watching the blood ooze out of the cuts gave her some momentary clarity and relief from the other, awful feelings. She made sure her clothes always covered the scabs.

Queer children's gender nonconformity makes them easy targets. Lonely, often desperate for attention, their depressions can easily be misconstrued as acting out. The problematic behavior further marks them as "different." Ever more alienated, they become more seriously depressed. Most ominous is that the depression, because it remains invisible, is never treated.

Border Crossing Blues

Enrique, thirty-four, grew up in Puerto Rico. For as many generations as they can remember, his family has lived in Manati, a village about 100 miles west of San Juan. Because his mother is the mantenedora, the local person who services the statues of the saints, she is well-known and respected in the town. As a boy, he helped her, bringing fresh flowers every day and arranging the bouquets the faithful brought. He also peddled small saints—santos—that his uncle taught him to carve. His uncle also taught Enrique how to be pasivo, that is, to be sexually receptive.

Enrique says that his family probably knew what was going on. His uncle had a reputation as a joledor, a stud, and Enrique's mother was happy it was Enrique and not one of his sisters. She was also happy because, from time to time, his uncle would slip some extra chabo into mother's apron pocket. Enrique says homosexuality was not a big thing: "No gay liberation.

No gay rights." And he adds, even though it was not talked about, it was not a secret. "At the festivals, there were always las mujeres locas, the drag queens. They would come at the end of the parade, after the caballeros and vegijantes. Us kids would make fun of them, but I knew right away I was one of them. So everybody knew everything and it was not necessary to talk about."

When he was twenty-nine, Enrique came to New York for work. A cousin who lived in the Bronx let him sleep on the couch and found him a job in a hospital cafeteria where he worked. Enrique says the cousin, his uncle's oldest son, was also activo, but his wife got angry when she caught them. She said things were different in America. Then she cursed him.

After the episode, Enrique began to have ataques de nervios at work. Sometimes he would feel dizzy and have to lie down. Other times, for no apparent reason, he would begin to sweat and tremble. His head would feel like a balloon. He was afraid that he was dying. Twice, during these attacks, he went to see a doctor in the emergency room of his hospital. Both times, the doctor took his blood pressure, told him he was all right, and sent him back to work.

Through a coworker, he got the address of a curandera. After she performed a limpia—a cleansing of bad spirits—the ataques became less powerful. He also prayed regularly to The Virgin. Eventually the bad spells stopped completely.

According to Dr. Francisco Gonzalez, the Medical Director of the Instituto Familiar de la Raza in San Francisco, homosexual behavior and identity is part and parcel of one's culture of origin. Strong family ties, the influence of the Catholic church, and highly differentiated gender roles structure the way many Latinos express their same-sex desires. As a result, recent immigrants may be doubly stigmatized. Already marked as different by language and skin color, they are also percieved as apolitical and rigidly role-bound—secretive instead of out and proud—by politicized, gender-flexing North American gays. The newcomers may find they have traded the comforts of a familiar environment and the support of a close-knit, loving family for a chilly reception by supercilious strangers with alien customs. Ironically enough, they may find that their depressions mark them—yet again—as outsiders.

According to Dr. Gonzalez, depression is as culture-bound as homosexuality. Western doctors, unaware of cultural differences, often believe that Latinos have a tendency to "somaticize" their problems. That is, they transpose mental and emotional problems into the physical sphere. Gonzalez challenges the assessment. What might be labeled somatization by western clinicians, he says, is in fact a holistic experience of the depression. Latinos experience their distress in their minds and bodies and spirits. Healing, to be effective, must address all dimensions of being. For Latino gays, it includes finding some cultural mirroring. "The chances aren't great," Dr Gonzalez adds a little wistfully, "that they will find it in the Castro."

Postpartum Blues

After the breakup, Terry says she couldn't eat or sleep. And she couldn't stop crying. She tried to keep herself busy by running mindless errands. And she always kept her two "bibles" with her: a book of affirmations for codependents and How to Survive the Loss of a Love (Colgrove, 1976). Whenever she stopped at a stoplight or waited in a line, she would pull one out and flip to a helpful passage. But, she explains, it wasn't the girlfriend part that broke her heart. It was losing her kid.

The irony was that she had never wanted a baby. She had fought Marisa tooth and nail. They had gone to couples' therapy over "the issue." Finally, Terry saw that there was no way out. So she made the best of it. She went through the online spermbank catalog, and even picked the donor: a second generation Italian-American who, from the specs, could have been a brother or a cousin. She was present in the delivery room and even though the baby wasn't the hoped for girl, she felt in love at first sight.

Sleeping, eating, all their recreation hinged on the baby's schedule. And of course—just as Terry had predicted—their sex life dwindled to an occasional quickie. But Terry didn't care that all her misgivings had come true. The pleasures of parenting, of watching her kid grow up, made it all worthwhile.

When Zach was two, Marisa announced that she was in love with someone she had met on the Net. They had been having online rendezvous for a year and half, and after a real life meeting, had decided to move in together. Marisa was going to move across the state to her new lover's hometown.

Terry sued for parental custody. The superior court judge ruled that she had no claim on Zach because she was not related to him through blood or marriage. Legally she was a "third party" and third parties seeking custody "had to prove unfitness or abandonment by the 'real' parent in order to challenge his or her rights."

After the ruling, Terry started planning her suicide. "I thought I didn't really deserve to live . . . I was convinced that I had done something wrong . . . that I hadn't been a good enough parent or lover. I knew that the woman she was leaving me for would be a better mom. She had a hotshot job. My imagination just went crazy. I drove myself crazy picturing them all together . . . A happy little family."

Terry credits a couple from their lesbian parent support group for sav-
ing her. They made her call her family doctor who, after an examination,
prescribed antidepressants. They also moved her into their house, made her
soup, and turned on the electric blanket for her in the spare bedroom. Their
month-long vigil really got her through the worst time. Terry says she knew
she had turned a corner when her suicidal thoughts changed to revenge
fantasies.

Over time, the homophobic customs, attitudes, and beliefs that
we encounter on an everyday basis have a confidence-eroding effect.
By the time legislatures or courts rule against us in immediate,
life-changing ways, our psychological immune systems are already
compromised. Instead of feeling outraged and indignant, we become
despondent. But the last straw is betrayal by an intimate. We are
even more likely to turn our anger inward if someone from our own
tribe, a partner we have shared our lives with, has used institutional-
ized homophobia to gain the edge in a private battle.

The Double Closet Blues

By using a series of codes, aliases, and passwords to disguise his
tracks, David has been able to leave his restricted RL (real life) and join the
gay cyberworld. Even if one of his siblings could turn on his computer, he
says they would never be able to read his files. Still, he says, he feels para-
noid all the time.

By any measure, David is an outstanding teenager. He is the junior
class president of the Mormon academy he attends and he won the Kiwanis
Club's outstanding citizenship award. He attends temple several times a
week and has organized a youth service group.

David is also an entrepreneur. In addition to all his activities, he has
managed to start his own deck-refinishing business. He is a responsive,
respectful son, and an exemplary model for his younger siblings. His parents
are delighted with him.

No one in the family suspects David of leading a secret life. Yet, since
he turned thirteen, David has been fantasizing about other boys. He imag-
ined what his classmates might look like naked. He pictured himself touch-
ing and kissing them. And he imagined them responding passionately.

David says it would kill his parents if they knew. His grandfather, a
church elder, has made it clear that that any form of premarital sexual
behavior is wrong. These injunctions even extend to sexual thoughts.

At first, David tried very hard to control himself. "I'm a Mor-
mon—I'm like, how could God possibly do this to me?" he asks. "My
mother's always saying how wonderful it will be when I find a girl I love,

get married, so she can have lots of grandchildren. And every time she says it I get really stressed and panicked. "

When he was fifteen, David bought his own computer. Hoping to find some companionship online, he typed "gay" and "teen" into a search engine. Almost immediately, he was in touch with a whole gay world: resource centers, advice columns, personals, chat rooms, message board, porn sites.

David says that for a while it seemed like a lifesaver. But every time he seems to be getting into a relationship, his cyber pal disappears. "His e-mail address just stops working . . . just like that. Maybe he moved. Maybe he wasn't real in the first place."

To protect himself from "cybercreeps and stalkers," David lies about who he is and where he lives. He even e-mails his cyber pals a phony photo of himself. "Hey," he says, "If I'm not real, why should they be?"

After he gets burned, David crashes emotionally. "I feel so sad and lonely sometimes. I'm sure I'll never meet anybody." Those are the times he has to push himself to get up in the morning. And, for a while, he stays off the Net. But isolation and the hope for some connection always drive him back.

Recent studies show that the average age most young adults identify as gay has dropped from twenty to fifteen (Egan, 2000). This accelerated coming out timetable has tremendous implications. At twenty, most young adults have left home. Consequently, the life of a twenty-year-old queer—though certainly not trouble free—is at least not subject to direct parental scrutiny. For the fifteen-year-old, the story is very different. Anonymity is not an option. His gay lifestyle puts him on a direct collision course not only with friends and schoolmates, but with mom and dad in the next room, or the kid brother who sleeps in the bed next to his. Consequently, he must guard his secret with particular vigilance.

The irony is intense. At the same time that the new technology allows David to show more of himself, he must become more adept at hiding himself—both online and off. The need to cohabit double closets puts gay youth at high risk for the blues.

Ghost Sickness

At fifty-one, Leah thought that she was incredibly lucky. She had a great job, wonderful children, an ideal partnership , and she was seemingly (finally!) at the end of menopause. Then Carol, her lover, was diagnosed with breast cancer.

There was no trace of malignancy in Carol's lymph nodes. After a lumpectomy, and chemotherapy, her prognosis was excellent. Leah, on the other hand, went into a tailspin. She could not shake her sense of impending loss.

Leah had grown up in an orthodox Jewish home. The oldest of six children, she had assumed the role of assistant mom, caring for her younger siblings and doing much of the domestic work. Leah's family was devastated when, during Leah's junior year in high school, her mother was diagnosed with ovarian cancer. Leah, who had been particularly close to her mother, found herself numb with despair. Unable to reveal her grief to equally stricken family members, she began to mother her siblings obsessively. Already an A student at school, she became even more zealous about her schoolwork. When it came time to select a college, she agonized for several weeks before deciding to stay home. She would get an office job, and continue as surrogate mother until her siblings were ready to go off on their own.

When Leah was twenty-six, her youngest sister graduated from high school. Leah realized that it was time to begin her own life. Though she felt awkward and uncomfortable about the prospect of dating, she knew that her father valued marriage and family. She accepted a movie invitation from Steve, a supervisor in her office.

She and Steve eventually married and by age thirty, Leah had two children of her own. Although the marriage was comfortable enough, and Steve was an excellent father, Leah began to realize that something was missing in her life. Her dissatisfaction led her to explore a women's support group at the reform synegogue in her neighborhood. There she first met Carol, an open lesbian with a child from a previous marriage.

Although she had never thought of herself as a sexual being, Leah found herself increasingly attracted to Carol. Having come out completely as a lesbian after only three years of marriage, Carol embodied a strength and spirituality that Leah had never known before. Leah and Carol's intimacy grew. Her relationship with Carol made her feel strong and worthy and complete for the first time in her life. She says the most difficult decision of her life was to ask Steve for a divorce.

During the fifteen years that they have been a family, Leah and Carol have never spent a night apart. Both agree that they are so attuned that they can read each other's thoughts. Such intimacy makes the thought of losing her soul mate unbearable to Leah.

In the days after Carol's diagnosis, Leah couldn't stop worrying. Did Carol have the best doctor? Could she tolerate chemo? Would the cancer come back? At night, Leah had recurrent nightmares about impending disasters. Unable to save Carol, her crying and thrashing would wake them both up.

It was Carol who finally urged Leah to get into therapy. Though she prides herself on her self-reliance, Leah was desperate enough to acquiesce.

She found the therapist warm and supportive. It was easy to talk about her growing up experiences. As she was describing the loss of her mother, Leah remembered that she had learned about her mother's diagnosis only by overhearing a conversation between her father and his sister. At the time, she also remembered making a decision not to cry. She didn't want to seem weak in front of her siblings.

Over the next month, as Leah allowed herself a much delayed grief reaction over her mother's death, she stopped fretting about Carol's care. She began to sleep well again. One night after a particularly emotional session, she dreamed that she was back in her old family home. Her mother appeared, and though no words were spoken, Leah felt her presence intensely. For the first time in months, she woke up with a sense of well-being.

Angst into Art: A Queer Postscript

Recovery from the blues seems to require us to come up with our own accounts—the whys and wherefores of our depressions. Some of us get help from outsiders, therapists or other healers who help us craft our stories. Some of us use other sources—literature or history—to understand and explain our sorrows. One underutilized source of possible meanings may come from within our own tribe. That is, other queers who have written about the blues may help us to develop our own unique accounts. We hope the following excerpts provide such inspiration . . . or, at the very least, a sense of being in eminent company.

> *Only I remain burning in the dusk*
> *After the sun has stripped the world of its rays*
> *Whereas other men take their pleasure, I do but mourn*
> *Prostrate on the ground, lamenting and weeping.*
>
> Michelangelo, 1522
> *Gay Roots*, 1993, p. 148

> *I know not how it is, I feel as if I was going to have an illness . . . My head seems heavy, as if it was too full & that this occasions a pressure over my eyes which makes them not bear reading. I am not right by any means.*

Anne Lister, 1821
I Know My Own Heart, 1992, p. 150

This is the Hour of Lead—
Remembered, if outlived,
As Freezing persons, recollect the Snow—
First—Chill—the Stupor—then the Letting Go—

Emily Dickinson, 1860.
The Complete Poems of Emily Dickinson,
1960, p. 162

My life is now full of emotional complications which make me
write good verse—at least a lot of it—but makes my mental
chart a series of dizzy leaps up and down, ecstasy one
moment—O dapple faun!—and consummate despair the next.
Never thought I could go through something like this again!
But never do you know! . . . Isn't it hell? But, oh God,
Stinkie, I wish you could see him in his blue tights!

Tennessee Williams, 1940
Tennessee Williams Letters to Donald
Windham, 1976, p. 8

Down, down, down into the darkness of the grave
Gently they go, the beautiful, the tender, the kind;
Quietly they go, the intelligent, the witty, the brave.
I know. But I do not approve. And I am not resigned.

Edna St. Vincent Millay, 1949
Middle of Winter, 1982, p. 157

I make myself cry, in order to prove to myself that my grief is
not an illusion: tears are signs, not expressions. By my tears,
I tell a story, I produce a myth of grief, and henceforth I
adjust myself to it: I can live with it, because, by weeping, I
give myself an emphatic interlocutor who receives the "truest"
of messages, that of my body, not that of my speech . . .

Roland Barthes
A Lover's Discourse, 1978, p. 182

I sometimes feel it is a Laocoön struggle between anger and
my life itself, as if anger were a witch who has had me in her
power since infancy, and either I conquer her or she conquers
me once and for all through the suicidal depression that fol-
lows on such an exhibition of unregenerate behavior.

Mary Sarton
Journal of Solitude, 1973, p. 27

For the next weeks, elation alternated with intense and utter despair. I was devoted to my wife and two children and was nearing completion of training in a profession that was prejudiced against and intolerant of homosexuals. I was excited by the prospect of expressing my sexual passion, but I could not conceive how the confines of my life would ever permit this.

Dr. Richard Isay
Becoming Gay, 1996, p. 28

The best way I can describe it is as a kind of distaste, or at least lack of enthusiasm, for the kinds of objects and experiences that other people seemed to get pleasure from: not just dolls and dresses and behaving the way girls (as opposed to boys) were supposed to, but something about the very nature of life itself—talking, eating, getting dressed, washing one's face—struck me as unbearably tedious. Perhaps, as with so much of queer life, it simply came down to a matter of taste . . .

Jane Delynn
A Woman Like That, 1999, p. 53

CHAPTER 5

Tips for Main Squeezes

How to Cope with a Depressed Partner

Something strange has happened, but you can't put your finger on it. Those wickedly funny quips—the ones you've always said he should turn into a comedy act—have stopped. So has that mad bedroom fandango, his way of letting you know that it was time for you to get up and take the dog for a walk. The affectionate neck-nibbles when you were hunkered over the kitchen sink, scrubbing the lasagna pan, have also stopped. You assume he's having a few bad days and try to focus on other things. But then, without any warning, he snaps at you about something inconsequential. Perhaps he found some sour milk in the back of the refrigerator; perhaps a bill came back because one of you forgot the stamp. He has also morphed into a TV junkie. Always scornful of couch potatoes, he now watches mind-numbing sitcoms for hours. All your suggestions for diversions—a walk on the beach, a weekend getaway—are ignored. After a while, you begin to feel lonely, desperate really, for any kind of connection (even an angry one). So this time it is you who snap. It happens after you can't stand the drone of the TV for another minute. But as soon as you see your partner's haunted expression, you regret your outburst. You feel guilty, confused, angry. Who is this person you have lived with and loved for years? Has your real partner been abducted by an alien spaceship? And what the hell are you supposed to do with this imposter who's been left behind? Eventually, you too start to feel lousy. You wonder if you're coming down with something.

It's easy to get caught up in a partner's funk. We cajole, distract, blow up—in short, try every strategy we can think of to get him to be "normal" again. Perhaps we attribute our partner's altered behavior to stress. We try to take over more of the household chores. Perhaps we decide that our beloved is just being a prima donna. Perhaps we try to outdo what we assume is a hissy fit by throwing an even grander one ourselves. The idea that a soul mate is suffering from depression may never even occur to us. And the depressed partner is probably not offering much in the way of clarifying information. He may not know he is depressed himself. He is certainly not in the mood to bare his soul. In fact, the non-depressed partner may be lucky if she or he hears an occasional grunt emanating from the vicinity of their gloomy girl- or boyfriend. With so few cues coming from a despondent mate, partners are in the dark. They have to guess what the person they love is thinking, feeling. It is easy to see why the partners of depressed people often slip into the twilight zone themselves.

Myths You May Have Heard

We believe that being informed about depression is the best way to cope with a withdrawn and melancholy partner. One good starting place is to examine the conventional misconceptions about depression. The following myths, adapted for queer partners, come from Dr. Mitch Golant and Susan Golant's book, *What to Do When Someone You Love Is Depressed* (1996).

Myth #1: Anyone can overcome depression with enough willpower.

From the outside looking in, it seems as though the depressed person lacks motivation. Well-meaning, but misguided partners are convinced that all that is needed is a little jump start. They try all the old incentives: everything from sales pitches about the benefits of fresh air and exercise to bribes. When neither wheedling, sulking, nor atta-boy encouragement works, partners may resort to sniping, shaming, or barking angry demands. Unfortunately, the underlying belief—that your partner or friend lacks the character or strength to pull himself out of it—is an inaccurate one. Imagine telling someone who had heart problems, "If you just had more guts, you could get rid of that pacemaker!" In fact, any sort of badgering only makes the situation worse. It amplifies the self-torture that the depressed person is already inflicting on himself. His internal voices only become more critical. The truth is that depression is an illness. Partners did not cause it. They cannot cure it.

Myth #2: It's all in your loved one's head.

Even the experts have trouble untangling the psychological and physiological aspects of depression. In the first place, depression—for many people—seems to have a biological component. The picture is further complicated by the fact that, in some instances, depressed people have underlying medical conditions. For example, changes in eating and sleeping patterns that usually indicate depression can also signal a thyroid dysfunction. Or perhaps a partner who seems uncharacteristically listless is anemic, or has a viral infection. To make matters even fuzzier, certain medical disorders are often accompanied by clinical depression. Examples of such illnesses include fibromyalgia (a painful, chronic muscle disease) and chronic fatigue syndrome. In addition, heart attacks, traumatic accidents and injuries, and strokes are often followed by depressive symptoms.

Because depression can appear in so many guises, and has so many possible contributing factors, it is important to resist any attempts to diagnose your partner yourself. But you can suggest that they schedule a consultation with their physician. And if you feel like being extra supportive, offer to go with her, or meet her for coffee afterward.

Myth #3: Depression is something to be ashamed of.

There is no doubt that many people view mental or emotional problems as weaknesses or as evidence of a personal deficit. Just a few generations ago, it was common for a family to be ashamed if one of its members "gave in" to a mental illness. Such a moral failing was evidence that the family suffered from inferior "breeding" or defective stock. In order to avoid social stigma, families would keep mentally ill members safely hidden away in "lunatic" asylums for decades. Until relatively recently, such asylums were little more than warehouses for the mentally ill—that embarrassing aunt or cousin nobody wanted to deal with. The mere threat of placement in these facilities was often enough to spark the spiraling sense of shame that frequently accompanies depression.

Amplifying the stigma associated with mental illness are the scores of melodramatic films and TV exposés of the grim—even nightmarish—conditions in mental institutions. Emblematic of these portrayals was the classic 1948 movie, *The Snakepit*. The title says it all. More recently, the Winona Ryder film, *Girl, Interrupted*, portrays a woman who is placed in a facility against her will and diagnosed inappropriately. Hollywood has hyped and sensationalized mental illness and mental asylums. Unfortunately, in some cases, mental health systems have lived up to their bad reputations. Terry Taylor, a nurse and passionate AIDS and gay rights activist, remembers when queer men were treated with electroshock therapy simply because they were gay. "I look back now and think about a time when the mental health system had some woefully wrong ideas about sexual orientation." Now, even though the majority of mental health practitioners no longer consider homosexuality a mental illness, the stigmatizing link between gayness and psychological dysfunction has never dissolved completely.

Gays and lesbians are not immune to the cultural biases about psychological problems. If your partner is depressed, she may even be more susceptible to these prejudices. Perhaps she is ashamed of her "weakness." Perhaps, in her gloomiest moments, she wonders whether her depression may have something to do with her gayness. Perhaps this negative self-assessment prompts her to isolate herself. She stops calling her friends who, in turn, stop calling her. Perhaps she tells herself that they no longer have time for her and, in fact, were only feigning friendship in the first place.

It is important for partners to be sensitive to the shame spiral in which their depressed partners may be caught.

Myth #4: Your productivity suffers when you're depressed.

We've heard it dozens of times, and when life seemed overwhelming, we've probably even made the I'm-going-to-pull-the-covers-over-my-head announcement ourselves. The notion that depression is synonymous with bedroom retreats and emotional paralysis is widespread. Again, Hollywood is partially responsible. The image of the hibernating hero or heroine has been featured prominently in plenty of movies. In *Men Don't Leave*, for example, Jessica Lange portrayed a woman recovering from the loss of her husband. Overwhelmed by financial problems and a move to a new city to search for work, she takes to her bed for days at a time. A stranger, played by Joan Cusack, forces her way into the slug-a-bed's apartment, opens up the shades, and pushes her into the shower in an attempt to "snap" her out of it.

While depression certainly causes some people to cocoon themselves in sleep and sloth, plenty of despondent people continue to be productive. In fact, the majority of depressed people remain functional and meet most responsibilities. Ironically, those who feel most overwhelmed may even become hyper-functional. In other words, your partner may be depressed *and* active—even hyperactive. He may have learned that staying busy is an effective way to ward off melancholy and fatigue.

Myth #5: Psychotherapy doesn't work.

This is an easy one! If the bad news is that your partner is depressed, the good news is that, in the majority of situations, she can look forward to getting some relief. Depression responds well to treatment. The type of treatment will depend on the severity of the depression. Many studies have shown that psychotherapy alone is an effective remedy for depression (Chambless, 1998). More severe depressions are often treated by a combination of psychotherapy and antidepressants. There is some evidence that these two modalities, in combination, enhance your partner's chances for recovery (Persons, 1998).

Myth #6: Antidepressant medications are worthless or dangerous.

It's hard to know what to believe. On the one hand, we are bombarded with stories about "miracle" drugs, cures for everything from AIDS to Alzheimer's disease. On the other hand, any second-grader can give you a rap about the perils of drug-taking. If you're hooked, your goose is cooked. Addicts, we all know, will lie, steal, even murder to get the substance they crave. In this contemporary morality tale, these lost souls end up dirty, sick, and homeless. They die alone. No one notices or mourns their passing. Yikes, we think. If we're not careful, it could happen to us!

Because both the pro- and anti-drug camps peddle their messages so relentlessly, most of us have settled the matter in our own heads by believing *both* stories. We picture legions of lab-coated chemists laboring over the frothy broths that will one day improve our lives. At the same time, we know that scores of Colombian coca growers are conspiring to ruin them. This two-tiered system is easy to misapply. For example, someone who wouldn't hesitate to take penicillin might balk at antidepressants because they fall into the "bad" drug category. Part of their refusal may be related to addiction anxiety; part of their reluctance may be due to a conviction that reliance on medications is a sign of fragility or inadequate willpower. After all, only weak people need such "crutches." But antidepressants are neither crutches nor sirens-in-a-syringe. For many people, they are a remedy for a real problem—the one remedy that offers the best chance of positive results.

A capsule summary of the history of Prozac is perhaps the best way to illustrate the to-ing and fro-ing in our heads and in the culture at large about the subject of medicating depression.

When Prozac was first introduced, it was heralded as a miracle drug. It was also simultaneously demonized—the target of bad publicity. According to a flurry of largely unsubstantiated reports, people who took the drug were likely to become suicidal or homicidal. Even though subsequent studies seem to substantiate the manufacturer's claim that the drug is more effective than any previous antidepressant, and has fewer side effects, the battle between the pharma-philes and the pharma-phobes continues to rage. The "better-than-well" pro-Prozac claims made in Peter Kramer's best-selling book *Listening to Prozac* (1997) have recently been challenged by the popular anti-Prozac tracts, Peter Breggin's *Talking Back to Prozac* (1995) and Joseph Glenmullen's *The Prozac Backlash* (2000).

Prozac has now been available for over a decade. Subsequent studies continue to prove its efficacy. Other drugs in the same family have also proven reliable, safe, and effective, and perhaps more importantly, non-addictive.

If your partner has decided to take antidepressants, it is important to monitor your own apprehensions. Are you nervous about addiction? Will you be scrutinizing him for telltale signs of an altered state? Are you going to expect him to get jittery between doses, to count down the minutes until his next "fix"? If so, your fears are unfounded. He probably *will* be waiting impatiently for the time to pass—not the hours until his next dose, but the months until he can get off antidepressants.

But perhaps you're in the other camp. If you've put your faith in miracle cures you might want to check out the following myth.

Myth #6A: Antidepressant medications are miracle drugs that will transform your life.

This is the flip side of Myth #6. Plenty of boomers and gen-x-ers who have come of age in the era of high-tech miracles and chemical transformations may be convinced that there is no problem drugs cannot solve. Want to lose weight? Become the life of the party? Have an erection? Find a permanent partner and make a million bucks? Well, just pop one of those magic bullets and your wish will come true. The fact is that antidepressants may not help your partner's mood. They do not work for everyone. Or, if they do relieve his depression, they may cause so many side effects that your partner may decide the trade-off isn't worth it. For example, a substantial portion of antidepressant consumers complain about reduced sex drive. A smaller proportion of people who take these drugs report other unpleasant side effects ranging from weight gain to sleep problems to headaches to an inability to feel the exhilarating highs they used to experience between depressive bouts. In short, antidepressants are not miracle drugs, and in some cases, they do not even help.

Seeing your partner experience unpleasant side effects or experiencing them yourself (if your partner's sex drive plunges) may make you a little less certain about claims of medical miracles. In fact, look closely at some of the data that "proves" the efficacy of antidepressants, and you may find that drug companies funded the study. In other words, a bit of skepticism is probably healthy. It will modify your own unrealistic expectations and help you be more sensitive to some of the choices your partner is facing.

Myth #7: All depressions are alike.

In chapter 1, we mentioned several different types of depression. The word *depression* itself has come to signify a variety of moods—everything from normal sadness to severe, clinical "depression" and suicidal behavior. Diverse people experience depression in diverse ways. Take the two gay authors, Emily Dickinson and May Sarton, for example. Emily Dickenson's poetry suggests that she often experienced life as flat and monochromatic:

There's a certain slant of light
On winter afternoons,
That oppresses, like the weight
Of cathedral tunes.

In contrast, May Sarton's journals reveal that she was in a constant state of volcanic upheaval. Both were experiencing depression.

Even people of the same age with a similar diagnosis of clinical depression vary. They may behave in totally opposite ways and will seem, despite identical struggles, to have nothing in common.

In the past, you may have suffered through the depression of a friend or parent. Perhaps you've been depressed yourself. Don't be surprised, however, if your partner's particular shade of the blues fractures all your preconceived notions about what it means to be depressed.

Myth #8: Depression and substance abuse aren't related.

As we discussed in chapter 3, there is a clear relationship between depression and substance abuse or dependency. It is important to remember that many substances ingested for recreational purposes are depressants; that is, they have a depressive effect on the central nervous system. People who abuse drugs and alcohol are therefore very likely to become depressed, and people who are already depressed are more likely to abuse drugs and alcohol. Substance abuse and depression are so connected, in fact, that many treatments for people in recovery from alcohol and other drug abuse and dependency specifically target feelings of depression. Consequently, abuse recovery programs often include support groups, individual psychotherapy, and a regimen of antidepressant medications.

For partners with depressed mates, substance abuse is a particularly sticky issue. Perhaps one of your favorite ways to unwind together is to go out and have a few drinks. If he is abstinent, how will you be able to enjoy your downtime together? Or, perhaps you've supported his addictions by covering for him when he couldn't get up for work, or finished his grad school term papers when he was in no shape to do it himself. If substance abuse is implicated in your partner's depression, then chances are you've played some role—albeit an unintentional one. The first step toward extricating yourself from an enabling role might be to go to an Al-Anon meeting. These meetings are free, in many cities gay or gay-friendly, and provide support and guidance for partners of substance abusers.

Myth #9: Depression is common in lesbians and gays because they are psychologically impaired.

We added this myth to the ones identified by the Golants because of our own clinical experience in the queer world. Despite much evidence to the contrary, there is a lingering belief among less informed Americans that gays and lesbians are mentally ill. Numerous studies disprove this contention. The psychological test scores of gays and non-gays, in study after study, are not significantly different: There are mentally healthy gays and mentally healthy heterosexuals. There are emotionally disturbed gays and there are, in equal proportion, emotionally disturbed heterosexuals. Being gay or straight does not correlate with mental health or illness. The same is true for depression. The rate of depression is comparable in both groups. As we noted in chapter 2, however, because gays and lesbians have to contend with a homophobic society, they may be differently depressed.

Myth #10 Depression is something that could never happen to me.

We've included this myth to counter a couples' dynamic that can develop when one mate becomes depressed. Over time, the blue partner turns into an "identified patient." In addition to being perceived as incompetent, she may get the blame for all the relationship problems. "If only you weren't so depressed, then . . ." goes the familiar refrain. Almost by default, the non-depressed partner becomes an exemplar of robust mental health. Because such a polarization is ultimately destructive to partnerships, we want to emphasize that depression is not an exotic illness. In the course of our lifetimes, most of us will experience some form of it. Just to prove our point, we'd like you to induce a mini-depression right now. The process is quite simple. Sit in a chair with minimal back support. Slump forward. Put your head in your hands and repeat over and over, "God, what an asshole I am. I am such a pathetic excuse for a human being. Someone should really put me out of my misery. Life is such a fucking joke. There is absolutely no reason for me to stick around." Continue in this morose vein for a few minutes. Then take your emotional pulse. When you see how easy it is to work yourself down into a funk, it will be easier to identify with your partner and to avoid the burdens that relentless mental health imposes.

To Help or Not to Help?

Now that we've cleared away some of the myths that distorted your understanding of depression, it might be useful to talk about some of the ways you can help. When someone you love is hurting, you may have to deal with your own share of critical voices. "Don't just stand there," they may screech. "Do something!" After all, if you *really* loved your partner, you couldn't just sit there and watch her suffer, because if you did, you'd be labeled (or label yourself) a bad partner, cold and uncaring.

What is the best way to help someone who is depressed? Should you try to cheer them up by telling them jokes? Make them breakfast in bed? Bring them flowers? While it is clear that showing support to someone who is depressed is critically important, some demonstrations of concern are more effective than others.

One of the first dilemmas you face is that your partner may not acknowledge that he or she is depressed. As we mentioned earlier, depression can occur very slowly over time, so insidiously, in fact, that changes may not be apparent until they are severe. Our first suggestion is for both of you to become aware of the formal symptoms of depression listed in chapter 1. There are other, less formal, but equally important markers of depression that you may notice.

Informal Signs of Your Partner's Depression

1. You notice that your partner is smiling less. It may even seem as if his smile muscles have frozen. His whole demeanor may have become uncharacteristically somber.

2. She has begun to complain about stomachaches and headaches.

3. He has begun to watch more TV.

4. Her alcohol or recreational drug use has increased.

5. He is wearing darker clothes.

6. Her sleeping or eating patterns have changed.

7. He has started to fret over details. Perhaps he has become obsessed with bills, work tasks, or even health concerns.

8. She stops taking care of herself. Chores are left undone. Personal habits are neglected. If your partner had been a fitness fanatic before, for example, she may stop going to the gym. Perhaps she stops jogging or meditating or walking the dog. She may neglect the activities which, in the past, she depended upon to reduce tension or energize herself.

9. You may notice that your partner seems reluctant to make or keep dates with friends. Perhaps she stops taking phone calls. If she was formerly the "social director" in your relationship, you may notice that she hasn't made efforts to schedule or follow through on planned activities.

10. The quality or frequency of sex changes. Perhaps your partner is less playful. Or he may be completely disinterested in sex.

11. The characteristic ways that your partner has expressed herself may change. Perhaps she cries more easily. Or if she cried easily and frequently before, she may stop completely. Perhaps she is less animated. Perhaps she speaks in a monotone. You may notice that many of the old highs and lows you shared are missing.

12. Your partner's customary chattiness has been short-circuited. Meals have become quiet and awkward events. Your attempts to start conversations may be deflected with a monosyllabic "yep" or "uh huh." The only topics worth discussing may be how life sucks and/or the obsessions mentioned in number 2.

13. Your partner complains that she has disappointed everyone—you, her friends, her co-workers. She seems unable, no matter what contrary evidence you present her with, to escape from this downward spiral of self-blame.

If you have a strong hunch that your partner is depressed, what should you do next? In our opinion, your next step depends on who recognizes the depression first and how the issue is broached. If your partner is aware of what has been happening to him or her, and tells you about it, you may be able to sit down together and, in a direct way, discuss the ways you can work together to improve the situation. As you finish the rest of this book, you will have a better grasp of ways to manage depression together and/or with professional assistance.

If your partner is unaware of her depression, however, or if she does recognize it but seems unable or unwilling to take steps to manage the problem, it may be a bit more challenging to address. We've put together a few suggestions to help those living with someone depressed. First, if you feel compelled to make any of the following comments, find a way to restrain yourself. (Counting to 10—or to 100 if necessary—may help).

Bad Things to Say to a Person Who Is Depressed

1. "Your problem is really getting on my nerves."

2. "Just pull yourself together!"

3. "Get the lead out, lazy."

4. "You're acting crazy, you really need a shrink."

5. "If you don't do something about this, I'm leaving."

6. "Look on the bright side . . . you still have your health (job, money, looks)."

7. "I think that it must be a nutritional problem . . . I've heard rutabagas twice a day are a natural antidepressant."

8. "Cheer up, things can't really be that bad."

When someone you love is depressed, it is tempting to try to rebut their scary (and many times distorted) statements. You want to reason with them, argue with them, confront them—anything to show them how wrong they are.

It is important for partners to realize that, no matter how ridiculous the depressed person's perspective seems, it is emotionally true for him in the moment. To deny or argue with his reality only confirms it. He concludes that he MUST be worthless—a total loser—otherwise he would be able to follow your exhortations to pull himself up by his bootstraps. Trapped in shame, he is even more unlikely to hear the between-the-lines message: that you love him and care about what he is going through. Direct confrontation—particularly if it comes in the form of an invalidation of your partner's feelings—doesn't work for someone suffering from clinical depression. It only serves to deepen the guilt he already feels for not living up to his (or your) normal standards. Nor is it useful to offer direct suggestions about actions to take. What the depressed person really wants is to be heard—to have his feelings acknowledged. When he has had a chance to express his anger, sadness, or loneliness, he may indeed ask for advice or help. At that point, you can think through the best options together.

How then should you talk to a partner who is depressed? Often, the most powerful thing that you can do doesn't involve talking at all, but listening. While it can be uncomfortable to hear someone you love disclosing their pain, your responsive and loving presence can be more reassuring than any particular words or advice you offer. In these situations, it is important to borrow a few tricks of the trade from psychotherapists. Trained to listen actively, they sit quietly, maintain eye contact, and employ an emotional sixth sense to understand and identify with the internal reality of the distressed person. By nodding encouragingly, or saying, "I understand what you mean," every now and then, the active listener signals that she is in tune with the distressed person. If it seems appropriate, partners might want to initiate some physical contact—perhaps holding the hand or touching the arm of her partner as she talks. Occasionally, the active listener might repeat some of what she hears back to her blue partner. Or she might say, "I know how sad that makes you."

Good Things to Say to a Person Who Is Depressed

1. "I hear what you're saying and I understand."
2. "I support whatever you need to do to take care of yourself right now."
3. "Anytime you need to talk, I'm here for you"
4. "We can get through this together."
5. "You sound exhausted . . . this must've been terrible for you."
6. "I'm so sorry that you've felt so lost. I can only imagine what that is like."
7. "I know it's hard when things don't go the way you think they should."

The key to empathic listening is to be sincere and to respond with care to the feelings—rather than the content—of the speaker. Reassurance and validation are key. Also remember it's not necessary to argue or contradict their distorted thinking or to fix the problem. It is important to be a stalwart and non-judgmental supporter.

Good Ways to Touch a Person Who Is Depressed

No doctor's visit or prescription is necessary for touch, yet physical comfort is probably the most potent antidepressant available to any of us. If you and your partner are used to exchanging plenty of affection, you might even up the ante a bit. Extra hugs, perhaps some impromptu shoulder-rubbing, a shared bath, or more time spent spooning before you both fall asleep are all good ideas.

But physical contact may not work for everyone. One depressed woman reported that mornings were particularly grim for her. She really couldn't get out of bed. And she couldn't bear to be touched. Though she was unpartnered at the time, concerned friends often stayed with her. During the worst stretch, one of these friends simply crawled into bed with her. She lay silently beside her. Eventually, when her depressed friend started to cry, the visitor was able to tune into her sorrow, and cry as well. For the depressed person, this sort of empathy was very powerful. Though far from exuberant, she felt much better afterward.

Even if we do not have such intuitive gifts, it is important to remember that mirroring the mood of your depressed partner can, at times, be as much of a comfort as physical touch. And don't be fooled by your partner's apparent indifference if you're simply hanging out quietly in the same room with her. Even your mere presence is comforting.

Sad Sex

Sex is much trickier. If your partner seems disinterested, your first instinct may be to try seduction—the maneuvers that always worked in the past. You dab on a little Issey Miyake, deck yourself in your most alluring silk pjs, turn down the lights. Perhaps you even make little moaning noises, and writhe a bit. All to no avail. Your partner's libido simply refuses to be goosed. What can be done?

The first rule is to take care of yourself. Use a vibrator, your hands, your fantasies. Make sure you're not climbing the walls. Any signs of desperation on your part will only make your partner feel worse. Then when you're perfectly satisfied, you might propose having what we call sad sex with your partner. The inspiration for sad sex comes from an Annie Sprinkle piece entitled "101 Uses for Sex—Or Why Sex Is So Important." (1996). On her list, Annie lists everything from sex as a laxative to sex as a good deed ("Give the needy an occasional mercy fuck"). Annie also lists sex as an antidepressant. We think that sad sex has great potential as an antidepressant. Sad sex means having sex with someone who is too blue to do much of anything. Perhaps she lies there passively. Perhaps she even cries. That's fine. Actually, it is better than fine. During sad sex, there are no expectations beyond the sorrowful presence of a partner. Sad sex can last a couple of minutes, or it can stop and start. One or both partners may be turned off. Orgasm is not necessarily the culmination of sad sex. Being close and sad together—coming together without coming—is the point.

If your partner is too sad for sad sex, we recommend some massage or an exercise that comes from a book by Kenneth Stubbs called *The Essential Tantra* (1999). In the exercise, the sad person lies down, closes her eyes, and relaxes. She then role-plays a rag doll—that is, she is utterly limp and passive. Randomly and slowly, you should lift, support, and move each of the rag doll's arms, then her legs, and finally her head. Using an arm as a starting point, gently explore all the possible movements in the rag doll's fingers, wrist, elbow, and shoulder area. After you have completed lifting and exploring both of the rag doll's arms, move your attentions to your passive partner's legs. When lifting or lowering a bent leg, support the knee joint. After lingering for a few minutes on each limb, move behind the rag doll's head, lift it slightly above the pillow and cradle it for a minute. Afterward, you can lie down next to your rag doll partner, and breathe synchronously with her for five or ten minutes.

If your partner is not willing or able to participate in any of the aforementioned activities, we recommend sneaky touching. For example, sit on the couch next to her when she's watching TV. Gradually ooze over so that your legs or shoulders are touching. Ooze over a little more. Or pick some imaginary lint off your partner's shoulder. Gently brush some more off. If she starts worrying that she has dandruff, stroke her hair while pretending to check for the unsightly stuff.

You get the drift. Use your imagination. The possibilities for sneaky touching are endless.

There are dozens of ways to bypass the anti-touch gendarmes (whoever they may be) and cop some comfort.

Treatment: A Couples' Approach

Up to now we've focussed on how depression affects the ways you characteristically interact with your partner. Treatment issues introduce a whole new element to twosomes. How will you feel, for example, if all your support and sensitivity don't make a dent in your partner's depression? Say he or she decides to get outside help. What if, after all your efforts, he starts singing the praises of his new therapist? Or what if, after months of tender solicitude, you are suddenly cut off from information about his progress? In the future, he informs you firmly, he will process all the information about his mental status with his therapist. If you have always been *numero uno*, chief confidante and cheerleader, you may feel replaced and more than a little jealous—though you might consider it bad form to mention it to anyone. Or, say the opposite is true: Your partner refuses to go to a therapist, and his funk is getting worse. We have a proposal that might be a solution to all of the above-mentioned partner quandaries: getting into therapy as a twosome.

As an adjunct or substitute for individual therapy, couples therapy isn't as farfetched as it sounds. In fact it makes a lot of sense. Depression may be an individual problem. But if the depressed person is partnered, it is also a couple's problem. And partnerships comprised of one depressed and one "helpful partner" often DO need help. During funky stretches, non-depressed partners often become ghosts, denying their own needs and walking on eggshells in an attempt not to tilt the depressed partner into deeper despair. But observing her partner turn herself into a pretzel only makes the depressed partner feel more monstrous. As she gets more depressed, the helpful partner contorts herself even more. In other words, without meaning to, helpful partners may be contributing to their loved ones' depressions. Such destructive couples' dynamics, which may have been in place for years, may continue even during recovery from depression. Even if the depressed partner does seek individual help for her depression, such dynamics may prevent the depressed person from ever improving. Couples therapy may also be the best bet for depressed, therapy-aversive partners. It can provide a face-saving treatment entry point. The identified patient is, after all, the relationship. And a depressed partner, ashamed or unwilling to get help for herself, might be willing to invest time and money to help her partnership.

There's another important reason to consider couples' therapy. It works! In a recent experiment conducted in London, 77 couples, each comprised of one depressed and one non-depressed partner, were divided into two groups. Half the couples received couples therapy. In the other half, the depressed partner was treated with antidepressants. The recovery rate of the depressed partners who were part of the couples therapy treatment group was better than the drug-treated group (Reany, 2000).

Though the experimental group was heterosexual, our prediction is that couples therapy would be just as effective for gay and lesbian couples.

Couples Therapy Part 2

Up until now we've been focusing on the couples in which one of the partners is depressed. But it is not unusual for both partners in a relationship to be depressed. What if, for example, it is clear that your partner needs support? If you are hanging by a thread yourself, you may be in no position to give it. In our experience, this couples' dynamic really ups the depression ante. You already feel unloved and abandoned yourself, and now you can add "unsupportive partner" to your already voluminous list of shortcomings. Your partner may have abandoned herself to the same orgy of frustrated yearning and self-blame. Under such circumstances there is no time to lose. It is very important to go to couples therapy. You could probably both use some assurance that, yes, you are still a couple despite the bumpy times. And at the same time the counselor validates your partnership, she will help you temporarily limit your expectations of yourself and your partner. Perhaps all three of you may collaborate on a minimal expectations agreement for, say, the next two weeks, with an option to renew. Perhaps you can contract to be hard-time roommates—lovers on hold—who, for the time being, can only wish each other the best. The particulars of the new agreement are not so important. What is essential, however, is that you and your partner are responding to the blues by consciously and actively adjusting your expectations of each other.

What If Your Partner Is Suicidal?

This part can be really scary. Your partner has been sinking more and more into the pits. You watch him drinking more or using street drugs as an escape. Or maybe he is calling in sick to work and sleeping all day and all night. He's lost weight. He looks alarmingly gaunt. He has stated, clearly, unequivocally, that he intends to kill himself. As a loving partner, what should you do?

First, ask him what it is that he thinks he needs. Listen carefully. If, after he enumerates all his ideas, and outside help is *not* on his list, ask if you can make a suggestion for him to consider. If he agrees, gently suggest that he might discuss treatment options (if he hasn't already) with his doctor, a counselor, or psychotherapist. If he refuses to seek treatment or cannot find the motivation to do so, share your concerns about what is happening to him and to you if the depression is left untreated. Ask again if there is any way that you can help him in the process of seeking the right treatment. If he again refuses, and it appears that treatment is needed (particularly if he is suicidal or otherwise doing self-harm directly or through inaction), it may be helpful to consider the following steps:

1. Call your partner's physician, psychotherapist, or clergy-person to ask for help. You may decide to call more than one of the above and create a "team."

2. Develop a plan with the team that includes a meeting where you will gently confront your depressed loved one about the need for assistance. It may be helpful to include any other close friends or family who may be concerned, but we recommend keeping the number small (five or less). Have an option ready, as a part of the plan, in case he refuses to acknowledge the problem or refuses to seek help.

3. Begin the meeting by letting the depressed person you love know that the team has gathered because they love him very much and have serious concerns about what the team has seen happening behaviorally. Give specific examples, such

as, "I've noticed that you have been stockpiling barbiturates," or "You've told me on several occasions that you can't go on and that you intend to kill yourself."

4. Once gently confronted about your (the team's) concerns, ask the person you love to make a specific plan with you regarding getting help. For example, getting into regular psychotherapy, talking to the doctor about trying an antidepressant, going back to twelve-step meetings, etc.

5. If he becomes defensive or uncooperative, you must be prepared to discuss your next step, which may involve transporting him to an emergency room for "official" evaluation by a professional regarding the need for involuntary treatment. This should be a plan that you've already discussed in number 2 and you should be prepared to follow through on. Let him know that the evaluation gives him the opportunity to cooperate with treatment, especially if he goes along peacefully, and there is the possibility that the professional may support his position that he is not depressed enough for direct intervention.

6. If there continues to be resistance and you are very concerned about imminent self-destructiveness, here are two specific options. First, you can call 911 and explain to the operator that you have someone with you who is suicidal and needs immediate help. In some cases, either a psychiatric emergency team (PET) will be dispatched to your location, or the police will arrive to take your loved one to a properly staffed emergency room. Second, you can call a local mental health crisis or suicide prevention line and they can talk you through the appropriate steps. Usually these numbers are listed in the phone book under names like "Helpline," or "Crisis Counseling," or call your local mental health center, usually listed in the county services section of your phone book.

7. If he does cooperate, it offers him the opportunity to get intensive emotional care and to begin to reverse a potentially harmful trend. Either way, it is important for you and the team to state that you have taken this action because you care about him and want to see him get better.

Making this type of stand may be one of the most difficult things that you've ever had to do. Your partner may get upset or even quite angry with you, particularly for what seems to him to be a "betrayal." While you owe your partner respect and the right to make their own decisions, in the case of suicidal depression, he may not be thinking rationally or safely and your action may mean the difference between life or death.

Partner Burnout

Your partner's well-being is not all that's at risk here. You may become overwhelmed and burned out. The first sign of burnout is a short fuse. An annoying fly, a persistent kitchen sink drip can send you into a rage. You are, after all, at the end of your rope. And you feel guilty. More than guilty. You are resentful, hopeless, anxious. You've done everything you can think of. You're doing all the cooking and cleaning. You're not appreciated. Nothing changes. You lose patience and then hate yourself for lashing out. You begin to exhibit signs of depression yourself. You run out of energy. You stop seeing friends.

Burnout is not limited to a flood of unpleasant emotions. Many people on the verge of burnout begin to experience headaches, cold or flu symptoms, stomach or bowel problems; they have difficulty sleeping. They complain of neck and backaches or even chest pain. Because burnout is so potentially harmful, it is important for people who live with depressed partners to take preventive action. Here are our suggestions:

Learning to Take Care of You

- **GET SUPPORT** wherever you can. Talking to friends and family or even getting your own psychotherapist can help relieve your sense of isolation and reduce stress. Depending on your location, there may even be support groups for caregivers of people with depression or bipolar disorder. Twelve-step programs like Al-Anon can be extremely helpful—they are free!

- **TAKE TIME FOR YOU** by continuing to have fun and laugh with friends. Understand that it is not only permissible but absolutely necessary for your own mental health to continue your usual hobbies, social activities, and friendships.

- **EXERCISE AND GET PLENTY OF SLEEP.** The best protection against stress is aerobic exercise. It enhances the release of endorphins and encephalins—your body's natural pain relievers. Your body also requires sufficient sleep to restore itself when it is depleted. Although you may be tempted to skimp on both exercise and sleep in order to better care for your partner, you will not be able to make it for the long haul (if necessary) if you neglect your own self-care.

- **MANAGE YOUR TIME** by assigning priorities to your daily tasks and stopping before you reach your limit. Try to live in the moment, recognizing that you are only human and can't possibly get everything done all the time.

- **TAKE A BREAK** and get support for yourself. Although being committed to your partner is admirable, this trait, along with conscientious care-taking and scrupulous house-hold maintenance, is a surefire recipe for burnout. Allow those who care about you help when they offer. Remember that allowing others to give to you is actually a gift to them.

- **STAY OUT** of the medication monitor role. This is particularly important if your partner is not taking antidepressants prescribed for him. It is not good for your partner or the relationship for you to assume responsibilities that are not yours.

- **LET GO** when it is obvious that the strategy you are using is not working. If you have a hard time keeping a sane perspective, rely on outside sources: Keep a journal you can reread at intervals; talk to friends; spend time alone.

- **SAY NO** when you need to. Taking care of you means saying no sometimes, even if it means that your partner gets upset with you.

- **PRACTICE ACTIVE RELAXATION** through techniques like abdominal breathing exercises, relaxation tapes, and listening to soft music. Also included in this category are times for spiritual refreshment through meditation, prayer, or other spiritual rituals and practices.

- **TAKE A SABBATICAL.** Do yourself a favor. Go away for an afternoon, a day, a week, or longer, if necessary. Nurture yourself. Get a massage. Stroll on the beach and look at the horizon. Read a trashy novel . Go dancing. Get in touch with your own bio-rhythms again.

Partner Homework:
An Advance Warning Exercise

Burnout comes from not knowing your limits. Name three major ways that you have been taking care of your depressed partner:

1)

2)

3)

Now, go through this list again and describe your bottom line. For example, if you do all the housecleaning, name what it would take for you to straddle the broom and head toward the moon, howling, "I'VE HAD ENOUGH!" Would it be if she brought home a new, very hairy pet? Would it be if you realized that you were going to be permanently stuck in the role of domestic maidservant?

Bottom line for 1)

Bottom line for 2)

Bottom line for 3)

Now, if you reconsider these bottom lines, you'll realize that they are probably not bottom lines at all. In fact, they represent the point at which you have crossed the line and entered the burnout zone.

Now, go back and think of some reasonable limits for these activities. For example, a reasonable limit for housecleaning might be when you have spent more than thirty minutes doing any unpleasant activity—vacuuming or dishwashing, for example

Reasonable limit for 1)

Reasonable limit for 2)

Reasonable limit for 3)

We don't expect miracles, but we recommend that you try to apply at least one of these reasonable limits in the upcoming weeks.

What About After the Depression Is Managed?

As we have mentioned elsewhere, depression is a treatable mental disorder. Even chronic bipolar disorder can be managed with a good regimen. Say everything has stabilized. You and your partner are on an even keel again. What is the aftermath of your partner's depression?

It depends. Was the depression a brief episode or one in a series? Is it a condition that, though treated, will persist in a less dramatic form? Will your partner be independent or will he continue to require extra support from you? Do you or your partner have residual anxiety or anger about what happened between you?

All these factors will figure into the time it takes for the couple to recover and find a new equilibrium. If the depression has ended, or is in remission, the well, but still-worried, partner may have trouble surrendering the care-giving role and resuming a more equal give-and-take relationship. Sometimes, the person who was depressed may resent the actions that the caregiver took to protect or assist them. The caregiver may continue to resent his partner for "causing" the problem, for the months of self-sacrifice, and even for the leftover financial mess the depression may have caused. Both partners may live in constant fear that another episode is just around the corner.

How does one begin the process of picking up the pieces and moving on? Here is another juncture where couples therapy may be helpful. At this point, it can provide a safe haven in which to explore the ways that your relationship was affected, the ways the roles were changed or reversed. Couples counseling is also a good place to play out "what-if" scenarios. What if it happens again? What if the depression is both chronic and treatment-resistant? How will each of you know? What will you do then? And then? Having an advanced warning system in place and a plan worked out beforehand can be reassuring. Your partner may be depressed again. But this time you'll be prepared.

CHAPTER 6

Monitoring the Minotaur

Self-Management and Self-Nurturing

We've done a grand tour of depression. We've probed the cultural aspects of queer depression. We've explored its chemical pathways. We've even approached the blues from the perspective of long-suffering partners. But, so far, we haven't actually visited the beast in its underground lair. We haven't seen him operating up close and we haven't explored the ways in which depressed people can take specific steps to protect themselves. In this chapter we'd like to outline a few self-help interventions—several mood-improving strategies that do not require professional or expert intervention. In fact, to try them out, you don't even have to get out of your pajamas if you don't feel like it. All you need is an adventurous spirit, a pad of paper, and a pen. Before we propose our experiment, however, we'd like to discuss the effectiveness of such self-help strategies.

Because depression has been such a ubiquitous mental health problem, its treatment has been singled out for particular research attention. The cure claims of various schools of psychotherapy have been subjected to rigorous scrutiny. The approach that consistently shows very positive results is called *cognitive behavioral therapy* (or CBT). The basic idea of CBT is simple: Negative thinking leads to negative feelings which, in turn, result in self-destructive or ineffective behaviors. Therefore, in order to feel better, depressed people must change their characteristic thought patterns. Cognitively-oriented psychotherapists help their patients do this by teaching them a series of thought-altering techniques. Because these techniques are straightforward, they are easy to convert into a few exercises—those bedroom slipper adventures we mentioned above—that you can practice on your own.

This chapter contains some ways to become aware of, and then change, negative thinking. We recommend that you experiment with these suggestions. Before we outline the techniques, we'll explain the underlying theory in more detail.

Cognitions, Beliefs, and Behavior

Dr. Aaron Beck, the major architect of cognitive behavior therapy, began his career as a Freudian psychoanalyst. In the course of his work, he observed that people who shared similar symptoms of anxiety and depression also tended to think alike. More specifically, he noticed that his depressed patients tended to focus more on the negative aspects of a situation than on the positive aspects. He also found that they tended to see relatively neutral or meaningless events (according to an unbiased observer) as negative and personal. Another important contributor to cognitive therapy, Dr. Albert Ellis, made very similar observations, but his emphasis was on *irrational beliefs*. He found that not only did people who were depressed tend to interpret benign events as negative, but they also held beliefs about themselves that were long-standing and were usually completely illogical or unreasonable.

Instead of continuing to try to help people who were depressed by analyzing the unconscious residue of early traumas (the Freudian approach), both Dr. Beck and Dr. Ellis tried a new approach. They reasoned that if people who were depressed had systematic ways of thinking that led them to feel inadequate or guilty, these thoughts were the most appropriate target for therapy.

Their theory makes sense. If you are consistently misinterpreting events in your world, or chronically underestimating or undermining your own capacities, chances are you are depressed. And if you can alter your negative thought patterns, your mood will probably improve. So how do you begin to recognize how and when your thoughts are producing your depression? And, if you can identify your negative mental mantras, how do you change them?

The Depression Triple-Decker

According to cognitive behavioral therapists, our thoughts are as multi-layered as coats of paint on an old barn. The first level, the primer coat, consists of our core beliefs. These are the lessons we first learn about ourselves, the world, and others. If family members are nurturing to us when we are still in our vulnerable unpainted state, our views are likely to be positive. Growing up with emotionally absent or abusive parents, however, will generate an opposite set of core beliefs. And, if we didn't conform to traditional gender expectations, our first contact with playmates, teachers, or neighbors may have cemented this negative primer coat.

According to the cognitive therapists, negative core beliefs fall into two categories. The first are beliefs about helplessness. Statements like "I am inadequate" or "I am a failure" might reflect such helpless core beliefs. The other set of negative core beliefs concerns unworthiness. "I am unlovable" or "I am bound to be alone" are examples of this set of core beliefs. Because these beliefs are so primal, and have been masked over the years by endless attempts to compensate for them, they are probably no longer consciously accessible to us. We can infer they are there, though, from the next coat of mental paint. This layer of thinking is comprised of conditional beliefs or reasonable expectations for yourself derived from those vintage core concepts. Say, for example, you are profoundly convinced, at your deepest level, that you are not lovable. Your conditional belief might be: "I'll never find a lover, and therefore I'll always be alone." Or perhaps it will be phrased slightly differently: "Someone may be idiotic enough to be with me temporarily but eventually he will come to his senses and leave."

Most of us are more aware of these second-coat thoughts than we are of the primer/primal core belief that generates them. Yet, even this second coat may be concealed, covered up by yet a third layer of mental paint. The outside coat, which we do have access to, consists of the nonstop mental patter most of us engage in when we're daydreaming or driving or waiting in a grocery line. Some of this automatic chatter may simply be a reminder to add dishwashing detergent to the shopping list, but some of it, in the case of depressed people, consists of self-deprecating remarks. This negative interior monologue is the logical consequence of the conditional beliefs that are, in turn, based on the core beliefs. An example may help clarify what we mean.

Let's call our example Michael. Say Michael, who happens to have a core belief that he is unlovable, has been invited to a party. As he gets ready, he berates himself for not remembering to pick up his clean shirts at the laundry. As he checks the mirror before leaving, he itemizes his other fashion flaws. His sweater is dorky. His jeans are grungy. He really should have planned ahead. He should look better.

Now, his dweebiness will be apparent to everyone. In the car, he tells himself he has the social graces of a banana slug. He won't know anyone. He is sure of it. He will never meet anyone who will want to date him. He will always be alone, and so on.

If Michael's depressing patter is contained, audible only to himself, what harm does it do? The answer is that it does a lot of harm. Michael's self-deprecating narrative is bound to lead to self-effacing behavior. In other words, Michael's negative self-talk will prevent him from initiating any conversations. Since wallflowers don't attract much attention, his demeanor at the party will only confirm his negative opinion of himself. Let's play out the scenario in more detail.

Michael arrives at the party. Already convinced that he is not going to make the grade, he stands on the sidelines, shifting uneasily from foot to foot. Or perhaps, spotting a bevy of hunky guests engaged in animated conversation, he sidles over. He hopes he can somehow blend in. But these men obviously know each other and their conversation already has plenty of momentum. Michael remains mutely on the fringes of the group. All the time, the automatic thoughts are throbbing relentlessly in his skull: "If I opened my mouth now, a big nothing would plop out. Or I would mumble mmmmfffff mmmmmfffff mmmmmffff. There is nothing to say. I never have anything to say anyway. Better just keep quiet. I must look like an earnest chipmunk standing here. Just as bad as the bald guy hugging his martini glass in the corner. No, I'm worse. At least he is buffed. Good God, they're comparing Mediterranean cruises. They're not only gorgeous. They're rich. I'm really out of my league."

Eventually, without talking to anyone, Michael scuttles toward the door, and, checking to see that his host is distracted, he slips out and goes home. When he unlocks his door, his apartment seems dark and quiet. He notices there are no messages on his answering machine. What's the point, he thinks. It's hopeless. Not only is he unworthy of the attentions of a lover—friends don't even call. No one ever calls. He is, he thinks, unlovable and unlikeable—a cosmic flyspeck.

Cognitive behavioral therapists would point out that the depressed person in the example managed to construe several neutral events—a group of animated party-goers, and later, at home, an answering machine—as proof of his inferiority.

Now, imagine for a moment how different the whole scene would have been if the self-doubting Michael could have tuned in to his pre-party negative mental chatter. Had he been aware of the way he was programming himself for a dismal outcome, he might have been able to tweak his thoughts into a slightly more positive direction. Before he left home, he might have focused on something he liked about himself. It wouldn't have to be grand; perhaps he might savor the Polo Sport he had just sprayed on; perhaps he might find a certain appeal in his crooked grin. If he hadn't been so predisposed to be rejected, he might have plucked up enough courage to talk to someone. In general, people who are approached respond positively. Chances are that, even if hadn't met Mr. Right, he might have had a pleasant conversation. Heartened by that exchange, perhaps Michael might have hazarded another overture. By the end of the evening, he may have pocketed a few phone numbers; at the very least, he would have felt more socially competent, and, therefore, more likely to accept other such invitations. Additionally, this new sense of social competency would percolate through all his mental undercoats. His conditional belief that he would always be alone might be shaken; and perhaps the effect would seep all the way down and modify—ever so slightly—his conviction about his unworthiness. And all these positive changes hinge on modifying, say, twenty minutes of pre-party mental chatter. But how to do it? The first step is to tune into the barrage of propaganda many of us unknowingly inflict upon ourselves. In his *Gay and Lesbian Self-Esteem Book* (1999), Kimeron lists the characteristics of these negative interior monologues.

1. They are typically experienced as brief self-statements, sometimes in the form of just a few words like "Stupid!" or "This will never work out." Such statements aren't always comprised of words. Some people conjure up negative images from the past, or anticipated, equally unpleasant future scenarios. Automatic words and images seem to pop up spontaneously. They occur so quickly that, unless you're paying close attention, they may escape conscious notice.

2. Because they originate in childhood, long before you had the ability to question or evaluate them, most images or automatic self-talk is experienced as the voice of reason. And what's more, these unassailable truths seem as familiar (and automatic) as breathing. Because they have a life of their own, it never occurs to you that you might have any power over them and that you can challenge or disprove them.

3. Automatic thoughts often include rigid rules hidden in the words "should," "always," "never," "must," or "ought to." Examples include, "I must never tell anyone that I am gay (or lesbian)." Many of the rules you lived by as a child helped you survive. In fact, in that environment they may have been

very adaptive. Yet, the same rules are unnecessarily restrictive for an adult who has the power to move freely in the world and make choices. In addition, the "should" statements set up unrealistic and unattainable standards. The resulting feelings of failure only reinforce helpless core beliefs.

4. While automatic thinking usually occurs in response to a specific event, you have deeper, core levels of beliefs that represent common themes. After you begin to recognize the many types of specific automatic thoughts you have, it will then be important to look for patterns or themes. Your self-worth will be a primary theme. So will your view of the world, and what you can expect (or not expect) from others.

The more we engage in this sort of self-talk, the more depressed we become. The more depressed we become, the more we chant these negative mantras to ourselves. They affect our psychology and our behavior; they probably even change our brain chemistry. In order to interrupt them, it is important to be able to recognize their twisted logic. In fact, we can sort most negative self-talk into the following six categories.

- **Catastrophizing or Negative Predictions:** This aspect of self-talk depicts a cataclysmic future. Even though there is no evidence for such a dire outcome, anticipating it creates anxiety and depression.

  Example: Driving to the party, Michael is certain that he will not meet anyone and will always be alone.

- **Overgeneralizing, Magnifying, or Jumping to Conclusions:** According to the precepts of automatic thinking, single events are never simply solo occurrences. Rather, they are part of a larger, usually very dismal picture. Words that are reflective of this process include "everybody" or "nobody," "never" or "always."

  Example: Because Michael felt he had nothing to add to a particular conversation in progress, he concluded that he never had anything to say.

- **Black-or-White Thinking:** Much of negative thinking is restricted to a binary system. In any given situation, there are two alternatives: yes or no, good or bad, right or wrong. Choices that exist somewhere between or beyond these alternatives often do not occur to depressed people.

Example: Because Michael cannot anticipate being the life of the party, he is a banana slug; because he is not Adonis, he is an earnest chipmunk.

- **"Shoulds" and "Musts":** When such words pop up, we are probably lecturing ourselves—giving ourselves harsh commands to achieve unrealistic goals. When they are not met, automatic talk shifts to a punishing round of name-calling. Other phrases that give away such harsh automatic thinking are "ought-to-be" and "have-to."

  Example: Michael tells himself that he should look better. He berates himself and tells himself he has the social skills of a banana slug.

- **Emotional Reasoning:** This sort of automatic talk is most likely to be experienced as absolute, gut-wrenching certainty. In spite of all evidence to the contrary, you know you have been rejected, or are disliked, or are about to be fired or (fill in the blank).

  Example: Michael knew, beyond a shadow of a doubt, that he would not pass muster at the party.

- **Filtering or Tunnel Vision:** This is overgeneralizing in reverse. In other words, instead of creating a negative scenario out of one event, depressed people—when confronted with a whole scenario—tend to zero in on one negative detail. In other words, they discount everything positive.

  Example: Michael reduces his whole friendship history to one relatively insignificant detail: In the hour or two he has been out, no one has left him a message; ergo, no one cares about him.

All of these thinking patterns have something in common: They generate emotional pain. In spite of their cumulative negative effect, they are hard to interrupt. As we've mentioned before, they have probably been in place since childhood. They seem as natural as breathing. Consequently the first challenge is to become aware of them.

Increasing Your Awareness of Negative Thoughts

If it were easy to recognize distorted thinking, you would've probably changed it by now. But as we mentioned before, automatic thinking often occurs at levels just below the surface of your awareness. The emotion that these thoughts have generated, however, is not at all hidden. In fact, it probably dominates your consciousness. It is these powerful, and usually negative, emotions that can clue you in to the fact that you have just had a thought that might be in need of some work. Next time you feel yourself shift from, say, boredom to anger or despair, ask yourself, "What have I just said to myself to create these feelings?" or, "What was I just thinking?" Or, ask yourself what element of the situation that you are currently in triggered the feeling. This type of process takes some practice. It isn't always easy to figure out what you were thinking only a few seconds before your mood change. At first, you may only be able to figure out your thinking sequence long after your emotional shift has actually occurred. But don't give up, once you finally get it, this process becomes much easier.

There may be some of you who live in a uniformly funky world. In other words, you cannot track the thoughts that shift your moods because your mood—alas—never changes. In these instances, it is important to use some outside cue to tune into your thoughts. If you live in a big city, when a noise—a siren for example—distracts you, tune into what you were just thinking. If you have an alarm watch, set its beeper to go off at certain intervals. When you hear the beep, make a mental note of the thoughts you were just having. In other words, your first task is to start to get a rough idea of some of your automatic thinking. Remember, we're not after a perfect record—just a general sense of what's going on in your head.

Taking Aim at the Culprits

After you start to get the hang of recognizing the thoughts that are causing the negative feelings, the next step is to begin to challenge them for accuracy or helpfulness. Here's where the writing pad and pen we mentioned in the beginning of the chapter will come in handy. It is helpful to write down the negative thoughts on a piece of paper. Draw a line down the center of the page, and write them down exactly the way you think them on the left side of the dividing line. Then, look at each one to determine, first, if it is indeed a distortion or if it is accurate and realistic. Use the list of distortions listed earlier in this chapter to categorize the type of distortion you are making. If you can't decide which distortion category it fits into, don't worry. What's most important is that you recognize that the thought is unreasonable, irrational, or distorted. After you've written down the problematic thoughts, write an affirmative rebuttal of the distortions on the right side. Just to make this process a bit easier, here are some specific tips—ways to challenge common thinking distortions.

Catastrophizing or Negative Predictions

On the left side, write down your dire predictions. Tell yourself that—as much as you would like to—you do not possess magical shamanic powers required to foretell future events. On the right side, write: *I am utterly powerless to predict the future.* You might want to write it more than once. Or draw twenty crystal balls. Then go back and, using a heavy magic marker, draw an X through each one. This exercise can be fun. It can also be a relief. Enjoy it.

Overgeneralizing, Magnifying, or Jumping to Conclusions

After an insignificant episode, you realize you have started to tell yourself that you are a loser, that you will never (fill in the blank). The first step is to, ever so briefly, become a lawyer, put yourself on the stand, and ask if this conclusion is really justified by the evidence. Chances are you will see immediately that it is not. In fact, such a conclusion is so overstated that it is patently ridiculous. But this is only the first step. This sort of automatic thinking is probably a replay of the way you were spoken to as a child. Bizarrely enough, it may be the only form of love that you experienced. (At least your parent "cared enough" to lecture you.) Consequently, it is not enough to simply understand the flawed logic of this kind of automatic talk. You must also find a way to invoke the person who first made dire predictions about your future and have a dialogue with him or her. You might want to conjure that person up in your mind's eye and recreate the negative scenes that transpired between the two of you so long ago.

This is a simple but powerful way for you to have a conversation between you and yourself, you and a significant other, or even between you and some*thing* that is troubling you. To have such a conversation, some people find it easier to actually sit across from an empty chair and imagine that part of yourself (or the other person or thing) is sitting in it. You can say whatever you want to the empty chair. You can switch and sit in it yourself, become the long-ago child, or the parent, and answer back.

If you have a difficult time feeling compassion for yourself but you know that you need it, imagine that a child about six or seven years old is sitting in the empty chair, feeling the way you are currently feeling—perhaps alone, scared, and confused. What are your natural impulses? Would you sit there and let the child cry? Would you tell her or him to shut up? You'll probably have an impulse to say something like, "You'll be okay," or "I'll protect you." Some people practice a form of visualization in which they imagine taking the sad or scared child onto their laps and hugging or soothing him. If you feel uneasy, you may need to imagine the child as a stranger, but eventually, as you become more relaxed, you can imagine the child as the emotional part of yourself or the child who needed hugging and more loving acceptance when you were growing up.

This is your opportunity to be angry or call a truce, to ask for comfort or compassion, or to give it. As stage manager, director, and script writer, you can do whatever feels good. Whenever you catch yourself in some punitive self-talk, we recommend that you pull the chair out, and put the original punishing parent where he belongs, and have a heart-to-heart with him or her.

Black-or-White Thinking

Down with dualism! Long live pluralities! One way of challenging the binary division of everything into right/wrong, good/bad, or beautiful/ugly is to give a positive spin to the negative half of your particular dualism. Say, for example, you've concluded that there are, basically, two types of people: Gorgeous Blond Sylphs and Ugly Fat Outsiders. Naturally, you feel you belong in the UFO category. To dissolve the depressing dualism and pump up your right-hand, positive-spin column, use some of the affirmations listed in Marilyn Wann's fabulous book, *FAT!So?* (1999) for inspiration:

I'm not tiny and helpless.

It gives me attitude.

People get out of my way when I'm in a hurry.

I have big, luscious breasts.

I have more body to tattoo.

I am loved for who I am.

I'm unique, not a cookie-cutter person.

I am more accepting of other people.

If your black-and-white thinking centers around some other aspect of your life or personality, explode your binary thinking by listing a half-dozen ways the negative half of the split could be viewed differently. List them in your positive column. The point here is that there are usually "grays" in life and that it can help to stretch your worldview to include them.

"Shoulds" and "Musts"

Now is the time to replace that perfect icon—the person you should be—with a "good enough" image of yourself. Consider the lofty standards you are expecting yourself to meet. Say, for example, you have set your sights on abs of iron and buns of steel. Write these goals down in your left-hand column. Then, in your positive column, write down a reasonable goal. For instance: "going to gym twice next week." Wow! Terrific. Now see, that wasn't so hard. If you have assigned yourself the improbable goal of finding a forever-after soul mate who also happens to be brilliant and beautiful, write that in your left-hand column. In your positive column, write "one date with a fairly interesting person." ***** (You get five stars for that one.)

If this is really hard for you, we suggest that some old parental messages are operating. To flush out the source of the problem, go back and try the empty chair exercise mentioned above in the overgeneralizing section. Work on making your self-expectations more reasonable.

Emotional Reasoning

Say you've pinpointed a tendency to be absolutely certain of worst-case scenarios: Perhaps you are convinced that your lover is about to give you the heave-ho; maybe you know that you are going to be fired first thing Monday morning; or perhaps you are certain that you have a terminal but undiagnosable illness. No amount of reassurance can persuade you otherwise. This is perhaps the most intractable of the distortions. You have probably successfully defied many attempts to snap yourself back to a more reasonable view, so we aren't going to suggest you argue with yourself anymore. Instead, we propose that you try a go with the flow approach—a strategy we call a "what then" narrative. To explain what we mean, let's use your partner desertion delusion as an example. In the left-hand column write, "My lover is leaving." Then pose the question, "What happens to me then?" Write down your answer on the right-hand side. Say you scribble, "She won't talk to me. She packs up. Calls the moving van. I stand by watching, broken-hearted. I plead. She doesn't look back." Repeat the question to yourself again: "What happens to me then?" Say you write, "I collapse on the floor, sobbing. I cry for hours until I fall asleep." Pose the "what then" question again. Keep writing down the answers to this question. Ask yourself "what then" until you shift a postcrisis view of events. You may have to pose the "what then" question to yourself (and answer it) 50 or 100 times. Be as patient with your miserable scenario answers as you need to be. You may, at some point, come to understand their origins and see that they have nothing to do with your present fears. At this juncture, unmanageable depression may change to an expressible form of sadness. Even if the repeated posing of the "what then" question elicits no particular insight or catharsis, it robs the original conviction of its original tyrannical power. As the story you are telling yourself changes, so will your accompanying feeling of powerlessness. In the process of making up the fictional what-thens, you will have broken—or at least loosened—the emotional stranglehold of your original conviction.

Filtering or Tunnel Vision

Say you realize that you can't stop replaying a coworker's insensitive, off-hand comment about something you've done or the way you look. Or say you've gotten a very good performance evaluation at work, but, days later, you are still focusing on the single "needs improvement" check mark. In your left-hand column, describe the experience that bummed you out. In your right-hand column, draw a pie chart. Have the chart represent your entire relationship with the coworker, or the whole performance evaluation. What percentage is negative? What part is neutral or positive? Chances are, if you look at the whole picture, most of your pie chart will be neutral or positive. If, say, it turns out that most of the interactions with a particular friend *are* negative, however, then have the pie chart represent all your interactions with all your friends. Now, what percentage of the pie chart does the negative exchange with this particular friend occupy? We are guessing that it will be a thin sliver. We hope that such graphic representations of the preponderance of positive or neutral interactions depicted on your chart will put this particular negative interaction in its insignificant and anomalous place. But, chances are, this is not a one-time occurrence.

If you have a general tendency to focus on the negative and discount the positive, you'll probably need a regular program of affirmation calisthenics. The first step is to generate some positive statements about yourself. Write the following headings on the top of the next four pages in your pad:

THINGS I'M GOOD AT

PERSONAL CHARACTERISTICS I HAVE BEEN COMPLIMENTED FOR

ACCOMPLISHMENTS I'M PROUD OF

EVIDENCE THAT I'M LIKED OR VALUED

Now choose one or two of these headings, and start making some notations on the page underneath. If writing down positive statements about yourself seems difficult, you might need some extra coaching. Books of affirmations are easy to find in libraries and bookstores. As well as jump-starting this process, they can be very useful guides in low moments. The same is true of inspirational tapes. Put one in your car tape deck whenever you start your ignition or, if you bike or bus to work, play the tapes on a Walkman. It's hard to focus on negative thoughts while you are being bombarded with positive messages. In particular, we recommend the tapes listed in the Resources section.

Once you've jotted down some positive statements about yourself, you might want to use a bright-colored Magic Marker to transfer the affirmations to index cards. Paste them all over: the bathroom mirror, refrigerator, anywhere else you linger for a few seconds during your daily rounds. Every time you put out the recycling, or do the laundry, refresh your affirmations. Put them in different places or substitute a new round. Every day, make a point of leaving some of these personal affirmations on your home or work voice mail. Send yourself an appreciative, loving e-mail. We don't expect you to be really fluent in the language of positive regard immediately, but we would like you to be a little less rusty.

Attention: Special Homophobia Alert

Internalized homophobia often acts as a distorting lens over events. Perhaps we can't stop ruminating about the way a driver cut us off after he spotted (we are sure) the rainbow sticker on our bumper. Never mind that we passed the same driver, ten minutes later, obviously pulled over by the cops for speeding. Or perhaps our internalized homophobia expresses itself in distortion number 2, overgeneralizations. Perhaps, after an unpleasant exchange with a gay salesperson or even an ex, we tell ourselves that all fags are silly queens or that all dykes are femiNazis. We fume. We rage. If we identify as gay ourselves, such mental muttering will not boost already sagging self-esteem. At times like this, it might be good to draw a pie chart or two, or to explode such black-and-white thinking by remembering how many of our queer friends defy such classifications.

In other words, each of the distortion categories we've listed can be a vehicle for internalized homophobia. And each of the exercises we've listed above can be modified to counteract our negative thinking about gayness. But internalized homophobia is only part of the picture. Homophobia also exists externally. And often times, our perceptions about the external manifestations of homophobia do not need correction. They are 100 percent negative and they are 100 percent accurate. What is the remedy for depression in these situations? Or what about the other times—the times when we can't be sure whether the homophobia is external, internal, or both. Is that new manager at work chilly with everyone, or does he just freeze up around queers? And what about the number 1 distortion on our list: catastrophizing or making negative predictions? If, say, most of your friends have died of AIDS, and all the survivors (including yourself) are HIV positive, is it really distorting reality to say the future looks grim?

What's the Difference

The split between justifiable depression and the self-doubts generated by distorted thinking are best summed up by an amusing postcard. The card shows two freeway signs. The sign hanging over the two left-hand lanes reads *Depressed for No Reason*. The sign indicating the two right-hand lanes reads *Depressed for a Good Reason*. In fact, there is a controversy within psychology over an idea called depressive realism. Some psychologists, including the cognitive behaviorists, believe that depression is caused by a pessimistic, distorted view of reality. This depressed-for-no-reason crowd believes that if such distortions can be corrected, then moods will improve. The other camp believes that depressed people may be *too* realistic. They simply don't share the optimists' ability to deny the grim nature of reality. Up until now, the recommendations we've made have been based on the cognitive behavioral view that depressed people distort reality in a pessimistic direction. Even though we think such distortions may account for some of the blues, they certainly do not account for all of them. When it comes to some things, social injustice, say, or personal loss, we choose to head in the direction indicated by the *Depressed for a Good Reason* sign. But what does it mean, exactly, in terms of rebound strategies? Are there any self-help antidepressants available for those of us who find ourselves in the two right lanes?

One answer we've found comes from a book called *Stop Smiling, Start Kvetching* (Held, 1999). The author, psychologist Barbara Held, maintains that facing the harsh realities of life can be demoralizing. But, she says, it can also be liberating. In the first place, you can drop all Pollyanna pretense. You can complain (or kvetch) to whoever will listen.

Over the years, Marny has come to peg herself as a "half-empty glass" kind of person. She has dealt with her inability to deny certain depressing realities by finding a similarly inclined friend. They get together every week for "kvetchfests" about a long litany of miseries: the latest incursions of the right wing, global warming, a friend's cancer diagnosis. Surprisingly enough, after these *oi vey* sessions, both feel, if not exactly exuberant, then much less depressed. Why?

Think about what is going on for a minute. Despite all the verbal hand-wringing, Marny and Jane are saying, "We are both in the stew together—as observers *and* casualties of the human condition." There is something ferociously comforting about this witnessing/commiserating combination. It is the reason that support groups, in which many of the members are suffering acutely, have such an uplifting effect. And think for a moment about social activism. What are political demonstrations, for example, but a large, well-coordinated, and vociferous protest—a to-whom-it-may-concern complaint. Even if they do not result in any change, there is something both soothing and empowering about saying (with a picket sign, a petition, or just by showing up on Pride day,) "Hey. I exist and I feel this way." The very act of complaining out loud to one person or in concert with a million is a form of affirmation, and, therefore, acts as a powerful antidepressant.

Homophobia Antidotes

In the first chapter, we made a distinction between endogenous (or internal) types of depression and depressions that were justifiable reactions to demoralizing events. This distinction corresponds to the great freeway divide between the no-reason-to-be-depressed left fork, and the good-reason-to-be-blue right fork. This split also corresponds to the distinction between internalized homophobia and the psychological effects of daily, direct discrimination. Internalized homophobia may cause us to undermine ourselves and distort situations in which we find ourselves. External homophobia may cause us to lose jobs, housing, and in some cases, our lives. What is unique, then, about queer depression is its double-tiered nature. It is both endogenous and reactive. *Most gay people who are depressed are suffering from both.* Queer blues consists of internalized, negative messages as well as reactions to very depressing external realities.

As a result, to be effective, the remedies for queer blues must also be two-tiered. We need to monitor our self-talk to see how and when we have become inadvertent double agents—unconsciously parroting the negative messages from our families and the culture. Then we must figure how to apply the thought-correcting strategies that prevent us from becoming our own worst enemies.

The second tier of remedies must address the corrosive effects of external homophobia. Making noise, kvetching, challenging, organizing, protesting, petitioning, marching, coming out once, twice, dozens of times—to the same person if necessary—are all ways of declaring that ERASURE IS NOT A NATURAL ACT. And furthermore, we will never, ever consent to it.

Learning the Art of Self-Nurturing Against All Odds

There is one remedy that is equally effective for both tiers of the queer blues. Self-nurturing is the most effective and important antidote to the homophobia in our everyday lives. It is equally important for the ravages of internalized homophobia. Unfortunately, there is a slight problem with such an eminently sane prescription.

Tell a depressed person to treat themselves lovingly, suggest that they give themselves some positive strokes or rewards, and they will stare at you uncomprehendingly. Or they may look as though you have just offered them a steaming bowl of moose gland stew. In other words, even though self-nurturing is a cheap, readily available and powerful antidepressant, it is not an option for depressed people. If they could have luxuriated in a bubble bath or strolled down a picturesque country lane when they felt blue, they would have. The fact is that those critical committees meeting in their heads have decreed that such time-outs are excessive, indulgent, and entirely undeserved. So the question is how to drug, decoy, or otherwise distract those vigilant committees? We have a suggestion. Even though it seems like a long shot, we think it's worth trying. Succinctly put, we recommend turning the tables on the committee, and putting them in the spotlight. Here's our slightly tortured logic.

Ghostbusting

As we mentioned before, we think the negative voices in our heads have a venerable history. In all likelihood, they have been passed down from generation to generation for centuries. If a family documentary could have been made 100 years ago, it might have revealed Great Grandpa admonishing Grandpa to be more manly. Or perhaps Great Grandma was scolding Granny for being such a sorry excuse for a girl, for being much too ugly to ever get a husband. Perhaps the abuse was physical. Perhaps it took the form of neglect. Whatever their modus operandi, these ghosts must be attended to before we can attend to ourselves. They must be reminded—clearly, firmly—that we no longer need their supervision. The best way to notify these ghosts that their tenure is over is by a form of communication they would recognize: a plain, old-fashioned hand-written letter. Perhaps there is more than one person in your past who deserves such a letter. Or perhaps you have a stubborn ghost who needs to be notified several times. The letters can detail all the ways you have been controlled or criticized in the past. If you feel like it, you can give the ghost credit for being well-intentioned, if misguided. You can say you understand that he was treated harshly by his father. Understanding and forgiveness are optional. But the central message of the letter—that the ghost is now off duty—is not. Firmly, unequivocally, tell the ghost that you are now able to take care of yourself and that you will no longer need his or her supervision. Period. Here is a sample letter:

Dear Mother,

First, I want you to know that I love you very much. I know you loved me, too, in the best way you knew how. You had such a hard time growing up. When you talked about your mother, I heard—more or less between the lines—that your mother was cold, uncaring, a no-nonsense sort of person who never approved of you. I know that you really had no support, and felt you had no choice but to get married yourself. I think you were always unhappy. And you hoped that, if you played your cards right, your kids would have more choices than you had. And that is where your disapproval came in. It was your desperate attempt to shape us up, to give us a shot at what you never had. But it was so powerful, much more powerful than you ever suspected. And, years after your death, your disapproval and disappointment are still reverberating in my head. Now I want to make peace with you, to let both of us off the hook. Wherever, whoever you are now, you can just relax. Your supervision is no longer necessary. I know it will seem strange at first. I may have to keep reminding both of us that you're not in charge anymore. But I'm going to be fine without you. I'm going to take good care of myself. In fact, my regime will be kinder and gentler than the one you have always imposed.

All the best,
Marny

Now, practice writing your own letter:

Dear _____

_____

_____

_____

_____

_____

_____

_____

_____

_____

_____

_____

_____

After you've written your letter, you might want to keep it around as a reminder. Or you may want to revise it, or dash off notices to some other tenacious ghosts.

Writing such a letter can be painful. It may also stir up painful old memories. And after you compose it, you might want to give yourself a pat on the back. You deserve it.

All Rewards Are Not Created Equal

Now you're ready to think of other ways you can reward yourself. Kim likes to save up for a professional massage or go for a mountain hike. Marny prefers dinners with friends and queer films. Rewards can include treats like special dates or trips. But they can also include less pricey adventures: people-watching at a local park, intimate time with a friend or partner, cuddling or playing with a pet, taking guilt-free time off from a project to read a novel or listen to music.

Mention treats and the issue of goodies is bound to pop up. Does a chocolate truffle constitute a treat? How about two or three? How about fourteen? Or how about a glass of wine? If one is good, aren't four even better—the long overdue debt to herself that the depressed person should finally repay? The problem is that certain quick fix treats, in the long run, can turn into depressants. So we want to encourage the development of a repertoire of non-depressing treats. Take yourself to a museum that you've always been curious about, or pick a good film to see alone (so that you can cry or guffaw without being self-conscious). Haul out the vibrator for a sensuous interlude with yourself or visit a flower market and sniff your way from the bromeliads to the bougainvillea. Take out your pad again and make a list of all the things you always told yourself you'd do, if only you had the time. Now, select one or two and, on your calendar, mark the day and time you'll do them. Now, take a moment and savor your accomplishment. You've actually made a date with yourself, planned something strictly because it appealed to you. Chances are it is an unprecedented gesture. But it is only the beginning of self-nurturing.

Advanced Self-Nurturing

Before we go on, we want to mention a common trap that novice nurturers fall into: Beginning attempts at self-care can easily turn into the old carrot and stick routine. Say, for example, the new self-nurturer rewards himself for a job well done. So far, so good. But what if the critical voice in his head, so recently deactivated, starts to stir again. It informs him that a job well done isn't good enough. It could be better. Much better. Soon, self-administered rewards for accomplishments turn into a system of bribes. When the bribes no longer serve as goads to greater achievements, the reactivated head committee may start wielding the same old stick. The predictable outcome of this scenario is a swift return to the blues.

An expanded definition of self-nurturing may help you avoid this pitfall. To nurture yourself means to attend mindfully to your needs—all your needs. Although positive strokes and rewards are part of this attention, self-nurturing includes much more. Comprehensive self-care includes nurturing your body, your mind, and something else more intangible: your spirit or your soul. Here are some specific tips for self-nurturing:

Listening to the Body

When we hear the phrase "body language," we tend to think in terms of postural signals: How, for example, sitting with one's arms folded indicates a certain reticence or how leaning forward signals receptivity. Such postural cues are a form of corporal communication. When we refer to body language, however, we are talking about a different kind of nonverbal conversation. It is a dialogue that goes on all the time between ourselves and our bodies and it consists of a series of internal cues about our need for sleep or food or exercise or touch. There are plenty of reasons not to attend to such messages. Often, they aren't convenient. If, for example, a work project isn't complete and a midnight deadline looms, we must find a way to bypass the fatigue signals and soldier on. Plenty of cultural messages also contradict our bodies' cues. The "instant pain relief" ads that pepper us whenever we turn on the TV or open a magazine instruct us to suppress—rather than listen to—our bodies' language.

Finding a reasonable balance between cultural expectations and our bodies' rhythms is a critical part of self-nurturing. The next time you have a headache or a stomachache, wait a few minutes before you rush to your medicine cabinet. See if you can decode the pain. What sort of pressures is your body responding to? Are you over-working? Do you feel lonely? Do you need to get back to the gym or start meditating again? Would a nice stretch or massage hit the spot? Are you holding back tears or anger? The answers probably suggest that your body needs more than Pepto Bismol. Is it possible to give your body some of what it wants? If you need to rest, can you close your eyes for ten minutes? If you have been focusing on a computer screen for too long, can you get up and stroll around? These are easy, beginning steps. You get the idea. Let your body be your guide. It is an excellent self-nurturing coach—the best you'll ever have.

But say you feel numb. You have no sensations at all in your body. Perhaps, after years of censorship, it has ceased sending all communiques and become mute. Nurturing yourself means renew-ing a dialogue with your body. In order to jump-start the conversa-tion again, you'll need a big sheet of paper: a butcher block–sized page will do. Draw a rough outline of your body. Be sure to include every part of yourself—legs, arms, neck, head, fingers, toes, joints, breasts, butt, stomach, genitals. Now, using your pencil like a Geiger counter, retrace the contours of your body very lightly and slowly. Let your pencil linger over certain parts. What messages are you picking up? Are you getting particular signals from your neck? Your stomach? Your back? Do you feel sad or angry as you retrace parts of yourself? What have certain body parts decided *not* to tell you?

The division between body and mind, or feelings, is obviously artificial. How arbitrary the split is becomes clear when you realize how easy it is to translate your bodily signals into particular emo-tions. The next part of self-nurturing involves their expression.

Emotional Expression

"Big boys and girls don't cry" is the most obvious example of emotion-discounting messages we heard growing up. But there were others, dozens of them. Sometimes they were wordless messages: simply the disapproving expressions of our parents when we complained or argued. The proper guides to action, we learned, were reason and logic. Feelings only got in the way.

As queer children and adolescents, we were particular casualties of this brand of chilly logic. After all, it is certainly "abnormal" and "unreasonable" to be attracted to the same sex. Concealment in one area spreads easily to others. Consequently, when it came to our emotions, many of us learned to be master-deceivers. Our skillfully wrought *façades du jour* kept us safe in plenty of situations. But they also put us at risk for depression. How, then, can we begin to express the emotions that we have learned to treat as dangerous emissions? The most nurturing answer we can give is to go slowly. The first step in the process is to reassure yourself about your entitlement to your own emotions. The following bill of emotional rights comes from *Stop Smiling, Start Kvetching*. Dr. Held points out that:

- You are entitled to see your problem as a real problem and, we would add, your feelings as authentic, legitimate emotions.

- You don't have to tell yourself that it's not that bad

- You don't have to convince others that it's not that bad.

- You are entitled to complain to others.

Since all your experience contradicts these tenets, we expect a little initial skepticism. But even though you don't believe in your rights at first, keep pondering them. Ultimately you'll see that they make a certain sort of sense. To test out these new premises, choose a situation where the stakes aren't too high. Nobody is likely to drop dead or leave, if, for example, you admit that you didn't love the film as much as they did. If you still feel shaky about going public with your feelings, we suggest you start to keep a journal. Keep it small enough to fit easily in your pocket or pack. Pull it out a few times a day and jot down your feelings. Or doodle them. They can be your response to certain events or just a log of your free-floating emotions. Proceed as slowly as you need to with this expression of less-than-positive feelings. They are the heart of your self-nurturing program. Now for the soul.

Soul, Spirit, the Time/Space Continuum, the Big Picture, Somewhere Over the Rainbow

We don't know exactly what to call this third dimension of self-nurturing, so we've tried every label we could think of. We hope that at least one of our designations for beyond-the-self will ring your celestial chimes.

Transcendent travel is another element of self-nurturing. Some people do it with art or music; others pray or chant; still others find it by reveling in the glories of Mother Nature. Even though each of these travelers follows a different route, they all seem to convene at the same point. Journey's end is marked by a blend of contemplation and awe, of serenity and ecstasy. You've probably been there yourself. But instead of stumbling upon it haphazardly, when you've fallen in love or watched a dazzling sunset, we're suggesting that you make this experience a central part of your new self-nurturing regimen. How? We don't know. We simply know that you have a capacity to experience such mysteries on a daily basis. One route that seems to offer easy access is meditation or some other form of regular spiritual practice. Another seems to be regular, vigorous exercise. Still another is taking regular time-outs to listen to other-worldly geniuses like Bach or Thelonious Monk. In short, nourishing your soul is as important as feeding your body.

Summary

We've touched on the basics of self-nurturing. Of course, your regimen will include many other activities: fun, sex, good times with friends. A successful regimen also includes sustaining these activities over time. Dr. Ellis has called this approach to self-care long-term hedonism. Try on the title. Can you savor the notion of yourself as a long-term hedonist? If so, wear the label proudly. We think it is a grand appellation—almost as good as being queer.

We've covered a lot. At this point, a summary of our main ideas might be useful:

Self-Help Guidelines for Every Day

First-tier interventions for negative thinking:

- When you find yourself feeling sad, insecure, angry, or confused, search your thoughts for self-talk that is discouraging, frightening, or irrational.

- Evaluate the self-talk for accuracy or usefulness and begin using mental strategies that contradict negative thinking.

- Think about what deep-seated beliefs about yourself are being activated by the situation, and if the belief is negative, try to counter it with a revised, more accurate statement about the self. For example, "I am cherished by my partner," in response to "I am unlovable."

- When you are challenging a negative thought, remind yourself that you are your own best guardian or the parent that you always wanted. Your new voice (or self-talk) is respectful of you, is wise and understanding, has endless patience, and believes in your absolute value to the world.

Second-tier interventions for homophobia:

- Tell yourself that you have the right to exist.

- When your right to existence is denied in any way, you have the right to protest.

- Your protest can be both visible and noisy.

- You are entitled to nurture yourself.

A comprehensive self-nurturing program includes:

- Positive strokes and rewards

- Tuning into and responding to body language

- Emotional expression

- Soul food

In the next chapter, we'll look at some more queer interventions for depression.

CHAPTER 7

Queer Psychotherapy
The Talking Cure

It's only natural to want to talk about the blues. And it seems to help. So, when we get in funks, most of us turn to friends, lovers, family members, and, of course, shrinks. High percentages of gay and lesbian blues-sufferers frequent psychotherapy offices in times of stress. But even though surveys show that such support is an effective depression remedy and a useful adjunct to immediate support networks, psychotherapy may not be every queer's cup of tea.

How to Choose a Therapist

One of the major stumbling blocks seems to be trust. How, some of us wonder, can we expect strangers to be loyal or to genuinely care about us? Money issues also loom large. If we already have confidantes, isn't it absurd to pay someone—a sort of "rent-a-friend"—to listen to our woes? Or perhaps psychotherapy seems problematic for other reasons: Perhaps it is too inconvenient or it seems apolitical—an individualistic solution for societal ills.

Some of the criticisms of therapy are justified. On the other hand, some downsides of therapy, examined in another light, may actually be plusses. It may be helpful, for instance, to talk to someone outside our immediate circle—someone who is not a friend or a lover. Perhaps a confidante's behavior has triggered the blues. Or perhaps friends' over-identification with the problem has resulted in unsolicited advice, futile rescue attempts which have only made the situation worse.

In other words, psychotherapists' outsider status—the very quality that disqualifies them as "family"—may be useful. Regardless of their theoretical orientations, psychotherapists have been trained to recognize boundaries and stay out of the stew—your stew. They are empathic, and at the same time they know that if they over-identify with their clients' hopelessness, they will compromise their ability to be agents of change. There are other reasons psychotherapists may provide additional help during the down times. First, they will have a particular theoretical framework—a specific way to interpet the blues. After poking and prodding your depression, trying unsuccessfully to make some sense of it yourself, it may be an enormous relief to let someone with more experience and expertise have a go at it. Secondly, a therapist will come up with a plan of action. Of course, one size does not fit all, and the therapist's approach will depend as much on your symptoms as it does on her theoretical orientation. Perhaps she will conclude that you need a good dose of nonjudgmental listening, and simply mirror your feelings. Perhaps he will confront you about self-destructive behaviors and help you make a self-protective pact with yourself. Perhaps, in the process of rummaging around in old memories, she will help you arrive at new insights. Perhaps the therapist, by acting as social critic, can pinpoint the ways in which you have internalized anti-gay, or anti-female, or anti-ethnic attitudes and help you make peace between previously warring aspects of yourself. The particular strategy that the therapist chooses may not be as important as the fact that you now have an ally—someone to support and guide you through your depression.

On the plus side, then, therapy can offer an outsider's neutrality, empathy, and a clarifying perspective. On the negative side, therapy can be costly and time consuming ... and it doesn't always work. Not all depressions respond to talk treatment and, furthermore, not all therapists are good at their profession. Psychotherapy consumers have some protection against ethics violations but, if therapists are licensed, there is little to protect clients from ineffective therapy. Perhaps the best protection against substandard therapy is to be well-informed. With such consumer empowerment in mind, we will explore the options and issues facing therapy seekers. We hope this brief guide through the therapy marketplace will increase the chances that individual psychotherapy, if you should choose that route, is a positive, helpful experience.

Psychotherapist Credentials

There are many different types of psychotherapists and levels of training. The basic types include psychiatrists, psychologists, and counselors. The term "psychotherapist" can refer to any of the three basic types of mental health professionals that we are describing here. Each of these has a corresponding state credential license or certification. Some practice independently and some may require ongoing supervision by a higher-licensed professional. In most states, individuals in training in each of these professions are allowed to provide psychotherapy or counseling services under the direct supervision of a licensed professional. This is usually a formal part of a training program or clinic. Psychotherapists who are in training are usually required to reveal that they have not completed their degree or licensure requirements and they are often referred to as residents, fellows, interns, practicum students, or trainees.

Even though the degree of rapport between clients and therapists seems to be unrelated to particular credentials or length of training, it seems important for consumers to be aware of training differences before choosing a therapist.

Psychiatrists

Psychiatrists are physicians who have attended medical school and have an M.D. (doctor of medicine) degree. As physicians, psychiatrists are the only mental health professionals who can prescribe medications. For many years, psychiatrists provided what most people think of as "talking" therapy. That is, they met with their patients for forty-five minutes to an hour and explored personal histories and interpersonal dynamics. With the advent of drug therapy for treating mental health problems in the 1950s, psychiatry became more biologically focused. Today, most psychiatrists' practices are limited to the evaluation and diagnosis of mental health, and the prescription of psychotropic (mood-affecting) medications. Typically, patients are seen monthly for a brief medication monitoring and support session. It is likely that today's health insurance environment, where quality care is often sacrificed for cost savings, has contributed to this change in approach. Since psychiatrists are typically paid at higher rates than other mental health professionals, many insurance companies attempt to limit the psychiatrist's role as much as possible. Often, in the role of medication providers, they will work in conjunction with another type of psychotherapist, who continues to use primarily talking and behavioral therapies for treatment.

The majority of psychiatrists are represented nationally by an organization called the American Psychiatric Association (APA), which oversees the training, ethical standards, and professional practice guidelines for psychiatrists in the U.S. This organization provides the most frequently used diagnostic guide in the country, called the DSM-IV (*Diagnostic and Statistical Manual of Mental Disorders, Fourth Edition. Text Revised,* 2000). In 1973, after reviewing available research data on homosexuality, the APA board of trustees decided that homosexuality in itself did not constitute a mental disorder, and the larger membership of this organization went on to vote to back the board's decision. In 1986, all references to homosexuality were finally removed from the DSM. In 1998, the APA's board voted to condemn therapy aimed at turning lesbians and gays into heterosexuals.

Psychologists

Psychologists are also doctors, though not medically trained. A psychologist has received a doctorate in psychology, which can be a Ph.D. (doctor of philosophy), a Psy.D. (doctor of psychology), or an Ed.D. (doctor of education) with an emphasis in psychology. Some psychologists, trained to be scientists and professors, do not see patients and are not licensed to provide psychotherapy. Though they received a Ph.D. or other advanced degree in psychology, they did not receive specific, supervised training in applying their knowledge in mental health settings. Those who are trained to provide psychotherapy are usually considered clinical psychologists, counseling psychologists, or educational psychologists. The term "psychologist" is regulated by the state so that people who refer to themselves this way must have passed a national and state examination. Therefore, other mental health professionals may have a doctoral degree but are not necessarily psychologists.

There are many areas of treatment in which psychiatrists and psychologists overlap. They are both equipped to make psychological diagnoses and to provide some form of behavioral and psychological treatment. They also both have doctoral degrees and can provide talking psychotherapy. Since psychologists do not attend medical school, they typically cannot prescribe medication as a part of their therapy. But as mentioned previously, they may work in conjunction with a psychiatrist who will prescribe and monitor medications. Psychologists are usually uniquely qualified to perform certain types of psychological assessments, including intelligence and learning disability testing, personality testing, and neuropsychological testing.

The hourly fees for psychologists generally tend to be less than for psychiatrists (although there are exceptions), but tend to be higher than for counselors.

Most psychologists are represented by the American Psychological Association, also known as APA. This organization also supports the view that homosexuality in itself is not a disease.

Counselors and Other Types of Psychotherapists

This term applies to a wide range of mental health practitioners with an equally wide range of degrees and training, and this category represents the largest number of practitioners. Most mental health counselors have a master's degree in some form of social science. These professionals are also typically trained in an academic setting where they have acquired either an M.S. (master of science), an M.A. (master of arts) in psychology or counseling, an M.Ed. (master of education) in psychology or counseling, or an M.S.W. (master of social work) with an emphasis in counseling.

To try to avoid some confusion, it is important to mention that the term "counselor" is sometimes applied to other types of helping professionals. They include alcohol and drug counselors, crisis counselors, peer counselors, school or camp counselors, financial counselors, vocational counselors, nutritional counselors, and spiritual counselors. These types of professionals do not necessarily have a master's or higher degree or any specific training in psychotherapy. Alcohol and drug counselors typically have some form of training to work with people in treatment for addiction, but the training varies widely from center to center and state to state, and alcohol and drug counselors typically are not trained in general psychotherapy practice. Any of the above psychotherapists may also be an addiction counselor or specialist.

Because the term "counselor" can apply to such a wide range of professionals, it is important to make sure potential helpers are licensed psychotherapists.

In some states, counselors with a master's degree can perform most, if not all, of the services offered by a psychologist, while in others, they may be restricted from performing certain duties that the state feels only a psychologist can provide, like the types of psychological testing that we mentioned before. Counselors are also not allowed to prescribe medications.

National organizations for counselors include the National Association of Social Workers, the American Association for

Marriage and Family Therapists, and the American Counseling Association. Like the two APAs, these organizations support the view that homosexuality is a healthy alternative to other sexualities.

Other Practical Issues

Licensure

Although licensing laws and procedures vary from region to region, most states have boards that control the licensing and credentialing of mental health professionals. Boards are usually appointed by the governor or elected by a state professional association. The primary function of such oversight bodies is to protect consumers. Board members set minimum standards that each professional must meet to qualify for his or her license. They also insure the safety of the public by not allowing people who are incompetent or otherwise unqualified to practice. They handle complaints and, in the case of therapist misconduct, they are empowered to issue reprimands, or to suspend or revoke licenses. The board typically takes action for both illegal acts performed by a mental health professional (such as rape) and unethical acts which may not necessarily be illegal, but are considered inappropriate (such as seductive behavior or coercion). Such board actions, as well as complaints that do not result in action, are a matter of public record and will be provided to consumers by boards upon request. Although state licensing boards attempt to block professionals who are not licensed from practicing, they have limited power over non-licensed professionals. The best that they can do in most cases is to prevent the person from providing services that are by law only to be provided by a licensed professional. Consequently, consumers who have been mistreated by unlicensed therapists must look elsewhere to redress their grievances.

Psychiatrists are generally licensed through the state medical board and psychologists are licensed through the state board of psychology. Master's level clinicians may have a separate board or they may be subsumed under one of the above two boards. In California, all licensed professionals, from contractors to beauticians, are licensed through the State Board of Consumer Affairs, with subdepartments for each unique profession. People with master's degrees in social work typically use the initials L.C.S.W. (licensed clinical social worker) or B.C.S.W. (board certified social worker) and in California, licensure is available for counselors at a master's or doctoral level, called an M.F.T. (marriage and family therapist). Other terms for nonpsychologist or nonpsychiatrist counselors include L.P.C. (licensed professional counselor) and psychological associate.

Professionals who are in training or are obtaining the required supervision hours for licensure may provide services in most states under the close supervision of someone who is already licensed in their field. Usually, this means that the patients of the person in training or supervision will be discussed with the supervising professional in detail on a regular basis. Sometimes, the trainee or supervisee will ask to tape record (audio or video) therapy sessions for use later with their supervisor. In most cases, the supervisor and the therapist in training will be studying the process in order to improve therapy. However, this may affect client comfort level, and if you are in the process of therapy shopping, you may want to ask if this will be something that your therapist does routinely. If taping or some other form of observation is used by your therapist in training, he or she is required to inform you that this is their practice beforehand. Psychologists who are not yet licensed but are accumulating supervised hours may be referred to by such terms as a psychological assistant (if they are working under a licensed psychologist's supervision) or as a "temporarily licensed" psychologist (where they are granted permission by the board to practice only under supervision).

Money Matters and Insurance

Fees that are charged vary and depend on the level of training and experience of the therapist. Psychiatrists generally charge the highest amount per hour, with psychologists charging the next highest and psychotherapists or counselors charging less than the other two. Typical fees can range from over $150 down to $75 per session.

There are exceptions to every rule and in some locations a highly specialized counselor may charge as much as or more than a psychiatrist. Prices also vary according to the local markets. University-associated therapists typically are on the higher end of the scale, but often are also involved in highly specialized training or research programs. Some therapists (and clinics, particularly training ones) offer some or all of their practice slots to patients who pay out of their own pocket on a sliding scale. Modification of standard fees are usually based on reduced income levels and can be as low as $5 to $40 per session.

Many insurance companies also offer outpatient mental health benefits. They may require members to pay a low co-payment for each session or companies may reimburse members for a portion of their out-of-pocket payments. Most HMOs offer limited mental health coverage. That is, they will only pay for a specified number of sessions per year. They may also have a lifetime cap on money that they will pay for mental health services. Some may only cover inpatient psychiatric treatment. Most require that you see a provider on their "panel" or list of approved providers. These therapists can be made up of a wide variety of practitioners from M.D.s to M.A.s, who have agreed to work within the guidelines of the company that contracts with them to provides services. The company typically has a mechanism in place to approve or deny the provision of mental health services. Mental health providers may be required to keep HMOs supplied with regular updates about the diagnosis and progress of therapy. Their continued authorization for services depends on the HMO's assessment of such information. The general guideline for an HMO or managed care company is "less is more"—the less therapy they provide, the more money they save.

Therapeutic Orientation

Every psychotherapist usually has a primary theoretical perspective or psychological theory upon which they base their practice. If you have never been in psychotherapy before, you may not have a sense of what type of approach makes sense for you. In some cases, the actual theoretical orientation of the therapist may be less important than how comfortable and supported you feel when you are working together. In many cases, a therapist will have a flexible range of therapeutic approaches that can be tailored to meet the specific needs of an individual client. For orienting purposes, we'll give brief summaries of a few of the major schools of therapy. Keep in mind that these are very simplistic descriptions and do not adequately describe the richness of each approach. It is also good to remember that there are many other forms of psychotherapy not included here, but that may be just as, if not more, effective as the ones listed . There also are subgroupings of therapies that fall within some of the categories listed below that are considered variants or revisions of the traditional approaches.

Psychoanalytic Therapy. Psychoanalysis was formulated by Dr. Sigmund Freud in the early part of this century. Psychoanalysts consider symptoms such as depression, anxiety, or maladaptive behaviors to be the result of an individual's unconscious efforts to solve emotional problems and achieve psychological harmony. Psychoanalysands (or people undergoing psychoanalysis) strive to discover the meanings of their symptoms and, through this understanding, resolve underlying conflicts.

According to psychoanalytic theory, present-day psychological and emotional difficulties have their roots in the formative childhood years, specifically as a result of conflict within the individual's relationship with his/her parents. Because psychoanalysts believe that unresolved conflicts from the original parent-child relationship will be transferred to present-day relationships, special attention is paid to the relationship that develops between the patient and the analyst.

A psychoanalyst is a mental health professional (typically a psychiatrist, but also psychologists and social workers) who has received extensive training after obtaining their license, including undergoing his own psychoanalysis.

In classical psychoanalysis, patients are seen four to five times per week and typically will lie on a couch. Recumbent, without the distraction of face-to-face interaction, the patient is invited to say everything that comes to mind. This process, referred to as "free association," presumably minimizes self-censorship and, thereby, allows for greater access to unconscious thoughts, feelings, beliefs, and fantasies. Psychoanalysis is a lengthy process that usually lasts two to five years, sometimes longer. Even if this form of therapy seems preferable, its length and expense make it impractical for most therapy seekers.

Many therapists obtain training in psychoanalytic techniques but do not pursue complete psychoanalytic education. They may practice a modified version of psychoanalysis called psychoanalytic psychotherapy. In contrast to patients in classical psychoanalysis, clients of these practitioners may only come to therapy once or twice per week. Although psychoanalytic therapy may be long-term, it is generally shorter than a psychoanalysis.

Other forms of therapy that evolved from psychoanalytic theory include psychodynamic therapy, Adlerian therapy, Jungian analysis, and self psychology.

Object Relations Therapy. Object relations therapy, along with self psychology and psychodynamic therapy, all spring from psychoanalytic roots. That is, they are concerned with the emotional and mental processes, often unconscious, underlying human behavior. Such intrapsychic dynamics, shaped in childhood, should be—these therapists believe—the primary focus of therapy. The therapist, by listening carefully and interpreting the material that the client discloses, facilitates insight and change. In contrast to the one-person focus of classical psychoanalysis, however, object relations therapy has a two-person focus. According to the tenets of object relations therapy, intrapsychic dynamics are inseparable from interpersonal relations.

Object relations therapists emphasize that, from birth onward, individuals need to bond, to form attachments, and to relate to others. Each succeeding developmental stage includes a form of relationship that serves as a postive feedback loop, to enable further intrapsychic development. In other words, it is a psychology that is concerned with the development of the self in relationship to others.

This form of therapy tends to draw upon a wider range of theorists than classical psychoanalysis. In addition, the theorists who departed from Freudian orthodoxies use a broader range of techniques than traditional psychoanalysts. They also tend to see patients less often than psychoanalysts, primarily on a once per week basis. Some object relations therapists work with clients on a short-term, problem-focused basis.

Cognitive Behavioral Therapy. As we discussed in Chapter 6, cognitive behavioral therapy (CBT) is an education-based approach to psychotherapy that focuses on learning to recognize and change thoughts that affect our moods. In the late 1950s and early 1960s the founders of this approach, Dr. Aaron Beck and Dr. Albert Ellis, developed CBT as an alternative to longer-term, unconscious-centered treatments. Initially, it was applied to people with depression. With its success, it has become the primary treatment for many different types of emotional, cognitive, and behavioral problems. CBT techniques include specific methods for countering unhealthy thoughts, and cognitive reframing (learning to think about a situation from a different perspective). Most cognitive therapists work on a short-term, problem-focused basis and assign between-session homework that includes keeping daily thought records, reading educational materials, and applying the strategies discussed in sessions to real life situations.

On average, most cognitive behavioral therapists work on a time-limited basis, usually four to twelve sessions for depressed and anxious patients, although resolution of some types of core issues may take longer.

A specific form of cognitive therapy includes rational-emotive therapy or RET (developed by Dr. Ellis), which focuses specifically on learning to recognize and change irrational beliefs and "should" statements.

Behavioral Therapy. Because behavioral therapy focuses primarily on changing observable behaviors, little time is spent discussing childhood or interpreting unconscious motivation. Behavioral therapists collaborate with their clients to design behavior change plans that reward desirable behaviors and eliminate undesirable ones.

Specific behavioral techniques include relaxation training, systematic desensitization (learning how to reduce specific fears or phobias), assertiveness training, and self-control procedures. As with cognitive behavioral therapy, this approach emphasizes setting and meeting measurable goals. Behavioral therapists work on a short-term basis—usually between four and twelve sessions.

Client-Centered or Rogerian Therapy. Dr. Carl Rogers, the founder of client-centered therapy, was one of the few theorists who gave self-esteem (or self-regard, as he called it) a central role in the formation of personality. He felt that childhood experiences often thwarted the natural self-actualizing tendencies of human beings. By providing empathy and unconditional positive regard, therapists could compensate for earlier developmental impediments. In such a corrective, nurturing atmosphere, clients could heal, become more revealing and authentic.

Mirroring—the accurate reflecting of client's thoughts and feelings by the therapist—is the primary technique of client-centered therapists. But more than any specific technique, Rogerians believe that the relationship with a caring, empathic, and unconditionally accepting therapist is the key to change. In terms of duration, client-centered therapy falls somewhere between cognitive behavioral or behavioral therapies and psychoanalysis. Typically, Rogerian therapists see clients on a once-a-week basis for courses of treatment that range from six months to several years.

Family Systems Therapy. In the late 1950s and early 1960s, a group of theorists and therapists that included Gregory Bateson, Virginia Satir, Murray Bowen, and Salvador Minuchin began to focus on social systems. They discerned that, no matter how chaotic or dysfunctional such systems might seem, they had an internal coherence or equilibrium. This innovative perspective led to a new way of viewing individual problems. Instead of considering the troublesome behavior of a family member through the lens of mental illness, systems therapists saw it as a way of maintaining the family equilibrium. In fact, if the symptomatic person were to leave the family, his role would be assumed by someone else, or somehow distributed among all the family members.

Systems theorists shifted the treatment focus from the "identified patient's " behavior to the behavioral rules and roles assumed by all the family members. The goal of therapeutic intervention is to change the dysfunctional homeostasis to a healthier balance. With that in mind, systems therapists reinforce mother-father bonds, and at the same time they try to undermine inappropriately triangulated or symbiotic unions between children and parents.

When systems therapists see clients individually, they maintain their contextual perspective. That is, the client is encouraged to see his role in the family and work toward establishing healthier boundaries vis-a-vis the larger unit.

Most therapists work with families or individuals on a once-a-week basis. Sessions may shift to alternate weeks or once a month. Depending on whether the sessions are individual or family, they may last from one to two hours. Therapists usually take a directive role, making suggestions that challenge or unbalance previous dysfunctional patterns, and giving individual or dyadic boundary-strengthening homework to be completed between sessions. There is no specific duration for systems therapy. It can take a couple of sessions or last for years. The ultimate goal is to help family members become less enmeshed and more autonomous.

Existential-Humanistic Therapy. Among the many contributors to this philosophical approach are Dr. Ludwig Binswanger, Dr. Medard Boss, Dr. Rollo May, Dr. James Bugental, and Dr. Sam Keen. These therapist-philosophers believed that it is appropriate for therapists to help their clients come to terms with the anguish—the painful choices—that is part of the human condition. Rather than a set of techniques, such a psychotherapeutic endeavor consists of a collaborative journey of personal discovery. To embark on such a journey requires the voyager to leave behind the familiar landmarks—the "truths" which provided daily life with its certainty and structure. It also requires voyagers to accept the lower as well as higher aspects of themselves, to face their ultimate aloneness, and, ultimately, to come to terms with death. When clients become more cognizant of the parts of themselves and the world that existential anxiety has caused them to avoid or deny, they become more self-directed, authentic, and open to new experiences.

In contrast to the highly differentiated therapist-client roles in most forms of psychotherapy, existential therapy is more conversational—a collaborative exchange between equals. Although existential therapy tends to be a long-term process, the duration and frequency of explorations vary from client to client. Subgroupings within existential psychotherapy include logotherapy and reality therapy.

Social Constructivist Psychotherapies. Constructivist therapies are based upon the premise that external, objective realities do not exist apart from perceiving subjects. In other words, "knowing" something—imbuing it with a certain meaning—is a function of the human mind. Social constructivist therapists maintain that since realities have been invented, they can be reinvented in ways that may be more beneficial for clients. Social constructivist therapy, therefore, widens the horizon of possible outcomes by renegotiating the meanings that clients attribute to certain aspects of their lives. Social constructivists use a number of very specific verbal techniques to reshape clients' perceptions of themselves. By asking certain questions, or emphasizing certain responses, they may accentuate or broaden an important aspect of the client's experience that had been previously overlooked. Or perhaps they articulate or organize material in a way that highlights previously invisible avenues of action. Rather than seeing themselves as belonging to a particular school of therapy, some social constructivists consider their techniques as a mind-set that can be applied productively to client-therapist interaction. Social constructivist therapies, like the existential approach, tend to be more conversational, and the length and frequency of therapy varies according to needs of the client. Subgroupings within social constructivist therapies include narrative therapy and reminiscence therapy.

Postscript: Psychotherapeutic Specialties. In addition to their basic theoretical orientation, therapists may advertise themselves as having a specialty or particular area of expertise. These specialties include working with people with particular diagnoses or emotional problems like depression, anxiety, chemical dependency, or stress. Some even subspecialize within larger diagnostic categories like postpartum depression, fear of flying, cocaine abuse, or post-traumatic stress disorder (which develops following a major trauma). Others help people who are not necessarily having emotional problems or a mental illness. These therapists may describe themselves as "growth" or "insight"-oriented specialists who work with issues like building self-esteem, coming out to yourself or to others, or learning to become more assertive. There are few rules that govern when psychotherapists can call themselves "specialists," but some have actually had formal training in their speciality or subspecialty, while others simply feel that they have sufficient experience in working with patients with particular problems to call themselves specialists.

Therapists also may advertise qualities about themselves that they feel might be attractive to various groups, such as acknowledging that they are themselves lesbian or gay (or lesbian/gay "friendly"), Asian American, Jewish, disabled, Spanish-speaking, and so on.

Eclectic Therapy. The handful of therapies that we have described barely scratches the surface of choices available to therapy seekers. In fact one A to Z handbook of psychotherapy lists 250 types, everything from Active Analytic Psychotherapy to Zaraleya Psychoenergetic Technique (Henrick, 1980). Adding to the theoretical melee is the fact that most experienced practitioners blend and borrow. Even though therapists may identify themselves as cognitive therapists, for example, they probably make liberal use of the client-centered technique of mirroring, and client-centered therapists probably use cognitive techniques. In addition to such technique swapping, there is a constant ferment in the field of psychotherapy. Old theories modified or combined with elements of newer modalities evolve quickly into new schools of thought. Cognitive therapy, for example, after it incorporated some of the elements of behavioral therapy, spun off a branch called cognitive behavioral therapy described earlier and in detail in chapter 6. Because of the overlap and cross-fertilization among therapists and among different types of therapy, most therapists, however they may label themselves, are in fact eclectic.

There is another way in which therapists, at least the good ones, overlap. In study after study, effective therapists—regardless of their theoretical orientation—behave very similarly when they are alone with their clients. That is, they are accurately empathic, non-possessively warm, and genuine. These findings suggest that the therapist that you feel most comfortable with—rather than one who has a particular degree or theoretical orientation—may be the best fit for you.

Is It Important to Have a Lesbian or Gay Therapist?

We would love to resolve the issue with a resounding YES. Then we could wrap up the chapter with a few concluding remarks, and, thereby assured of the appropriate choice, you could narrow your search to gay and lesbian therapists. Unfortunately, sharing a same-sex orientation does not guarantee a good therapist-client match. Choosing a gay or lesbian therapist does have certain advantages. If you are a first time therapy consumer, for example, it may reduce your anxiety to know that the therapist is at least comfortable enough to acknowledge his or her sexual orientation in public.

Chances are, if the therapist advertises him- or herself as a gay or lesbian therapist, he or she will have first-hand experience with some of the issues that you need to discuss. A gay or lesbian therapist is also are likely to have had other clients who are also gay or lesbian. Consequently, he or she is experienced dealing with gay or lesbian issues in therapy. In addition to personal experiences and previous work with lesbian or gay clients, the therapist may also have studied the psychotherapeutic theories and research regarding healthy gay and lesbian development.

But queer therapists are not automatically the best fit for queer clients. After all, the term "queer" represents a whole cluster of styles, ethnicities, genders, sexual practices, tastes, social environments, and political beliefs. For example, there is no guarantee that a gay or lesbian therapist isn't going to be conservative and closeted. Despite sharing queerness, such a therapist might not be the best match for an Act Up member or a Lesbian Avenger. Or, an openly gay therapist might be problematic for someone who is very nervous about taking his or her first baby steps toward a gay identity. There is also the matter of access. Queer therapists may be hard to find in rural areas. And, conversely, they may be too easy to find in cities with a high-density gay population and intersecting social circles. Who wants to run into their therapist at parties and concerts, or worse yet, find out that your shrink is an ex of your new flame?

Class and ethnicity are also factors. A gay therapist, if he is white, may not be the best choice for an ethnic minority client who may also be gay. According to psychologist Bev Greene (1997), most mainstream therapists, even if they are gay, have not had any specific training about the general characteristics of their minority clients' cultures. Consequently, they are often oblivious to the interplay between ethnicity, class, race, and sexual orientation. In some cases, the therapist, afraid of seeming insensitive to racial discrimination, may be reluctant to urge ethnic minority clients to assume greater personal responsibility. As a result of cross-cultural illiteracy, people of color may have a particularly hard time finding a culturally sensitive queer therapist.

Finally, it is important to recognize that the sexual orientation of the psychotherapist alone does not automatically insure the possession of legitimate credentials, the high quality of his or her work, or even his or her ability to be empathic.

Even though we cannot give a resounding thumbs up to all matches between gay or lesbian clients and gay or lesbian therapists, we do recommend—unequivocally—that you find a gay or lesbian *affirming* therapist. Regardless of his or her sexual orientation, such therapists share the conviction that the choice of a lesbian or gay identity is positive, normal, and healthy. In addition they know that negative messages, lack of role models, and discrimination lead to low self-esteem, relationship difficulties, and ultimately depression.

In short, it is important to find a supportive, empathic therapist who is skilled at understanding and treating homophobia-related depression. Even though all the problems you bring to therapy will not be gay-related, a gay-affirming attitude should underpin and shape every exchange within the therapy relationship.

How Do I Go About Finding the Right Therapist?

Finding a therapist that will fit you and your budget might seem somewhat daunting at this point. If you live in a large metropolitan area, your choices may be overwhelming. In Los Angeles County for example, a recent compilation revealed that there are over 12,000 licensed psychotherapists in the county, not including psychiatrists! On the other hand, if you live in a rural area, your choices may be quite underwhelming. Kimeron became acutely aware of this problem when he found that he was one of only two openly gay psychologists in a relatively conservative Southeastern city with a population of over 400,000. Now that he lives in San Francisco, he is an "ordinary" psychologist who is one of many openly lesbian and gay psychotherapists.

While finding the right therapist may take some time and several false starts, here are a few recommendations for where to begin.

Check with local or state professional associations for psychiatrists, psychologists, or counselors. Most will have a referral directory with the therapist's specialties listed, including gay/lesbian issues, self-esteem, etc. If you can't find a local or state association, check with the national mental health organizations listed at the end of this chapter for local resources.

Ask your primary care doctor. Most physicians have referred many of their patients to psychotherapists for various life crises and emotional difficulties and usually they hear back from the patient at a future visit about whether the interaction was positive or negative. The physician then typically begins to send referrals to the psychotherapists whom patients report back on most favorably. Sometimes, the physician will prescribe an antidepressant, but only under the condition that you also work with a psychotherapist of some type.

Contact local gay or lesbian organizations such as switchboards, community leaders, or AIDS service groups. Often, they have referral listings of gay or lesbian professionals, but if they do not have a formal listing, they may be able to provide you with a helpful lead. If you live in a rural area, try calling the nearest urban area for lesbian or gay resources since they often will list resources that extend beyond the urban area itself. You also may try calling a general crisis line or local community mental health center for leads on lesbian and gay (or L/G affirmative) counselors.

Check online. If you type "gay psychotherapy" into most search engines, you will come up with lists of gay and lesbian psychotherapists in several major cities. Links will lead you to other organizations with other listings. Also use search engines in queer online organizations like PlanetOut. Local newsgroups can also be a source of referrals. For example, BA-SAPPHO offers lesbians in the San Francisco Bay Area a way to exchange announcements and queries. For more info on how the list works, send e-mail to: majordomo@queernet.org and in the body type "info ba-sappho".

Look in lesbian, gay or other "alternative" newspapers for advertisements by psychotherapists. Often, queer, or queer-friendly, psychotherapists will make themselves known to the community through local LGBT resources. Even if they are not queer thmeselves, the fact that they would seek out these kinds of formats suggest that they are comfortable with queer issues.

Go to the Yellow Pages in your phone book and look under Psychotherapists, Psychologists, or Physicians (with a Psychiatric specialty). Often, you will find listings that are large enough to include at least some information about the therapist, their specialties, and their approach. While some will actually list lesbian and gay issues in their listing, others may use language that suggests that they may be open to working with gays and lesbians, such as "specializes in women's issues," "sexual identity work," "alternative lifestyles," or "HIV support." Also in the Yellow Pages under Psychologist, Psychotherapist, or Psychiatrist, there are often ads for psychotherapy referral services. These organizations are usually made up of a large network of local psychotherapists who financially support the referral service phone number, advertisement, etc., and who benefit from it by having callers directed to the therapists within the service. They typically also list their specialties and theoretical approaches for callers with those specific requests. Keep in mind that just because one referral service does not have someone listed with your special request, they are usually not a complete listing of psychotherapists in your area. You may need to try another (or several) referral services before you find one that meets your needs.

Ask your close friends or family members if you are comfortable doing so. Sometimes you can get great leads from people who have either been in therapy themselves or know someone who has been. It is not necessary to disclose why you might be thinking about therapy nor is it necessary for them to know that the referral is for you personally. If you feel that the person you ask may be insensitive with the knowledge that you asked, don't ask them! You have a right to your privacy about this issue.

How to Pay for Therapy Using Your Insurance

Years ago, it was common that health insurance covered mental health visits no matter whom you decided to see. Psychotherapy was commonly provided on a long-term basis with few goals other than to make the client "feel better" or "healthier" and there was often no definitive way of knowing when therapy was completed. With rising costs of care, however, both in the medical and mental health fields, large insurance companies and employers began to search for ways to control costs associated with treatments of all kinds. The term "managed care" was coined to try to provide quality mental health and medical care in a cost effective manner, thereby increasing the company's profitability. Insurance companies that adopted a managed care model began to oversee the types of psychotherapy and treatments that could be provided as well as the number of visits that seemed appropriate to address the client's needs.

In addition to overseeing the way psychotherapy was conducted, some companies began developing "provider panels," or lists of specially approved psychotherapists who have contracted with the insurance company to provide care to the company's subscribers. On the good side of this strategy was the assurance that the clinicians were well-trained and qualified within their field of practice. On the not so good side, some believe, was that in order to become a panel member, a clinician must agree to practice according to the guidelines of the managed care company and to accept the rate of service the managed care panel was willing to pay them.

From a client's perspective, the good side is that typically co-payments are lower than full psychotherapy rates. There are drawbacks as well. You can only see a psychotherapist on the panel to get the best coverage by insurance. The managed care company typically limits both the number of sessions allowed per year, and specific types of problems or diagnoses may not be covered.

If you are covered for mental health services by a managed care company or health maintenance organization (HMO), there are several ways to try to improve your chances of finding a successful match with a psychotherapist. First, if you have a good working relationship with your primary care doctor and she or he is a provider with the same company, ask for a referral to a mental health clinician that she or he recommends. If you prefer a psychotherapist who is gay or lesbian, let your primary care doctor know about your preferences. If your primary care doctor does not know specific clinicians and their strengths and/or weaknesses in your situation, call your managed care company directly and ask to speak with someone who can help you find a suitable clinician. Often, the psychotherapists on the provider panel have indicated areas of specialization or interests that will indicate any expertise with queer issues and/or depression. Don't hesitate to ask for an openly lesbian or gay psychotherapist or someone with expertise in this area. Even if the company does not keep track of this information at the time you ask, the feedback will be useful for them in understanding the needs of their members.

If you have had previous and positive experience with a psychotherapist, but this clinician is no longer covered by your insurance plan, ask him or her to look over the provider panel list for the names of colleagues that they recognize and recommend to you. At minimum, they may be able to at least make suggestions about which clinicians may not be a good fit for you, even if they can't recognize one that would be a good fit.

If you are not comfortable asking your managed care company for a gay or lesbian psychotherapist, you can contact the organizations at the end of this chapter to obtain referrals to queer professionals. Then search your provider panel lists for their names. Sometimes panel lists are not updated and you may want to call your managed care company directly to see if a particular clinician who has been recommended to you has been added to the panel recently.

If you do obtain a recommendation of a clinician who is on your provider panel and has experience with your specific concerns, it would still be appropriate to follow the same interview strategy we mention in the next section. At the end of your interview, if you still don't feel comfortable with the clinician, ask for names of other clinicians who may be a better fit within the panel.

Finally, if you have had no luck in finding a comfortable psychotherapist within your provider panel, some managed care plans will allow you to see providers outside of the provider panel but with a higher co-pay on your part. Although more costly, it may ultimately provide you with the quality care you need.

How to Interview a Potential Psychotherapist

In *Dykes with Baggage*, a new anthology about the lighter side of queer psychotherapy, there is a piece called "Techniques for Testing Your Therapist." Cassendre Xavier, the author, writes, "I require focus from my therapist. Focus and an iron hand. I'm the queen of non sequiturs and changing subjects when the subject gets a little uncomfy" (Xavier, 2000). Therefore, the first hurdle Cassendre places in front of potential therapists is "The Compliment Test." Cassendre suggests that you pay your therapist a compliment. If she dwells on it too long, ditch her. Test number two is the "Sudden-Observation-of-Décor Test." After Cassendre makes an off-the-wall observation about an on-the-wall poster, her therapist observes that she has changed the subject and wonders if she'd like to talk about that. (This therapist has passed the test with flying colors.)

If therapists have passed the first two tests, they may proceed to the third: "The Great Boundary Test." This is when the client proposes that she go to the therapist's house for a sleepover. "Of all the tests, " Cassendre writes, "this is my favorite . . . Simply because of the various shades of red and pink their faces get and all the new deep-breathing exercises I learn from watching them."

It probably is important for both you and your therapist to do some mutual interviewing before you decide to work together. Some of you may like Cassendre's scoping out methods. Just in case you prefer a more direct approach, however, here are some questions to ask potential therapists either by phone or in a face-to-face interview.

- *Ask directly if they are gay/lesbian or gay/lesbian affirmative.* If they are not gay/lesbian themselves, or refuse to answer the question, ask how they feel about gay and lesbian sexual orientation. Ask what they think causes sexual orientation. And, finally, ask if their attitudes have changed over time. This answers to these questions should tell you whether or not they are gay/lesbian affirmative.

- *Ask about their experience in working with gay issues and/or your specific problem.* For example, you may want to know if they have worked with gay/lesbian people who are depressed.

- *What is their therapeutic approach or theoretical orientation?* Do they believe that homosexuality represents an abnormal (or pathological) developmental process or do they believe that homosexuality is one of many normal developmental paths for sexuality?

- *Ask about their training and credentials.* Are they a psychiatrist, psychologist, counselor, or something else? Are they licensed or credentialed through the state? It also may be helpful to know if they belong to any professional organizations, since these, along with the licensing boards, provide some avenue for complaints if you were to feel that the therapist was inappropriate or unethical. You can also call state licensing boards before seeing a therapist for information on past complaints filed about that therapist.

- *Ask about how long they expect therapy to take and how often they expect you to meet.* While most therapists cannot give an exact estimate, most can give you an average number of sessions, based on their past or current experiences with patients. You can also ask if they generally provide short-term (weeks to months) therapy or more long-term (months to years) therapy.

- *What other expectations do they have for their patients?* It will be helpful later to know their appointment cancellation policies, scheduling systems, and payment methods (cash, check, billing, etc.).

- *Ask how much they charge per session.* This may be a good opportunity to discuss whether they accept your insurance or whether they are on the approved provider panel for your managed care company. They may also provide a sliding scale to a portion, if not all of their patients, based on income and ability to pay.

- *Ask about their view of using medications as an adjunct to treatment.* Some therapists do not believe in the use of medications as an adjunct to psychotherapy and others frequently support the use of them. Most psychotherapists believe that there are occasions where medications can be beneficial when they are combined with talking therapy. Although you may not have an opinion about this issue, it may be helpful to know the therapist's view about it. If they do not prescribe medications themselves, you should ask whom they refer their patients to for such prescriptions.

- *Observe how they respond to your discussion of your sexuality.* Look and listen for nonverbal cues that they are affirmative/nonaffirmative or uncomfortable with certain topics. Are they supportive, unconditional, empathic, easy to talk to? Are there uncomfortable pauses? Are you aware of an immediate physical attraction or an immediate negative response that might inhibit you or interfere with developing a trusting, professional relationship?

What Are the Limits to My Confidentiality?

Most psychotherapists strive to keep the therapy environment safe and the information discussed secure and confidential. In order to make it easier for you to talk about painful emotional issues, they realize that you must be able to trust that they will not use the information against you or otherwise harm you. Most therapists will attempt to protect your right to privacy and most professional mental health organizations consider it unethical to violate a patient's right to confidentiality unnecessarily. Most will also only provide information to other people outside of the therapy situation with your written permission.

There are exceptions to the confidentiality rule. These exceptions include situations in which the therapist has a legitimate reason to believe that you are going to harm yourself or someone else. Specifically, a therapist may break confidence if you:

- Say you are going to kill yourself.
- Say you're going to kill or hurt someone else or damage their property.
- Are unable to take care of yourself due to a mental or medical illness (like being unable to feed yourself or get clothing or shelter because of confusion or hallucinations).
- Are abusing a child or dependent adult.

In most states, not only are psychotherapists ethically allowed to break a confidence in order to either get help or warn the victim, but they are mandated by law to report certain activities. Most often, psychotherapists are required to report suspected abuse of a child (regardless of whether you are the abuser or you have knowledge of someone else abusing a child) to the state's Child Protective Services; they could lose their licenses or face other legal penalties if they do not make this report. Psychotherapists have also been found guilty of neglecting to warn victims of crimes by their patients when the patient revealed to the therapist that they intended to harm a specific person. Most now feel compelled to call both the police and the victim to warn them if a patient makes a specific threat to harm a specific person or persons. Some states require the report of elder or disabled/dependent abuse to the appropriate investigative agency, and a few require the report of domestic violence or spousal abuse.

Most laws attempt to clarify under which specific conditions a mandated report is required. For example, if a patient says angrily, "I am going to take my gun and shoot my boss this afternoon!," and the therapist believes that this is indeed a serious threat, then he or she must obviously warn the boss that she or he is in danger. On the other hand, if you were to say jokingly, "I feel like strangling someone!," but had no one in particular in mind, or with exploration made it clear that you did not intend to actually act on those feelings, then the therapist would not make a report since a specific person or persons were not identified.

In the case of a suicidal threat, most therapists feel some responsibility to protect you from harm, even from yourself, particularly if they feel that you are acting irrationally or because you feel overwhelmed emotionally. Most will attempt to keep you from harming yourself until you are feeling less emotional or depressed or are thinking more rationally. They are usually allowed to provide basic information about you, your history, and your situation to emergency care providers who may become involved so that they can better care for you during this time. Some psychotherapists have the authority to begin an evaluation for admission to a psychiatric hospital if one should be deemed necessary because of potential self-destructiveness or harm to self or others. Most therapists, however, will attempt to prevent psychiatric hospitalization and help resolve such feelings on an outpatient basis with your cooperation.

Managed Care and Confidentiality

An important exception to confidentiality involves insurance companies' access to records. In most cases, because they pay for services, insurance companies feel they have the right to review the notes your therapist may keep or to discuss your case with your therapist. Many psychotherapists feel that this attempt to monitor care is an intrusion into their patients' right to privacy. If they do not acquiesce, however, they will not be paid for the services they render. You are in the same position. You will be asked to sign a release of information statement that allows the insurance company access to your records. If you refuse to sign, chances are, your treatment will not be authorized. The only sure way to avoid this intrusion is to find a way to pay for your services yourself, through a reduced or sliding scale fee arranged with the therapist.

If you cannot afford to pay out of pocket, here are several suggestions:

1. Talk to the therapist about how much information they provide to the insurance companies and how often. Sometimes, the therapist only has to provide an indication that you are benefiting from therapy without going into specifics. Ask them to provide as little information as possible to meet the minimum requirements of the company.

2. When selecting an insurance company, ask about their mental health benefits and what their policy is regarding obtaining psychotherapy notes, records, or talking directly to therapists. While you are there, ask them if you must see only a provider within their network or if you can use your benefits with any psychotherapist. You may need to look at other insurance options if you feel that the company is too controlling. You and your psychotherapist are most likely the best judges of the progress of your treatment.

3. Ask your therapist to keep your best interests in mind when they are keeping notes, documenting visits, or communicating with insurance company case managers. Most psychotherapists are already ethically bound to keep your best interests at heart, but a reminder will not hurt.

What if Your Therapist Says or Does Something Inappropriate or Unprofessional?

As we have mentioned previously in the chapter, if you are seeing a psychotherapist who is licensed or certified by your state, he or she is bound to follow both ethical and legal mandates. If you feel that you have been violated or harmed in some way, you may choose several options. If it seems to be a relatively minor disagreement or misunderstanding, you may feel comfortable confronting the therapist directly about their behavior. You may be able to resolve the issue to your satisfaction through discussion and then feel you can continue therapy together. You may also decide that you cannot work together and it would then be appropriate for your therapist to refer you to someone else. Another option is to get an opinion from another mental health professional about the situation and your options.

If you feel that the situation is serious, you then have several options. You can file a formal grievance against the psychotherapist to the state licensing board for that professional. Most boards have a specific process for filing complaints against the licensed psychotherapist. You can also file a complaint with the therapist's professional organization, such as the American Psychiatric Association, the American Psychological Association, or the American Counseling Association. You can also file legal charges against the psychotherapist if they have broken the law. Some behaviors are considered unethical, like disclosing personal information outside of therapy without your consent (and when it is not one of the exceptions to confidentiality that we mentioned earlier), but it is not illegal to do so. Other behaviors, like coercing a patient to have sex, is in some states both unethical and illegal.

The following is a basic summary of the ethical principles of psychologists:

1. Psychologists do not exploit the trust of their patients (including attempting sexual contact).

2. Psychologists avoid situations which might be construed as a conflict of interest that would impair their professional judgment.

3. Psychologists should acknowledge the limits of their experience and knowledge and whether they seek supervision or consultation from other experienced psychologists when necessary.

4. Psychologists respect the diversity of their patients' backgrounds, including race, gender, ethnicity, and socioeconomic background, and get training to provide adequate services to these groups.

5. Psychologists provide a portion of their services to clients where they receive little or no financial compensation.

6. Psychologists maintain an awareness of their own personal problems and try not to let them interfere with their ability to provide services to patients. If they cannot control these personal problems, they refrain from providing services until these problems have resolved.

7. Psychologists protect the confidentiality of their patients as much as possible, except in the case of a danger to self or others or with the patient's written consent.

8. Psychologists are encouraged to end therapy when it becomes obvious that the patient is no longer getting benefit from it, and they refer the patient to another psychotherapist if necessary.

Duration of Psychotherapy

To the uninitiated or to those who have seen too many Woody Allen movies, therapy can seem like an interminable process. In fact, the average course of treatment is less than ten sessions. The amount of time that you can expect to spend in therapy will depend on the issues on which you choose to work, the goals you have for change, the type of therapist you select (and their therapeutic approach), and your financial and/or health insurance status.

You and your therapist may also decide to shift gears midstream. Perhaps the crisis that brought you to therapy has been resolved. But other longstanding issues that have contributed to your depression have surfaced, and seem fruitful to explore. At that juncture, it is not uncommon to shift from a short- to a long-term perspective. The question is, how long is long? Again, this depends. There will always be life crises—problems which you prefer to hash over with someone who, by now, you trust. Some people find it useful to continue in therapy indefinitely. Others, however, may feel as though the benefits of therapy are diminishing. They want to leave, but perhaps they are reluctant to bring up the possibility with their therapist. Perhaps they are afraid of being "bad" patients; perhaps they are afraid they will be accused of not digging deep enough. We cannot emphasize how important it is to voice your wish to end therapy (as well as your anxiety about bringing up the whole subject). But say your processing of the subject of termination with your therapist does not change your desire to leave. Your therapist may respect your wishes and begin the process of saying goodbye. Or he may tell you that termination would be premature. Like finding a good match, this is another ticklish consumer-beware juncture. Therapists may not always be in the best position to gauge the appropriate conclusion for therapy. In the first place, most therapist training—when it comes to matters of termination—is sadly deficient. Therapists learn how to connect with clients; rarely do they get any direct training in how to part from them. Secondly, because therapists in private practice depend on clients for their income, they may be biased in favor of longer term therapy. Finally, clients' departures may stimulate therapists own separation and loss issues.

In short, when it comes to ending therapy, clients must trust their own instincts.

Spiritual Sources of Depression

Earlier in this book, we discussed many different factors that contribute to developing the blues, including biological, social, and psychological factors. For many queer people, however, the pain and alienation they feel can be better described from a spiritual perspective. Rev. Mel White, director of Soulforce, a group devoted to nonviolent protest of religious and cultural oppression of our queer family, believes that depressed GLBT folk suffer from depression because they have heard it over and over again that God doesn't love them. He feels strongly that these "pseudo spiritual" roots of depression must be pulled up and new seeds of genuine spirituality be planted and nurtured. We couldn't agree more that queer spirituality is vastly underestimated as a contributor to unhappiness and depression. While we do address self-nurturing in general in this book, if you are interested in more about this topic, Kimeron spends a significant amount of time providing specific suggestions for healing and nurturing the spiritual side of yourself as a healthy queer person in *The Gay and Lesbian Self-Esteem Book*. We also recommend the book *Coming Out Spiritually*, by Q Spirit executive director Christian de la Huerta.

For those of you who identify spiritual disconnection or alienation as a potential source of your depression and who wish to explore these issues with a psychotherapist, we have included the next two sections as both a warning and a guide. Don't forget to protect yourself against spiritual violence along the way!

What About "Religious" or "Spiritually Based" Psychotherapists?

Some psychotherapists emphasize their religious orientations. They may advertise themselves as Christian psychotherapists or pastoral counselors. In some cases, the psychotherapy practiced by such counselors is really thinly disguised recruitment into a cult or religious sect. Consumers should be careful to distinguish between such solicitations and the advertisements of other groups of therapists who also announce their spiritual orientation. These are gay and lesbian or gay-affirming therapists who are religious and feel that they are in a good position to help gay and lesbian clients understand that not every religious person is homophobic. These therapists feel that advertising as a religious psychotherapist is also a way for gay and lesbian clients with a spiritual orientation to feel more comfortable initially, much like therapists who advertise as bilingual or gay or lesbian. Some clinicians (in contrast to other practitioners who focus on feelings, thoughts, or behaviors) believe that the spiritual side of human beings is an important area to address. These approaches do not generally promote specific values or beliefs , but rather encourage patients to nurture and validate individual experiences of spirituality and healing. Keep in mind that a trained and licensed psychotherapist who addresses spirituality as a part of a broader approach to therapy is very different from someone who has no legitimate credentials and yet calls him- or herself a spiritual counselor, guide, or healer. Use great caution when approaching any untrained and/or uncredentialed professional.

"Ex-Gay" Ministries and "Reparative Therapies"

The most dangerous group of religious psychotherapists are those who purport to "change" sexual orientation from gay or lesbian to heterosexual (or gay/lesbian to "celibate"). These types of "orientation change" therapies are promoted primarily from a religious perspective and are often called "ex-gay" ministries. They include such fringe groups as Exodus International and Transformation Christian Ministries and they are supported by the right-wing Christian Coalition. The basic premise is that being gay or lesbian is a sin and that through prayer and religious counseling, sexual orientation can be changed. Such therapists assert that your depression (or any symptom that you disclose) comes from the fact that you are following the "wrong" path. They insist that if you change your sexual orientation, your depression will go away.

Many lesbian and gay people who go through these programs end up either dropping out or experiencing significant emotional distress. Most have low self-esteem prior to entering these programs and are therefore vulnerable to misinformation and the extreme forms of emotional abuse characteristic of the "reprogramming." Trainers attempt to teach gays and lesbians to ignore their inclinations and to behave as if they felt attracted to the opposite sex. In order for participants to "act like heterosexuals," they are instructed to walk, talk, and dress in "gender appropriate" ways.

None of these programs can provide objective and unbiased evidence that they actually create change in sexual orientation. From time to time, however, they do showcase a "successful convert." To continue to behave in socially acceptable ways, the "convert" must attend regular meetings or prayer groups, or check in with a sponsor. Many so called "ex-gays" find it impossible to maintain the charade. Even after marrying an "ex-lesbian" and obtaining a salaried position within a well-known religious organization, a recent poster boy for the ex-gay movement was caught visiting a Washington, D.C. gay bar.

An extremely small minority of psychotherapists continue to believe that homosexuality is a result of abnormal development and that they can change sexual orientation through "reparative therapy." These professionals are not sanctioned by any legitimate professional organization. Some have been ousted from legitimate professional organizations for reports of unethical or harmful forms of treatment. Although some claim to have successfully transformed gays and lesbians into heterosexuals, none have collected credible evidence that the change lasts over time.

The American Academy of Pediatrics, the American Psychiatric Association, and the American Psychological Association have issued statements suggesting that conversion therapies for gays and lesbians may not only *not* result in change in sexual orientation, but can actually provoke psychological harm. For more on this topic, author Andrew Sullivan (1998) examines in detail the arguments of the reparative therapists and exposes their weaknesses in his book *Love Undetectable: Notes on Friendship, Sex and Survival*.

In response to the reparative movement, there are now organizations to assist and support "ex-ex-gays" that help lesbians and gays recover from the trauma of trying unsuccessfully to change their sexuality and being subjected to cultlike anti-gay reprogramming. Our recommendation is to avoid "ex-gay" ministries and "reparative" therapies altogether. Being gay/lesbian is not a sin or an illness.

National Mental Health Practitioner Organizations

Each of the following organizations have subcommittees on gay/lesbian issues and may be able to help you locate a professional in your area. They can also provide information on professional ethics and grievance procedures.

American Association of Sex Educators, Counselors and
   Therapists
P.O. Box 238
Mt. Vernon, IA 52314
http://www.aasect.org
FAX (319) 895-6203

American Counseling Association
5999 Stevenson Avenue
Alexandria, VA 22304-3300
http://www.counseling.org
(800) 347-6647

American Psychiatric Association
1400 K Street, NW
Washington, DC 20005
http://www.thebody.com/apa/apapage.html
(202) 682-6325

American Psychological Association
750 First Street, NE
Washington, DC 20002
http://www.apa.org
(202) 336-5500

National Association of Alcoholism & Drug Abuse
   Counselors
1911 N. Fort Myer Dr. Suite 900
Arlington, VA 22209
http://www.naadac.org
(703)741-7686 or (800)548-0497

National Association of Social Workers
750 First Street, NE Suite 700
Washington, DC 20002-4241
http://www.naswdc.org
(202) 408-8600

CHAPTER 8

Medications and Other Biological Treatments

Queer Psychiatrists Speak Out

This book wouldn't be complete without including strategies for managing the biological components of the blues. Whether your depression started with biological triggers or they developed later as the severity increased, clinical scientists have added powerful tools to the options you have in your management plan. In this chapter, we've chosen to do something a little different to help you decide which tools may hold the most promise. Since neither of us are specialists in the area of medications or other biological approaches to depression, we decided to go to the experts.

After a brief overview of the available medical treatments, we are going to introduce you to two queer psychiatrists who specialize in lesbian and gay issues including depression in their practice: Dr. Nanette Gartrell and Dr. Todd Cornett.

We sat down with Drs. Gartrell and Cornett and interviewed them from the perspective of someone who had no prior history with antidepressant treatment. For the interview, we had two goals: first, to help you get as much information about when and how antidepressant medications are used, and second, to provide the information in a comfortable, conversational way. Many people who are depressed either don't have the energy or don't feel prepared to ask even basic questions about a new treatment, and it is clear that many overloaded mental health care professionals feel compelled to get to the bottom of things rather quickly. Our interview is a way of helping you get the information you need to make an informed decision.

We strongly encourage you to have a similar conversation with any physician who is prepared to prescribe medications for you so that you feel comfortable in making treatment choices. Before we get to the interviews, let's take some time to talk generally about medications and other biological ways of managing depression.

Medications for Managing Depression

As we discussed in some detail in chapter 3, there are often changes occurring within the brain that correlate with the psychological, emotional, and physical symptoms that you may be experiencing. Antidepressant medication can be very effective in reducing the discomfort and giving you the energy you need to solve some of the problems that either caused or result from your depressed frame of mind. Most Americans know the name of at least one antidepressant medication, with Prozac at the top of the list. Beyond knowing the name, however, many people have a good deal of misinformation about how these medications are used and how they work.

When Prozac was first introduced in the U.S., the media reported on some stories about people who became suicidal or aggressive after they had begun the medication, which prompted a bit of hysteria about the drug early on. Later, many of these stories turned out to be both false and misleading, based on hearsay and the fears of the public at large. We now know it to be a stable and highly effective medication for the treatment of depression. In this chapter, we hope to clarify some common misconceptions and provide you with a basic understanding of how these medications can be beneficial.

Although you may assume that all "psychiatric" medications work in similar ways, the term "antidepressant" refers to a unique class of medications. Other medications that have gotten popular press include Valium, Xanax, and Buspar, which some people assume are cut from the same pharmaceutical cloth as antidepressants. These three in particular, however, are not antidepressants at all, but are in the *anti-anxiety* medication camp. Antidepressants work in a very different way from other psychoactive drugs that also work in the brain.

In 1996, the queer-friendly comedy troupe Kids in the Hall released their first movie, called *Brain Candy*, a hilarious parody of the pharmaceutical industry and America's quest for perfect happiness in a pill. In it, a greedy drug company speeds up the production of a promising new antidepressant that creates total happiness in the taker. Soon, the drug company is making billions, selling truckloads to a gullible public. The whole country gets "happy" and the inventor of the pill becomes a celebrity . . . that is, until the first side effects begin to appear. We won't spoil the rest for you.

Many people have the illusion that an antidepressant can make you happy. Far from it. Antidepressants are not happy pills and do not create a sense of euphoria. What they do instead is to generally reduce the intensity of some emotional pain, begin to normalize the disturbed biological depressive symptoms (such as sleep problems and low energy level), and restore some of the ability to experience pleasure and enjoyment. Antidepressant medications seem to restore certain parts of the nervous system to a more normal state of functioning. Once the normal biological state is restored, nerve cells begin to function normally again, thereby allowing depressive symptoms to begin to resolve. Because this process takes some time, often you will not begin to see the benefits of taking an antidepressant for several weeks. The time it takes for the medication to work will depend on your body's chemistry, the medication itself, and the dosage.

In general, antidepressant medications increase the amount of the neurotransmitters serotonin and norepinephrine available for communication between nerves. As mentioned in chapter 3, electrical impulses travel along nerve cells until they reach the end point of the cell axon, or terminal button. Because nerve cells don't actually touch, but are divided by a gap called a synapse, the electrically stimulated cell communicates with the next cell by sending chemicals (neurotransmitters) through the gap in tiny containers called vesicles. Like a note put in a bottle by a child and released on a pond, these vesicles will drift over to the next cell. Once the vesicles reach the next nerve cell, the loading dock accepts them and the neurotransmitter inside can continue the communication to the next nerve cell and so on, until the emotional areas of the brain have been activated.

In many depressions, however, this process appears to be disrupted in two ways. The first problem is related to a process known as "reuptake." When a cell releases a bunch of vesicles carrying neurotransmitters into the synapse, it is normal for some of the vesicles to be sucked back before they get too far away. The reuptake process appears to malfunction during depression, reabsorbing far too much of the released neurotransmitters before they have a chance to move across the gap and stimulate the next cell. This means that communication in the brain is not functioning properly, resulting in depressive symptoms. Most antidepressants decrease the reuptake of the neurotransmitters in the synapse, thereby allowing the vesicles to get where they need to go.

The other problem that can occur during depression is when the cell that is receiving the vesicles filled with neurotransmitters either begins to turn away the incoming vesicles or becomes less sensitive to the chemicals after they have successfully traversed the divide. Both reuptake in the communicating cell and decreased receptivity in the receiving cell interfere with normal nervous system processes. Either process appears to make people more prone to depression.

The good news is that even without treatment, these biological malfunctions can spontaneously reverse themselves in many types of depression. The bad news is that in untreated depression, this spontaneous reversal can take anywhere from months to years. The other good news is that antidepressant medications can be highly successful in reversing the biological symptoms of depression.

However, all antidepressants are not created equal. As we discussed in chapter 3, there are multiple types of neurotransmitters that may be involved in the experience of depression. Currently, there are four basic classes of antidepressants. Each class, chemically distinct, operates differently. These are norepinephrine antidepressants (tricyclics), serotonergic antidepressants (selective serotonin reuptake inhibitors or SSRIs), monoamine oxidase inhibitors (MAOIs), and others, which are unique (or "novel") antidepressants unlike existing antidepressant medications. It is typical for psychiatrists to switch among the classes of antidepressants if their patients don't respond or have uncomfortable side effects. The psychiatrist's selection of a particular antidepressant will be based on her experience of familiarity with a particular drug as well as the patient's sex, age, health status, depressive symptoms, and previous courses of treatment. Occasionally, a psychiatrist will augment antidepressant medication with a second medication. Such additional medications may include lithium, buproprion, or even a thyroid hormone. Sometimes tricyclics and SSRIs are used in combination.

When we were considering how to divide up our general descriptions of most commonly marketed antidepressants, we encountered some problems. Some of the drugs are grouped together based on their chemical design (like the tricyclics/heterocyclics), while some are grouped according to the effect they have on the neurotransmitters (like the SSRIs and MAOIs). Several individual drugs are so unique that they could have their own classification. We decided therefore, for simplicity's sake, to group the common available medications into four main categories: heterocyclics, SSRIs, MAOIs, and "Other Novel or Atypical" agents, which includes the unique drugs that can stand in a class all their own.

Heterocyclics

These drugs (which include tricyclic antidepressants) were the most commonly prescribed antidepressants for over 25 years and helped millions of people. They have been used not only for depression, but also for other conditions as well, such as bed-wetting, bulimia, chronic pain, and sleep problems. They appear to work primarily by increasing the amount of either serotonin or norepinephrine in the synapse. Some block the reuptake of serotonin; others block the reuptake of norepinephrine; and still others block the reuptake of both. Some commonly prescribed heterocyclic antidepressants include amitriptyline (with the brand name Elavil), nortriptyline (Pamelor, Aventyl), Doxepin (Sinequan), imipramine (Tofranil), and desipramine (Norpramin).

In addition to increasing the levels of serotonin and norepinephine in the synapse, these medications also block certain acetylcholine synapses. These side effects, called *anticholinergic effects,* include dry mouth, blurred vision, difficulty urinating, sexual problems, and constipation, and can vary in intensity and discomfort level. Other potential side effects include abnormalities in the cardiovascular system, such as variation in blood pressure and abnormal electrical activity in the heart. Still other side effects include fatigue, sleepiness, weight gain, and tremor. Despite the potential negative consequences, many people have been helped with tricyclic antidepressants, particularly when managed by a competent psychiatrist or other physician. Keep in mind that, because we are not physicians, we have vastly oversimplified this information. You can get more detailed information from your doctor.

SSRIs

The name of this class of antidepressant describes what it does. SSRIs are selective serotonin reuptake inhibitors, which means that there is little to no effect of the medication on levels of norepinephrine. Over half of all new antidepressant prescriptions in the U.S. are for SRRIs. Because they target limited chemical processes in the brain, they tend to have none of the anticholinergic effects that can make tricyclic antidepressants uncomfortable to take. They also appear safer generally, especially in terms of cardiovascular side effects. They have been used for problems other than depression. SSRIs have had some success in treating panic disorders, obsessive-compulsive disorders, personality disorders, and even migraine headaches.

SSRIs also cause unwanted side effects, albeit mild and often only temporary ones. They include nausea, headache, insomnia, nervousness, and sexual dysfunction. In people with bipolar disorder (even if not previously diagnosed), SSRIs can provoke manic symptoms such as thought-racing, euphoria, and excessive energy. Commonly prescribed SSRI antidepressants include fluoxetine (Prozac), sertraline (Zoloft), paroxetine (Paxil), and citalopam (Celexa).

As we mentioned in chapter 3, researchers hypothesize that too little serotonin causes depression and too much causes mania. If that were the whole story, we could simply give a depressed person more serotonin and he would get better. In fact, we know that brain activity is regulated by over fifty different neurotransmitters, such as norepinephrine, GABA, histamine, and acetylcholine, which interact in highly sophisticated ways. It is now known that SSRIs also act by making receptors less sensitive and that they affect serotonin receptor subtypes that are unrelated to mood. Celexa, one of the more recent SSRI antidepressants, appears to cause fewer side effects than some of the older SSRIs because it was designed to affect only the serotonin receptor subtypes that deal with mood and not with those that affect sexual functioning, nausea, etc. For this reason, it is considered to be *even more* selective than the other currently available SSRIs. Even though the original serotonin hypothesis was simplistic, SSRIs have been highly effective in treating the typical person who is depressed.

MAOIs

MAO, short for monoamine oxidase, is an enzyme that breaks down the neurotransmitters. Sometimes, a cell may malfunction, which leads to an overproduction of MAO, which in turn breaks down the neurotransmitters necessary for nerve–to–nerve communication in the synapse. Therefore, drugs that reduce the amount of MAO (called MAO *inhibitors*) subsequently increase the amount of serotonin, norepinephrine, and dopamine in the synapse. These drugs are typically used for people with depressions that don't respond to other antidepressants such difficult-to-treat patients tend to oversleep, overeat, and feel extremely fatigued. MAOIs cause many of the same anticholinergic effects as tricyclics but the side effects are often less severe. Just as they break down neurotransmitters, they also break down certain food compounds, especially the amino acid *tyramine*, which is found in beer, wine, aged cheese, bananas, avocados, canned meats, chocolate, and liver. Tyramine causes the release of norepinephrine from nerve cells that regulate blood pressure. People who take MAO inhibitors cannot break down this amino acid, making them susceptible to sudden surges in blood pressure and possibly even stroke, and must therefore avoid foods that contain tyramine, as well as nose drops and cold remedies, which may cause similar problems with blood pressure.

Common MAOI medications include phenelzine (Nardil) and tranylcypromine (Parnate).

Other Novel or Atypical Antidepressants

Bupropion's brand name is Wellbutrin. It's unlike any other type of antidepressant. It does not act exactly like a tricyclic, an SSRI, or an MAOI drug. It blocks some of the reuptake of norepinephrine and serotonin, but it also appears to inhibit the reuptake of dopamine as well. If you recall from our discussion in chapter 3, dopamine is one of the three neurotransmitters involved in the experience of depression. In order to boost available dopamine levels when a depression is particularly stubborn, some psychiatrists use Wellbutrin to augment a tricyclic or SSRI regimen. One advantage of Wellbutrin appears to be that people who take it are less likely to experience impairment in sexual functioning. The most common side effects are gastrointestinal, including mild nausea and dry mouth. One of the more uncomfortable, although rare, effects may be that it causes agitation, insomnia, or shakiness in some people. Over time, these negative side effects appear to subside in most people.

Mirtazapine (Remeron) is also a unique antidepressant that stimulates the release of the neurotransmitters serotonin and norepinephrine. It also keeps nerve cells from eliminating serotonin. It has been referred to as having noradrenergic selective serotonin activity, or NaSSA. At lower doses, mirtazapine is sedating and is often used when a person is depressed with anxiety and is having difficulty sleeping. Some people find that Remeron makes them drowsy and dizzy, and increases their appetite. Interestingly, at higher doses, Remeron seems to be *less* sedating. Its most troubling side effect is often reported as weight gain.

Venlafaxine XR (Effexor XR) selectively keeps nerve cells from eliminating serotonin and norepinephrine, and to a lesser degree, dopamine. It is believed that initially, Effexor acts like an SSRI, but at higher doses, it blocks norepinephrine reuptake, making it a both a serotonin and selective norepinephrine reuptake inhibitor (or SNRI). At doses over 300 mg, it also appears to have some dopamine reuptake blocking actions. It has most of the same side effects mentioned for the SSRIs and also may induce constipation, sweating, and dry mouth. At higher doses, it may increase blood pressure.

Nefazadone (Serzone) interrupts serotonin activity, but again, is not considered an SSRI because it also blocks the part of a serotonin receptor that causes insomnia, anxiety, and sexual dysfunction in regular SSRIs. An advantage then is that it tends to cause fewer sexual side effects than other SSRIs and may relieve some anxiety and insomnia. Common side effects include drowsiness, dizziness, dry mouth, and nausea.

Reboxetine (Vestra) is the first selective norepinephrine reuptake inhibitor antidepressant, in that it acts only on norepineprhine and not on serotonin or other systems that cause anti-cholinergic effects. The benefits of the first SNRI over other antidepressants have not yet been determined, but it offers promise for depressions that may not be as responsive to current medications. Currently, it is only available in Europe, but it is expected to be released in the U.S. soon. Because of its limited release here, clinical research continues to determine its benefit-to-side-effect ratio.

St. John's Wort is not technically a medication, since it is not controlled by the Food and Drug Adminstration and it is an over-the-counter herbal product. It has, however, been shown to be effective in treating mild depressions. It appears to work like an SSRI or an MAOI, but the research has not shown it to be effective with moderate to severe depressions. DHEA (or dehydroepiandrosterone) is another non-prescription chemical sold in health food stores that has been associated with beneficial mood effects. This chemical is an abundant adrenocortical hormone in humans and may be involved in regulating mood and sense of well-being. Currently, the exact way that DHEA may enhance mood is not well understood, but early studies suggest it has promise as another tool for managing depression. Much more study is needed to evaluate the potential for risk, particularly if someone takes it over time. As with any product that can affect mood, we strongly recommend that you consult with a physician before beginning it. We've included a table of common antidepressant medications with both chemical (generic) and brand names, recommended therapeutic dosage ranges, and possible sedation and anticholinergic levels by Dr. John Preston from his book, *You Can Beat Depression* (Preston, 2000).

Keep in mind that the biochemical explanations that we have provided here are very basic, very general and even at this printing, may be becoming obsolete. The pharmaceutical industry is constantly developing new drugs to increase effectiveness while reducing side effects.

We also recommend the books *Consumer's Guide to Psychiatric Drugs* by John Preston, Psy.D., John O'Neal, M.D., and Mary Talago, MS., R.Ph.; and *Prozac and the New Antidepressants* by William S. Appleton, M.D., included in our References section.

Common Antidepressant Medications

Generic	Brand	Therapeutic Dosage Range	Sedation	ACH Effects[1]
Imipramine	Tofranil	150–300 mg	mid	mid
Desipramine	Norpramin	150–300 mg	low	low
Amitriptyline	Elavil	150–300 mg	high	high
Nortriptyline	Aventyl, Pamelor	75–100 mg	mid	mid
Protriptyline	Vivactil	30–60 mg	low	mid
Trimipramine	Surmontil	150–300 mg	high	mid
Doxepin	Sinequan	150–300 mg	high	mid
Maprotiline	Ludiomil	150–300 mg	mid	low
Amoxapine	Asendin	150–400 mg	mid	low
Trazodone	Desyrel	150–400 mg	mid	none
Fluoxetine	Prozac	20–80 mg	none	none
Bupropion SR	Wellbutrin SR	150–400 mg	none	none
Sertraline	Zoloft	50–200 mg	low	none
Paroxetine	Paxil	20–50 mg	low	low
Venlafaxine XR	Effexor XR	75–350 mg	low	none
Fluvoxamine	Luvox	50–300 mg	low	low
Nefazodone	Serzone	100–500 mg	low	low
Mirtazapine	Remeron	15–45 mg	mid	mid
Citalopram	Celexa	10–60 mg	mid	none
Reboxetine	Vestra	4–8 mg	low	none
Phenelzine[2]	Nardil	45–90 mg	low	none
Tranylcypromine[2]	Parnate	20–30 mg	low	none
Hypericum[3]	St. John's Wort	600–900 mg	none	none
SAM-e[4]	SAM-e	400–1200 mg	none	none

[1] ACH effects (anti-cholinergic side effects) Include: dry mouth, constipation, difficulty in urinating and blurry vision.

[2] MAOI (MAO-Inhibitors). Unique class of medications. These require a strict adherence to dietary and medication regime.

[3] This over-the-counter herbal product has some research support of effectiveness in treating mild depression. It is not, however, effective in the treatment of moderate-to-severe depression.

[4] This over-the-counter product has some research support of effectiveness in treating depression. It must be taken with a vitamin-B supplement. SAM-e is the abbreviation for S-adenosylmethionine.

Reprinted by permission of Impact publishers. See copyright page for details.

What Other Biological Treatments Are Available for Depression?

Lest we seem too eager to have you standing in line at your local pharmacy, we thought it best to talk about other options for managing the biological aspects of depression either without medications (by your choice) or in case they are not helpful in your situation.

Exercise Regular exercise is one of the most powerful tools available for decreasing depression, at least in part because it increases the level of certain chemicals, namely endorphins, serotonin, and norepinephrine, in the brain. Boosting the levels of these chemicals reduces depressive symtoms. The most effective forms of exercise for depression appear to be slow, sustained aerobic activity, such as riding a bike, swimming, or walking, as well as brief, but more vigorous aerobic exercise such as dancing, calisthenics, and sports like tennis, basketball, and running.

Exercise has other benefits as well. It improves sleep quality, reduces tension, promotes better general health, and if your exercise occurs in a class or other organized setting, it increases your opportunity for social contact. If you have a health condition that may be affected by an exercise program, check with your doctor on ways to exercise that will be safe for you. People with particular physical problems may benefit from the supervision of a certified athletic trainer, physical therapist, or exercise physiologist.

Light Therapy We mentioned earlier that there appear to be depressions that follow a seasonal pattern. Although the causes of seasonal affective disorder (SAD) are not yet known, researchers theorize that some people become depressed when their exposure to the sun is limited. Because the sunlight is less direct in the winter, SAD often begins during the late fall and winter months. The symptoms seem to go away in the spring and summer.

One helpful approach, if you have SAD or perhaps a light-reactive depression, is to spend an extra hour outside each day, even on cloudy days. Some researchers and clinicians now prescribe special "light boxes," consisting of bright, fluorescent bulbs (in the wide spectrum, 2500 lux range), for their patients to sit in front of during winter months for one to two hours per day. There is some evidence that this treatment may in fact be helpful for people diagnosed with SAD, but more research is needed.

ECT Nothing conjures up old horror movie images faster than electro-convulsive therapy or ECT. In Dr. Betty Berzon's heartfelt and very personal foreword to this book, this oft-misunderstood and seemingly torturous treatment occupied a central role as she described her own struggle to help people with depression. Even in the early days of ECT, however, it was only applied as a treatment for conditions unresponsive to other therapies. The treatment itself involves passing a brief electrical current through the patient's head through electrodes placed on one or both sides of the scalp. The electrodes produce a *brief electrical discharge* (BED), usually no more than a few seconds. A BED is a repetitive firing of neurons in the brain. BED changes the brain chemistry in a way that appears to relieve depressive symptoms (and other emotional disorders) temporarily. Some studies have found that ECT stimulates the endorphin system and may alter the same neurotransmitters affected by antidepressants. Even after many studies of ECT, researchers are still not sure how ECT actually works, but it appears that the seizure itself is the key to relief from symptoms. The process is monitored by EEG (electroencephalogram), which detects changes in brain wave activity. The ECT equipment allows the doctor to control the amount of electricity passing through the brain very precisely. The person undergoing the procedure is made comfortable with sedation and then given a light general anesthetic and a medication to temporarily paralyze the muscles (to prevent muscle strain and spasm).

ECT is much safer and more easily tolerated today than in the early days. It still is often a treatment of last resort for severely depressed people who have not responded to psychotherapy and several tries with antidepressants (or for health reasons who cannot take them). At times people who need quick relief from depression so severe that they are suicidal or unable to take care of themselves are also offered ECT. A typical course of treatment consists of six to ten treatments and is generally administered two to three times per week. The only professional qualified to administer ECT is a psychiatrist trained in the procedure, although they are often assisted by an anesthesiologist and psychiatric nurse.

If the person doesn't have adequate follow-up treatment, such as psychotherapy or medications, ECT's effect often begins to wear off after several months. Sometimes a patient may get maintenance ECT on a regularly scheduled basis as an outpatient, or, to prevent relapse, at the first signs of a returning depression.

The most troubling side effect of ECT appears to be memory disturbance, although it is usually temporary. It happens mostly after two-sided electrode placement ECT and can begin as soon as the person wakes up after the procedure. For example, a patient can have problems remembering names, phone numbers, addresses, and dates. Memories of things that happened in the weeks leading up to and following the ECT may be hard to recall. People often forget the ECT procedure itself but, in general, the memories return in several days or weeks. A very small percentage of people have reported permanent problems in learning new information or remembering old information after two-sided ECT. Other side effects can include dry mouth and headache. It is generally not indicated for people with brain tumors or cardiovascular disease, but these factors will be weighed by the psychiatrist conducting the treatment. More detailed information can be obtained by speaking with a psychiatrist familiar with the procedure or with a representative of a hospital where the procedure is administered.

rTMS Repetitive transcranial magnetic stimulation (rTMS) is a new, ECT-like procedure that is still under development, primarily at Columbia University in New York and the Medical University of South Carolina in Charleston. During the procedure, a handheld coil creates a magnetic field that is passed through the head, which generates a small electrical current in the brain. Unlike ECT, the procedure does not cause seizures. Two early studies found that rTMS led to a reduction in depressive symptoms without memory loss in severely depressed test subjects. This technique sounds promising but it is much too early to know if the results of the preliminary tests will hold up. Much more study is needed in order to determine its effectiveness.

Vagal Nerve Stimulation Another very recent experimental therapy for depression undergoing experimentation through a large, collaborative study between twenty leading medical institutions, including the Stanford Mood Disorders Clinic, is known as vagal nerve stimulation. This so-called "brain pacemaker" is a small battery-powered electrical device implanted below the collarbone that delivers electrical signals intermittently to the vagus nerve, which then transmits the signals to the brain. These signals then seem to improve mood as well as stop seizures (it was originally developed to control epilepsy) through a process that is not well understood at this point. So far, results seem promising, particularly for people who have not responded to other types of treatment for depression. Much more research is needed to examine potential side effects or other problems with the devices.

Acupuncture Although acupuncture has been around for thousands of years, it has not yet been completely accepted in Western medical circles. It is an ancient form of Chinese medicine whose goal is to boost the body's natural healing powers by restoring the normal flow of "qi" (pronounced "chee"), or bioelectric energy. Qi follows body pathways called meridians, with designated points along the path believed to correlate with particular organs and tissue in the body. These specific points are stimulated by tiny, thin needles that are inserted and twisted; in some cases, an electrical current is passed through the needle to the specific point. Practitioners believe that acupuncture does not create side effects or damage to tissue. It is occasionally combined with Chinese herbs and used for a wide variety of problems, from infertility to chronic pain to mood disorders.

Experienced practitioners of acupuncture have reported success in relieving depression, but Western physicians have only recently begun to take an interest in the practice of acupuncture. One study by Dr. John Allen at the University of Arizona–Tucson randomly divided thirty-eight severely depressed women into three groups, one to receive eight weeks of acupuncture twice a week specifically for depressive symptoms, the second group to receive general acupuncture treatments, and the third group receiving no acupuncture. The results were promising in that the first group reported a significant reduction in depressive symptoms compared to the two other groups at the end of the eight weeks. This was only a preliminary study, but it does hold promise for future research (Granet, 1998).

Without much more scientific evidence to back up the claims, Western physicians will likely remain unconvinced of the effectiveness of acupuncture as a treatment for depression, but early results look promising for acupuncture as an adjunct to other depression treatments. If you decide to try acupuncture, talk to your primary care doctor about her prior experience with it; she may be able to refer you to qualified professionals in your area. We recommend that you see an acupuncturist who is a diplomate of the National Certification Commission for Acupuncture and Oriental Medicine and is licensed or certified by your state.

Although a thorough discussion of vitamin, herbal, and nutritional approaches to managing depression is beyond the scope of this book, we do have two excellent and comprehensive resources to recommend, *The Physician's Desk Reference for Nutritional Supplements* and *The Physician's Desk Reference for Herbal Medicines*. Both provide unbiased, evidence-based information about potential benefits, side effects, and appropriate dosages of widely available over-the-counter products.

Conversations with the Authorities

Even knowing basic information about antidepressant medications or other biologically based treatments, the thought of trying something new can be intimidating. It also may be difficult to ask your treating professional all the questions that you might want to because of time limitations or forgetfulness (due to depression of course!). We decided therefore to try a little experiment with two of our psychiatrist friends who were willing to humor us.

Dr. Nanette Gartrell is a psychiatrist and a lesbian, in private practice in the San Francisco Bay Area. She has been in practice for twenty-two years and in the San Francisco Bay Area for the past twelve.

Dr. Todd Cornett is also a psychiatrist and queer, practicing in San Francisco since he trained at the University of California at San Francisco in the early '90s. He has a private practice in San Francisco and Oakland.

When we were discussing how we would like to go about exploring the questions that our readers might have about the biological treatment of depression, it was sometimes hard to imagine a way to talk about side effects and drug interactions that would be accessible and user-friendly. Finally, it occurred to us that it might be interesting to sit down and interview them about the various medical alternatives for treating depression. The following is an edited transcript of those interviews.

Authors: First, we'd like to thank you for being here. Let's begin with each of you describing the typical person referred to you for treatment.

Dr. Gartrell   I treat healthy lesbians who have unipolar depressions
(NG):   or anxiety disorders. All of my comments will apply to this population—a very narrowly defined group. I mostly see psychotherapy veterans but medication "virgins." With rare exceptions, folks who come to me have never been on medication before and they're considering it for the first time, either at the recommendation of another therapist—their own therapist who is not an M.D. and can't prescribe—or a primary care doc, or their lovers/friends/family.

Most of my psychopharmacology clients come in sort of feet first—quite reluctant to take medications. They had hoped to manage their dysphoria without psychopharmacologic intervention.

I recommend antidepressants to clients who have a history of an anxiety disorder or unipolar depression that has been persistent despite psychotherapy with a competent therapist. The case for pharmacology is even stronger if the client has a blood relative with a similar disorder. The degree of impairment as a result of the mood disorder varies from client to client, as do the lengths and varieties of other treatment strategies previously tried.

Dr. Cornett (TC):   My patients tend to have an undertreated, complicated depression, and usually he has already tried medications, so that issue has already been resolved in his mind. For instance, what does it mean to take medication? What does it mean to have medications recommended by the therapist or the primary care doctor? Those are big issues, but by and large, they have usually been resolved by the time he sees me because the real issue is he's doing everything he can to get better . . . why isn't he getting better?

Actually I see a fair amount of patients with anxiety disorders, a fair amount of depression, some HIV-related—not the anxiety of having HIV per se, although certainly there are patients where that is their presenting problem, but just the effects of HIV on the brain can precipitate mental illness, and that's why they will come to my practice. What's interesting, though, is the severity. It is pretty much moderate to severe, and if it continues untreated, there is a really great risk of where the symptoms will go on to take on a life of their own and could result in hospitalization or something like that. That is why my interventions tend to be pretty aggressive because, by this time, the symptoms are pretty severe.

Authors: Will you talk a bit about how queer issues intersect with depression? In other words, in your opinions, are lesbians and gay men more prone to depression than straights?

TC: No. I think that there are some unique situations in dealing with one's sexuality in this particular society that cause a lot of extra stress, but I don't think that gay people are at any greater risk than the general population for major mental illness. I think that if somebody is predisposed to depression, the stresses of being gay can bring about that depression. That needs to be acknowledged and dealt with in the profession. I think that if somebody is having difficulty coming out or they've been kicked out of the house because they *have* come out to their family, and then they find that they're depressed, I don't think that people in medicine should say, "Oh well, that explains why he or she is depressed; anybody would be," or something to that effect, and [then] that depression goes untreated. It's kind of like when somebody is given the diagnosis of cancer and then becomes depressed. A lot of times, the doctor will say, "Well, of course this person is depressed. Anybody would be depressed." But then nothing more, like an evaluation for medication or a referral to a psychotherapist, takes place.

NG: Living as an outcast in a homophobic world is extremely stressful. Stress can lead to depression and anxiety and substance abuse and so on. Any individual in an outcast group is likely to experience psychological distress that over time can have a cumulatively negative effect. Our brain's biochemical mechanisms presumably just get worn down by experiencing chronic stress and distress. One can have the healthiest blood relatives in terms of brain biochemistry, and yet experience a personal tragedy or long-term distress that creates a biological depression. I consider a depression biological if a client has a favorable response to an antidepressant.

TC: Just out of curiosity, do you think that gay people are at greater risk for major mental illness?

Authors
(Kimeron
Hardin):   I don't think they're necessarily at risk for a major mental illness, but I agree with you that we have a lot more stressors than non-gay or lesbian people. I think that we have a relatively homophobic society, and like you said, if there are genetic or early environmental predispositions for stress, living in a homophobic society would certainly bring that out. I do think that gay and lesbian depression is different because of the fact that living as an oppressed sexual minority is different than living as an oppressed racial minority because we can hide it, and so then there is a lot of energy and anxiety that revolves around whether you should be out or whether

you shouldn't and always being very aware of who is around and what information can be shared. Marny and I believe that the depression that results from a situation like that is unique [and it's] coupled with living in a culture that continues to say that you're "second class," from the government to religious organizations along with your family and other aspects of the culture.

TC: Right, I agree. In my experience, I don't think the incidence of depression is any different, but certainly the experience of that depression is different.

Authors: How would you describe your philosophy about using medications in psychotherapy in general?

TC: I think that most depressions can be adequately treated with psychotherapy. When it becomes more than just mild or moderate depression, then I think medications should seriously be considered, and that's usually when I become involved in the process. Almost all of my clients are in therapy with a psychotherapist. If the therapy is not progressing as a therapist would like, the thinking is that with the additional support of medication, maybe the therapy can then proceed.

Authors: So one marker is [that] they have already been in psychotherapy, talking psychotherapy, and that is not progressing, and so then you might consider adding some type of medication.

TC: Right. The medications are effective in mild and moderate depression as well. Of course, the medications are not without their own risks and benefits, so you want to carefully evaluate if the medications are going to be indicated or not because you're adding on another layer of intervention, and that additional layer is going to have its own potential problems and expense.

I also tend to feel comfortable working in conjunction with other types of mental health professionals who are doing psychotherapy with the client while I handle the medications.

Authors: When would you use medications for mild depression? For example, in what case?

TC: If there has been a long history of several episodes of mild depression and the depression, despite the best efforts of the patient and the therapist, continues. If there are specific target symptoms that respond to medication, like problems sleeping or with low energy, then that also would argue for a trial of antidepressants in a mild depression.

NG: My threshold for prescribing antidepressants is much lower than it used to be in the era that I was trained, because we have medications that are so effective and so useful to treat a variety of conditions and symptoms. My goal is always to prescribe the lowest therapeutic dose of a medication. After starting with a subtherapeutic dose and slowly inching up, I hold the dose at the lowest therapeutic dose and wait six weeks to observe the outcome. Most of my clients are able to stay at the low end of the therapeutic spectrum for the particular medication they're using. Being fortunate enough to benefit from low doses of a medication reduces the likelihood of troublesome side effects.

Authors: At what point would you prescribe an antidepressant medication for an acute loss, such as with someone who has just had a death of a lover or close friend? At what point does it become abnormal grieving?

TC: That gets into the concern that some people have that the medications somehow subtract from the experience, that they somehow alter the experience for the patient so that it becomes an inauthentic experience, which doesn't actually happen in reality. What I use as a yardstick is the degree of distress. If someone is so depressed that they cannot function, how can they do the work of therapy if they can't eat, if they can't get out of bed, if they can't even look after themselves? If the symptoms are that severe and that quick, then it could be that the support of the medication, even just for a short period of time, could be helpful. The accepted practice is that the symptoms need to persist for more than two weeks to qualify as a depressive episode. I think that the definition also is that if somebody has been grieving for more than two months, then that would cease to be thought of as normal bereavement and depression should be considered.

Authors: It sounds like you're on the side of alleviating symptoms that are very distressing and uncomfortable as much as you can.

TC: Yes.

NG: When clients experiencing a severe loss are referred by another provider, it's typically because that provider feels as though the normal grief response is extreme— too incapacitating in some way or too prolonged. If the client and I agree with that assessment, I'll prescribe an antidepressant. I believe that psychotherapy should be tried first for a major loss, before considering any form of medication. I am reluctant to prescribe medications before psychotherapy in such circumstances, because experiencing tremendous sadness is a normal response to an extreme loss. There are a lot of positive experiences that come from mourning—including learning how to do it better the next time.

Authors: We've heard that approximately 80 percent of all medications used for psychiatric issues are prescribed by physicians who are not psychiatrists, like general practitioners and family medicine physicians. Could you comment on that?

TC: Usually, when people are considering antidepressant medication, they don't immediately think of going to a psychiatrist, but they talk to their primary care doctor, who will have tried an antidepressant or two. If those don't work, then their physician will refer the person to me. By the time someone is referred to me, he or she has probably already been on medications that haven't worked.

Authors: Why is that? What are some of the typical problems that may have led to the failure of the antidepressants?

TC: Misdiagnosis or underdiagnosis or inadequate treatment, in my opinion.

Authors: Okay, tell us more about that.

TC: Sometimes it happens that there is a complicated depression that could be manic depression or it could be due to a general medical condition such as HIV or thyroid disease. Often there is an undiagnosed substance abuse problem that hasn't been asked about and therefore isn't addressed. Then there are the unaddressed, untoward effects of the medication, which decrease compliance, and so the doctor thinks that the medication isn't working, but that's because it's not being taken, and of course, the doctor doesn't know that because the doctor hasn't asked about that. So, usually something like that is going on, and if not, then there has been proper diagnosis and prescribing of medication, but the trial has been inadequate, either in length or in dosage.

Authors: Do you find that in most cases there has been an underdosage or the amount of time that they tried the medication was too short?

TC: Oh, yes. Unfortunately, the perception is that with current antidepressants, one dose fits all and continuous reassessment is not required. So a lot of times, the primary care doctor, because she or he only has fifteen minutes with this patient every six months, starts the antidepressant at one dose, and then there is really no follow-up assessment on whether the dose needs to be increased or if there is even an adequate response. If it's a mild to moderate depression or if it's uncomplicated and if the primary care doctor is pretty savvy, then a lot of times, a referral to a psychiatrist isn't needed. Or maybe what will happen will just be that the psychiatrist will be consulted for one or two visits to lend expertise so that the medication becomes more effective, then the primary care doctor just continues to prescribe the medication [at the psychiatrist-prescribed level], which is fine. I actually think that that is a great use of resources, and I think that it is acknowledging the fact that medical costs are prohibitive and a burden and that not everybody can be referred to a specialist for everything. And it is the job of the psychiatrists to educate our colleagues on how to manage moderate depression in the primary care setting and when to appropriately refer to a specialist.

Authors: What would initial visits look like if you were starting someone on an antidepressant?

NG: I discuss the various kinds of medications, their expected therapeutic effects and side effects. They all have fairly equivalent efficacy, but their side effect profiles vary. Because the selective serotonin reuptake inhibitors (SSRIs) are extremely helpful for both unipolar depression and anxiety disorders, and have the best side effect profiles, I usually recommend starting with

an SSRI. Again, most of my clients are psychopharmacology "virgins," so the SSRIs are a good starting place.

I explain in detail how SSRIs work, and I provide
literature on the various medication choices. I tailor the
particular medication choice according to the expected
side effects. I attempt to use expected side effects in a
way that might benefit a particular client (such as
selecting a more sedating medication for a client who is
having difficulty sleeping), and avoid medications
whose side effects would be very detrimental to a particular client (for example, not utilizing medications that
are known to inhibit sexual functioning with any client
who would find that intolerable). I start with extremely
low doses in order to minimize side effects that occur
with increasing doses too rapidly. I recommend starting
slowly and taking a longer time to get to a therapeutic
level, because having fewer unwanted side effects
makes the adjustment easier on clients. However, it
takes a full six weeks [on] any dose to get to the therapeutic effect of that dose.

Authors: What are some of the most common side effects that
you observe in your patients on antidepressant medications?

NG: Well, since I tend to use SSRIs most often I'll limit my
comments to those medications. Gastrointestinal disturbance is one of the most common side effects of SSRIs;
however, it can be eliminated almost entirely by having
the client take the medication on a full stomach. In
terms of sexual side effects, which a sizable number of
women taking these drugs encounter, I have found that
Celexa in low doses (20 mg daily) produces much less
sexual dysfunction than the other SSRIs. I've not only
had tremendous success switching lesbians who were
taking the older SSRIs to Celexa in terms of improving
their sexual functioning, but I've also had a lot of success with first time antidepressant usage by women
who report that their sexual functioning is not significantly impaired or not impaired at all on Celexa. Very
occasionally I run into somebody who has the same
kind of sexual dysfunction that I see with the older
SSRIs on Celexa. For many of my clients, Celexa has a

sedative effect that has helped them sleep. Those that find it more activating take it in the morning. Among the other SSRIs, Prozac tends also to be activating, so I have clients take it in the morning. Zoloft can be either activating or sedating, and I've found that most clients find Paxil sedating. Again, SSRIs need to be taken on a full stomach to avoid GI [gastrointestinal] disturbance.

TC: I try to stay away from the SSRIs and SSRI-like medications with my sexually active patients because there is such a high incidence of the sexual side effects. In men, the sexual side effects can be anything from the libido being quashed by the antidepressant, if it's not already quashed from being depressed, to difficulty achieving and maintaining an erection to having problems achieving orgasm to retrograde ejaculation. That's where the sperm is directed into the bladder, rather than out through the urethra, which is a very disconcerting experience. While tricyclic antidepressants are highly effective with elevating mood in someone depressed, they tend to have the most side effects like sedation, dry mouth, and also sexual side effects, which tends to make people stop them sooner.

Authors: Tell us about your thoughts about combination drug therapies for depression that moderate serotonin, norepinephrine, and dopamine.

TC: I think that the fact that multiple neurotransmitters have been implicated in depression and that psycho-pharmacological theory is becoming much more sophisticated effectively dispels the myth that one pill fits all. I believe that there are multiple causes of depression. I also think that there are many different types of depression. The more we find out about depression, the better able we will be to characterize whether a specific subtype of depression will likely respond to a serotonin-modulating agent, as opposed to one that works on norepinephrine or dopamine or whatever else we discover. In fact, I find that in the more severe depressions, I often have to use one or two agents that modulate all three well-established neurotransmitters in order to finally get a significant response. Effexor plus Wellbutrin hits all three of those neurotransmitters, so if my client has not responded to anything else, I will use that kind of combination.

Authors: Are there any potential risks from taking antidepressant medications for lesbians who are thinking about getting pregnant or gay men who are considering becoming a father?

NG: I discourage my lesbian clients from being on psychopharmacological agents while they're pregnant. I encourage them to become as fit as possible prior to pregnancy. That means working out, taking vitamins, eating healthily. I then taper them off medication before they start inseminating. I don't believe that SSRIs are safe to be taken during pregnancy or breast feeding. There are studies that show that they do appear in breast milk. I do not recommend taking a medication that affects brain biochemistry when a fetus is developing. It doesn't make theoretical sense and I think the little bit of evidence that exists suggests that it's not safe. I was recently informed of a case in which a woman taking Zoloft during her pregnancy delivered a baby with no ears.

I also had a client who came to see me on Prozac, six months pregnant, who had had a fetal demise at seven months while on Prozac during her first pregnancy. The fetus had expired after a cyst rupture and bleeding. The second fetus also had abnormal cyst formation, and had to be delivered two months early because the cysts were growing quite rapidly. She had taken Prozac throughout both pregnancies. This client is currently pregnant for the third time, and she's off all medications. She's been running marathons, eating very healthily, and she's not on Prozac. So far, the fetus is completely healthy and there are no cysts. If she has no problems with this third pregnancy I will write up her experience as a case report. Her experiences so far are strongly suggestive of possible risks associated with taking SSRIs during pregnancy.

TC: There is no evidence that these medications are any more deleterious to the sperm than placebo, but of course we can't be 100 percent certain. In medicine, you can't be 100 percent certain, and you always have to be aware of the absolute and relative risk. If somebody is thinking about becoming a father and they want to maximize the natural component of the process, then they would want to be off all medication, but if the antidepressant is keeping them from being depressed and able to function and take care of themselves, then that may be more important than this theoretical risk that the medication may have on spermatozoa. The antidepressants actually present other problems in trying to become a father in that they can have direct effects on the plumbing of the sexual organs, and so that needs to be addressed. Sometimes we have to be creative in adjusting the dose or taking additional medication to counter the side effects or to find a totally different antidepressant.

Authors: Is postpartum depression more likely with somebody who's been on antidepressants and has been off during the pregnancy?

NG: It's definitely something that I would worry about. If a client's depression is severe enough postpartum, I recommend stopping breastfeeding and starting medication. It's really up to her to decide how severe her depression is and when she will accept psychopharmacological intervention. I do whatever I can to help depressed clients make it through pregnancy without medication.

Authors: What about clients who complain that they feel as though they have lost the peaks of life, of emotional experiences by being on antidepressants? Have you heard people complain about that?

NG: Some clients describe feeling as though their emotional experiences are flattened by antidepressants. That's a complaint that I sometimes hear from clients taking SSRIs. Such clients say they can't cry as easily when they're sad, or can't sob when they want to, or that they don't feel ecstatic very often on SSRIs. Those who don't want to operate within that limited emotional spectrum may be tapered off their medication to see how they do without it. As long as the client has been taking the medication for at least six months, I completely support tapering off medication to evaluate the ongoing need for it.

TC: I have certainly heard them express concern that that may happen. I have had a couple of patients comment that with the more stable mood, they don't experience the ups and downs as dramatically, and they are very thankful for that because this being all over the map in terms of their mood is really causing a lot of problems in their life. The unstable mood is contributing to their depression, let alone just having a depressed mood. There is still a healthy range of emotional experience, and it's still possible to be very, very happy and also to be very, very sad while taking antidepressant medication. But some people miss the drama of the really high highs and really low lows. It's interesting, I think, that that speaks more to their dynamics and their way of relatedness with others and with the world, but I haven't had anybody stop medication because their peaks are not as high and their valleys are not as deep.

Authors: What is the average amount of time for your patients to be on an antidepressant?

NG: I keep clients who have had a single depressive episode on an antidepressant for six months from the time that the drug is effective. Most people choose to stay on antidepressants for about a year before tapering off. I don't recommend tapering off unless the immediate horizon of a client's life is fairly smooth. It is always surprising to watch the transformation in clients from an initial reluctance to consider antidepressants, to an unwillingness to discontinue them. They feel so much better on medications, and they become fearful about returning to their previous dysphoria. I can't tell you how many times newly medicated clients have said to me, "I realize now that I've been depressed my whole life. Is this what 'normal' feels like? I have never felt this good in my life." So the first hurdle is the willingness to start medications; the next hurdle is anxiety about stopping them.

      I recommend taking antidepressants at least long enough to treat the current depressive episode (a minimum of six months), and then tapering off if that is the client's preference. I reassure clients that if they don't feel comfortable after discontinuing the medication, they can restart it. Most clients experiment at some point with going off—hoping that they can do as well off as on. A sizable number do fine after discontinuing. Overall in my practice, I would estimate that maybe half my clients stay on antidepressants chronically, and the remainder discontinue them, and are either off for a long time, or indefinitely.

TC: That's a good question. I'm actually asked that a lot by the patient when they're trying to discern if medication is still worth a try. People fall into three camps, more or less. One is that they just need the medication for this depressive episode, and then that's it. They won't have another depressive episode for the rest of their life for whatever reasons. The other camp is where they will need to take medication, but periodically. So many times during their life, they will have a severe enough depression that will require medication. Then there is the third camp where their biochemistry is such that if they don't have an antidepressant, they are going to be depressed. So therefore, they need to take the medication for very, very long periods of time. Since the people in my practice tend to need the services of a psychiatrist more frequently, most of my patients fall in the last two groups.

Authors: Do some chronically depressed clients need antidepressants forever? If so, are there any potential risks with taking an antidepressant long-term?

NG: Some clients need medications chronically because they have chronic intolerable symptoms. Many people worry that SSRIs are creating a kind of dependency. Currently, there is no hard evidence to support or refute that worry. Lesbians who have biologically depressed blood relatives, and who have had repeated episodes of biologic depression in their own lives already, may need ongoing antidepressant treatment to provide the quality of life they are seeking. Sometimes when such individuals go off antidepressants, and then decide to resume treatment, they have difficulty achieving the same level of symptom relief that they had during the initial treatment. Sometimes such individuals end up needing multiple medications to achieve symptom relief. Nobody knows why this is the case, but clients who have this experience find it quite distressing.

Of course I am very concerned about the health and safety of all clients for whom I am prescribing medication. The SSRIs have been around for twenty years, and there are people who have been taking them without ill effects for that amount of time. In terms of long-term antidepressant use, there has always been a great concern about potential dangers. I have been puzzled about why people don't express the same concerns about other kinds of medications that are taken long-term, such as hypertensive or diabetic medications. Perhaps that is because most people still consider antidepressant use optional, and they consider hypertensive or diabetic medications mandatory. But the fact is that plenty of people start antihypertensives in their forties and stay on those medications until they die, some forty-plus years later. The same questions about long-term use are rarely raised. I think questions about long-term medication use should be asked about all medications, not just psychotropic medications.

I can only say that I hope there are no long-term negative effects from taking antidepressants, but we can't know that until they have been around for many more decades. We have learned over time that SSRIs are not the weight-loss panacea they were thought initially to be. Some clients gain substantial amounts of weight on them, and they find that quite distressing. Many people lose weight initially on SSRIs. Weight usually stabilizes after a period of time. However, some folks gain a tremendous amount of weight on these drugs. I don't know what happens to change the metabolism in the individuals who gain a tremendous amount of weight with long-term SSRI use, but that's a side effect that no one is happy with.

I explain to clients that we will all hear about long-term negative effects of pharmacologic agents at the same nanosecond because we live in the information technology era: We'll all see it simultaneously on the Internet and on the front pages of every newspaper. If any long-term problems develop with SSRI use, we'll deal with them the moment we learn of them.

In the early '80s, there was a scare about lithium causing kidney toxicity. Psychiatrists began monitoring kidney status on all clients taking lithium. The antipsychotics and mood stabilizers have a whole variety of short- and long-term side effects that are worrisome and we're all concerned about. Basically it's a scary thing to prescribe medications when you can't be absolutely certain about their long-term use or their immediate side effect in any one person.

TC: Yes, everybody is different, so it's really difficult to come up with global statements that are helpful. I do have patients that have been on these medications for years and years and years. Actually, I have some patients that are in their seventies and have been taking antidepressant medications since they came out on the market in the '50s, but they haven't had a depressive episode for decades. They feel that the medications have a prophylactic effect, and actually there is some evidence in the literature that there is a prophylactic effect with antidepressant medication. It certainly lessens the severity of the depression when it does come.

Authors: Do people develop a tolerance to antidepressants and need stronger and stronger doses?

NG: Some clients do need larger doses over time. Unfortunately, we lack the technology to determine whether that is a matter of tolerance or a worsening of their condition. I treat very healthy lesbians, and few of them become treatment-resistant (that is, needing larger and larger doses of antidepressants, or multiple medications to treat their dysphoria). Sometimes when clients have an acute life stress, they need to increase their antidepressant dose temporarily. I have some clients in my practice who have been on the same dose of an SSRI since SSRIs became available in the U.S.

TC: That certainly does happen although rarely; sometimes the medications poop out, sometimes called "SSRI poop-out syndrome." That's always difficult because you don't know if the patient is more depressed, and that's why the medication is not working, or if a tolerance has developed to the medication, or if this is a side effect from too high a dose of the medication. It depends on one of those three things to determine if you go up or down in the dose or change medication. It's tricky and complicated, but there certainly is enough anecdotal evidence to suggest that there is this phenomenon with SSRIs. Generally speaking, though, no, I don't find that I have to gradually forever increase the dose of the antidepressants. Generally speaking, I don't find that once somebody is on an antidepressant that they have to be on an antidepressant for life.

Authors: Sometimes queer people who have lived in an urban gay environment for a long time, perhaps in their forties or fifties or older, have experienced a lot of losses, multiple losses, due to AIDS. They're a survivor, so to speak, suffering from what's been called Global AIDS Loss. Does that kind of depression seem different?

TC: Yes, I do see that. A lot of times, the patient will be HIV-positive and somehow manage to survive the early days of the holocaust, and there is an incredible amount of guilt and despair. What is striking is that there is really no forum for that to be acknowledged in the gay community, and I think that that is a huge, huge cause of depression in this age group.

Authors: Do you treat them in any different way than people who might have a reactive depression to one loss or a stress reaction or relationship issue? Or do you still follow the same steps: psychotherapy, medication, and then other intervention if necessary?

TC: It goes back to thoroughly looking at why somebody is being referred to me. It could be that in addition to depression, there are elements of PTSD (post-traumatic stress disorder). There could be elements of another mental disorder going on, and because everything is so confusing and overwhelming, it is difficult to discern or to tease out. I would approach such a patient with having a mind-set to have a thorough understanding of diagnostically what's going on, and this diagnosis drives the treatment. The diagnosis is got at with a very thorough history-taking. So, to answer your question, if this is a particular type of depression that warrants a different type of treatment—only if there is more going on than just depression.

Authors: Speaking of HIV, what about gay men who are on HIV cocktails? They're taking a significant number of HIV medications. What experience do you have in interactions or any problems that taking that amount and type of medications could cause?

TC: The cocktails are a mixed blessing in that they certainly have clearly prolonged life, but they are not without their own side effects, the least of which is that many of them interact with antidepressant medications. What I found is that since there are so many antidepressants on the market, if the patient is willing to endure the trial and error aspect, there are antidepressants that can be taken with the myriad of HIV medications and where the side effects are not debilitating such that [they] prohibit the taking of the antidepressant medication. Some of the newer antidepressants are easier to take with the HIV medications, with fewer drug-drug interactions, but it does entail my close collaboration with the HIV doctor.

I would steer away from medications that are known to cause GI upset or have interactions with the HIV medications that cause nausea. But unfortunately the antidepressants have to be taken in pill form. We're anxiously awaiting new formulations of antidepressants that can be absorbed through a patch, a nasal spray, or an implant, because there certainly is a need.

Authors: Do either of you find that queer people are more rebellious than others in your practice about the idea of taking pharmacologic agents? Does being a queer psychiatrist help?

TC: Interesting question. By the time they come to see me, they pretty much have resolved any conflicts or concerns they have about taking medication, but those can certainly come back. Part of my job is to address their concerns. I do my best to address them as they come up because it does mean there is stigma being attached, and there is risk of bruising one's ego even more by having to say, "My depression is so bad that it requires the intervention of medication." My thinking about it is that if somebody had high blood pressure that required medication after all other interventions had failed, most people are not too particularly upset with that. In other words, he doesn't feel that he's a bad person because his hypertension requires medication to be treated. The same way with diabetes. A diabetic doesn't think that he's a bad person because he requires insulin. So I try to reframe the situation along those lines to help the person deal with any concerns he has about taking medication or the stigma of taking medication.

My patients seem to be more comfortable in dealing with a gay-identified physician. I think that if it's important to them, then that makes them more comfortable. When I first started practicing, I thought that it would be a big issue, and I wondered about how would I deal with this in my practice. Basically, I think that the patient is looking for a sympathetic ear and somebody who is not going to get all bent out of shape because he's gay, and that's more likely going to happen with a gay physician than not. But beyond that, it's not really that big of an issue in the practice. I hope that my empathy regarding sexual orientation comes through in treatment, but I also hope that I'm just as empathetic with my non-gay patients as well.

NG: Well, first of all, it helps to be a lesbian physician treating lesbian clients. Secondly, many of my clients are referred by other lesbian therapists so they've already gone through the machinations of whether they're going to consider a physician's recommendation about medications. But thirdly, I am not a person who pushes clients to take medications. I consider it my responsibility to educate clients about antidepressants and then let them decide. It's really up to them to choose whether they want to take them or not. I don't strong-arm anyone into taking them.

Authors: Does therapy go differently with patients after they're on antidepressants?

NG: Some clients come to me for medication and psychotherapy, having worked with various other therapists previously. If they have never been medicated, and it seems that they are highly likely to benefit from antidepressants, I sometimes suggest that we wait on psychotherapy until the medication has taken effect in order to see what the remaining issues are. Very often, successfully medicated clients are much less obsessional, less negative, less pessimistic, and their agendas for psychotherapy shift accordingly. Occasionally I've had a client decide she didn't need psychotherapy at all after the antidepressant kicked in. I'm happy to help clients save time and money by postponing the psychotherapy and reassessing the need for it after achieving a successful response to antidepressants.

TC: I would say yes, it can improve the quality of therapy for a variety of reasons. I think that some of the antidepressants have an effect of slowing down negative self-talk and the obsessional thinking which tends to perpetuate depression. If the negative self-talk is ameliorated or ends completely, that can only be helpful. Certainly when the patient starts feeling better physically and mentally he can attend to the work of psychotherapy, and he is not overwhelmed, and he can tolerate looking at what is going on that makes him so unhappy.

There is some folklore out there that an antidepressant will blunt the emotional work the person can do, because people won't work through their issues as fast because they're not as emotionally motivated by the pain they feel with depression. And that may be true for somebody that needs the severity of the symptoms to motivate them to examine their life or if it's just too risky for a variety of reasons, including psychological reasons, for somebody to contemplate taking medication. For those kind of people, who feel that they can't get motivated to make changes because their dark feelings are essential to getting better, taking medications is an unacceptable alternative.

For most people however, just by having the severity of the symptoms diminished, he or she is able to proceed in the therapy better, and therapy becomes beneficial. Therapy is not inexpensive, and if you're stuck in therapy, then it can get not only expensive, but it can also prolong your suffering needlessly. Just to recap what we had said earlier that the full range of emotions are still there, and one can still feel quite sad while taking an antidepressant, and the patient is still having an authentic experience.

Authors: What about the process of coming off of an antidepressant? Is that a difficult process when you and your client decide that it's time to come off?

TC: It depends on the agent. Some antidepressants are eas-
           ier to stop than others. I think it's a good idea to start
           low and go slow in the beginning, and then when the
           decision is made to come off, to also do that in a slow,
           stepwise fashion that decreases the risk of withdrawal.
           Even then, it can be an unpleasant experience.

NG: As I stated earlier, I also recommend tapering off the
           medications when both my client and I agree that the
           time is right. That is usually at least six months after
           they have reached therapeutic effectiveness. Many cli-
           ents can discontinue the antidepressants and feel just as
           good or better (if they no longer have side effects) as
           they did while taking them. Others feel substantially
           worse when they stop medications and may need to
           continue taking them indefinitely if they have chroni-
           cally intolerable symptoms of depression.

Authors: It is possible to just stop taking an antidepressant sud-
           denly?

TC: It is possible, but it's not wise. Certainly such a decision
           should be made in conjunction with the prescribing
           physician, and to stop suddenly is going to raise the
           risk of a withdrawal. A stepwise fashion is going to
           minimize the unpleasant side effects, if any, of coming
           off the medication. It doesn't need to take months; it can
           occur just over a period of a few short weeks.

Authors: What about herbal remedies such as St. John's Wort?

NG: St. John's Wort actually has been shown to be quite
           effective in a lot of studies in Europe and [is] particu-
           larly useful for people with mild to moderate depres-
           sion. And I've used it extremely successfully in some
           women, and for any who come to me who have not
           tried it, I'm happy to have them try St. John's Wort first
           and talk with them about what we know about St.
           John's Wort. And I even had a woman who needed a
           substantial dose of SSRI in order to control her depres-
           sion successfully switch to St. John's Wort and do
           extremely well. St. John's Wort seems to be a safe drug
           with few side effects for most people.
               St. John's Wort is packaged as a nutritional supple-
           ment. It is difficult to find a consistent amount of the
           active substances in the various products on the market.

One company produces a capsule that can be taken twice a day, b.i.d., rather than the traditional three times a day, t.i.d. This compound has been helpful for clients who have difficulty remembering the middle-of-the-day dose.

TC: The problem with herbs is that since they're not held to the same standards that pharmaceutical agents are, it's difficult to do definitive research, but there certainly is enough interest out there that they certainly bear thoughtful consideration, and certainly they have the weight of millennia of experience. It turns out that St. John's Wort possibly has a component of an antidepressant, so that would explain chemically why St. John's Wort works in mild to moderate depression. I certainly wouldn't prescribe it in a severe depression. I don't think it's potent enough, and it's not without its own risks as well. It can theoretically interact with other antidepressant medications. So I usually have the patient stop taking that before we move on.

Authors: What about the effects of hormones on depression? Can you tell us about factors unique to being a man or a woman that affect mood?

NG: Certainly menopause is a time when hormonal factors can have a major role in mood difficulties. Clients at this stage of life may inquire about taking hormone replacement therapy (HRT) and antidepressants. I believe that nutrition is the place to begin. I recommend eating phytoestrogens in the form of soy or flaxseed to supplement the declining levels of natural estrogens produced by the body. If women are having difficulty with anxiety or depression at menopause, despite eating phytoestrogens, as long as there is no family history of breast cancer or other contraindications, they may consider hormone replacement therapy. If neither nutrition nor HRT relieves the symptoms, then we consider an antidepressant.

Younger women who suffer from severe premenstrual dysphoria may also benefit from SSRIs. Some women take SSRIs daily in order to decrease their PMS; others take a higher dose just prior to the onset of PMS and continue just until the symptoms abate. There are some new data indicating that taking SSRIs only on the days a woman is experiencing extreme PMS can also be helpful.

TC: I have several patients who, for whatever reason, suffer from low testosterone levels, and the way that that has played itself out is in precipitating and exacerbating clinical depression. The antidepressant and the psychotherapy are somewhat helpful, but you need the addition of the testosterone in order to have a full recovery. Of course, testosterone is not without its own risks and benefits, and steroid use over a long period of time can be quite dangerous. So again, the risks and benefits of this have to be weighed, and also the reason why he has low testosterone levels to begin with needs to be addressed. I would only prescribe testosterone in someone who had demonstrated low or below-average levels of testosterone and would not give it to someone who is depressed who had normal amounts of testosterone. There is not any evidence that suggests that testosterone by itself is the preferred antidepressant.

I do have some patients who fall into the low-normal category, and I'm more comfortable prescribing them testosterone, especially if it proves to be helpful. There could be a relative effect. It could be that they were at high–normal and then, for whatever reasons, they're now low–normal, and that is what's exacerbating the depression, but according to the laboratory values, they don't have low testosterone.

It is theoretically possible, but as yet unproven, that a normal functioning person who has some kind of metabolic disease or a drug-induced phenomenon where the testosterone level is reduced, in itself, plays a role in precipitating a depression. There is precedent that depression in a perimenopausal woman is a well-recognized phenomenon because of similar fluctuations in hormones around that time.

Authors: We would assume, speaking of hormones, that thyroid function would be something that you would assess in your initial evaluation.

TC: Yes. I can't tell you how many times that, as part of the initial workup, I have uncovered undiagnosed hypothyroidism, especially in young women. It's an easy blood test that's not ordered frequently enough.

Undiagnosed hypothyroidism can look a lot like depression, and that's why you would encourage nonpsychiatric therapists to recommend that their clients get a good physical or at least have that potential assessed before trying to treat depression right off the bat. Depression due to an underlying illness is going to be much more difficult to treat if that underlying illness is not addressed. Not to mention the potential harm that could come if the underlying medical problem is not treated.

Authors: How much attention do you pay to nonmedication approaches to the biological aspects of depression, like diet, exercise, light therapy ... those kinds of things?

TC: A great deal of attention. I feel that my job as a physician is to encourage the patient to do as many beneficial things as possible, rather than just taking medication, because usually the depression is so severe that it really does take a multi-pronged approach. I think that exercise helps the antidepressants work better. Now, I don't have any scientific proof to that, but just in my experience, I find that patients who either are already exercising or start exercising after taking the medication have a better response which could be a result of the combination of the two things or it could just be the fact that he is just doing more healthy and life-affirming things. The important thing is that physicians should comment on one's sense of well-being and how to improve upon that, and usually that requires more than just medication. Sometimes, especially with my clientele who are pretty savvy, they've already tried the healthy diet and exercise.

There are other biologic interventions other than just medication, like light therapy for seasonal affective disorder or ECT (electroconvulsive therapy) for really, really severe depression that doesn't respond to medication.

Authors: Would you tell us more about that? Let's start with light therapy. When do you prescribe this for your patients?

TC: One would think in San Francisco, which has so much cloud cover, there would be more people suffering from seasonal affective disorder because the theory behind seasonal affective disorder is that the less direct sun-

shine one has, the more likely they will have this particular type of depression. So the way to treat it is to
expose the patient to light within certain wavelengths.
But it doesn't occur any more frequently here than elsewhere at this particular latitude. It is a well-known and
well-described phenomenon, and the response to the
light therapy is quite dramatic when it works, and not
too expensive. As it is somewhat faddish right now,
there are a lot of companies out there producing light
boxes that don't seem to work, but there are a couple of
reputable companies, and I do prescribe their products.
I have a few patients that this is the only thing that
seems to work, and their schedule is such that they can
devote the time that's required for light therapy, usually
a couple of hours a day.

Authors: Have you ever tried light therapy with someone who
has tried other things and seems to be resistant to antidepressants?

TC: No, I haven't. I know that there are psychiatrists who
do try that. I know that the light therapy is indicated for
seasonal affective disorder, so certainly if I make that
diagnosis and that's the patient's preference, we would
go that way. I probably would be a little bit more hesi-
tant to use it for other types of depression because there
is not as much evidence and science behind that as
there is with seasonal affective disorder. Light therapy
does have some cost associated with trying it (i.e., pur-
chasing a light box), and it's not without its own risk.

Authors: What about the importance of improving sleep in managing depression?

TC: So many times sleep is disrupted when one is
depressed, and it's not just from a guilty conscience. It's
because of the biochemical effects of depression. It actually interferes with one's normal sleep–wake cycle. In
fact, I can often tell when an antidepressant takes effect
because the patient reports that they're having vivid
dreams once again and that they're waking up rested.
Indeed, this is a biological marker for antidepressants
when they're being tested and the research is being conducted. Poor sleep is a major component of depression
and is often overlooked. The sleep is disrupted, and the
prescribing of a sleeping pill often is thought to be

enough, but I will always go over with the patient good sleep hygiene or sleep habits. We go over good habits that help in restoring normal sleep, and almost all of those do not require medication.

Depression can also start following sleep disruption due to stress, like frequently changing work shifts. The body's circadian rhythm can be disturbed which can certainly affect other biological processes.

Authors: What do you think about the medications that are commonly prescribed now, like Ambien and Sonata, that are used for helping with sleep?

TC: As an adjunct and for the short term, they're great. Sometimes that's just what the patient needs in order to restore normal sleep–wake cycles, and for a short period of time at the proper dose, I think they're worth the risk—because they also are not without their own risks in terms of tolerance and addiction. The newer sleep medications are a little bit cleaner in that they have a more desirable pharmaceutical profile, which means that they have high efficacy and low incidence of side effects. They are very targeted toward helping you sleep and they don't have a lot of other effects that you would not want. And they leave the system quickly. The newer sleep medications do that, which is helpful.

Authors: For example, do you tend to use them with someone who has difficulty falling asleep, rather than someone who falls asleep just fine but they wake up at 2 o'clock or 3 o'clock and can't go back to sleep?

TC: Yes, and actually sometimes with the latter, those meds are helpful as well. Certainly they are not helpful for somebody who has no difficulty falling asleep and sleeping through most of the night, but then they wake up really early before they have a chance to be rested. If they wake up at 4 or 5 A.M. and then can't go back to sleep, then sleep medications are not helpful. They are usually better for people having difficulty falling asleep, with some newer meds better for waking up in the middle of the night.

Authors: Dr. Cornett, we know that you have training and experience in using electroconvulsive therapy, or ECT. Since a great deal of stigma is associated with it, would you say a few words about this procedure?

TC: When I first was learning about psychiatry in medical school, I wanted to know how something as horrible as ECT, at least as how it had been portrayed in the media, anyway, had been allowed to exist and be practiced. Then I quickly learned that this image existed because it sold movie tickets and that nowadays, the ECT, which is technically called modified ECT, is not the form of torture that it is in most of our minds. It actually is a very humane and effective treatment for depression, especially depression that is life threatening and hasn't responded to medications. Sometimes ECT is more effective than medication, but because of the expense and the stigma attached with it, almost always medication is tried before. What do you do with somebody who has failed every antidepressant and has lost fifty pounds because they have no appetite and they're in such distress that they really seriously think suicide is an option? And I do see these people. I'll see them in the emergency room when I'm on call and saw them in my training. Such a person could be a good candidate for ECT. Because of the laws, they almost always have to give their consent, so there is a lot of education and collaboration with the patient and with the family in making this recommendation. It's not a panacea, and it's not without its own risks as well, but there are times when the potential benefits outweigh the risks.

Authors: That brings up another question, at what point do you think that inpatient hospitalization is an option or necessity?

TC: If the person has become dangerous to himself or to others and he cannot control these impulses. Depression can be a fatal illness, and suicide is a real risk in people who suffer from depression. I don't think that this is talked about enough. Clearly, suicidal thinking can be an indication for hospitalization. Sometimes the depression will become so bad that the patient is unable to care for himself, and when they're this disabled, they oftentimes will need to be in the hospital, at least to give the medications a chance to take effect. Sometimes if the medications are not helpful or have serious side effects, that could precipitate a hospitalization. That needs to take place in a psychiatric setting because of the expertise that's involved in dealing with a psychiatric illness as well as with the medical complications. Sometimes hospitalization is helpful for diagnostic purposes if somebody has come to the attention of a mental health professional and presents a real diagnostic dilemma and there are concerns about the person's safety or ability to care for himself. Sometimes the safe and secure environment of the hospital is required.

Authors: Any last thoughts about gay or lesbian issues and depression that we haven't covered?

TC: My hope is that your readers will realize that the depression that develops from coming out is just as responsive to medication as the depressions of the general population and that we're just as effective in treating depressions that have their roots in those issues.

Just in the last ten years that I've been doing this, I've witnessed an incredible explosion in the amount of knowledge about the biochemistry of depression. With time, I am very confident that these medications are going to get better and cleaner and that the side effects, which now can be annoying, will become less and less so. In fact, if you compared the medications now to the first generation of antidepressants or tricyclics and MAO inhibitors, the side effects are have been reduced significantly. This is why I think they're prescribed more, and I believe that with time, those side effects will become even less problematic. I also want to point out that supportive psychotherapy only enhances the effect of the medication.

Authors: Dr. Gartrell and Dr. Cornett, we want to thank you both very much for your warmth, insights, and help.

CHAPTER 9

Befriending the Black Dog

Putting It All Together

In chapter 6, we referred to depression as the Minotaur. In this chapter we'd like to downgrade the monster to a more companionable beast. Winston Churchill referred to his bleak moods as the "black dog." We have decided to borrow his jaunty designation for the blues.

Despite our fondness for canines, our efforts so far have been directed toward banishing the black dog. We've advised you to discipline it and drug it. We've recommended teaching it to play dead, or, without so much as a backward glance, simply abandoning it. But here's a novel proposal: What if we treat the black dog more respectfully? What if we make friends with it, even admire some of its finer points? To be sure, it is a grim, mangy creature. But every dog has some positive qualities. And every dog deserves to have its day.

Our sympathetic surge comes in part from our desire to promote a more holistic view, in part from our own clinical experience. First we want to explain what we mean by a holistic view of the blues.

Holistic Views of the Blues

Because psychotherapy is a stepchild of Western medicine, counselors are likely to focus on the causes and cures of their patients' presenting problems. Critics of this medical model point to its obvious limitations. After all, they argue, a person is composed of more than the inflamed problem for which he is seeking relief. Shouldn't a proper assessment include *all* the physical and mental and spiritual aspects of the person? Shouldn't it include, as well, his or her social context? After all, isn't it often true that particular symptoms reveal more about the biases of society than they do about the patient? Lesbian and gay critics, in particular, point out that the culture-blind quick-fix approach can lead to abuses. Therapists often become society's soft police, trained to sniff out and snuff out so-called "deviant" behavior.

We agree with these criticisms. But our advocacy for a non-pathologizing, less compartmentalized approach isn't based solely on holistic theories of human behavior. We've learned firsthand from clients to look at the big picture. In some instances, the blues—painful as they are—serve adaptive, even positive functions. The withdrawal and hibernation that so often characterize depression can reduce our exposure to environments that have grown increasingly toxic. The corrosive self-doubt that plunges us into despair can also provoke "aha!" insights we might never be privy to in happier times. The blues can stimulate long-overdue bouts of reflection, as well as compassion for ourselves and others. Perhaps Kelly's story can illustrate the blessings, often indirect, sometimes bestowed by the blues.

Kelly is the youngest child and only daughter in an Irish-Catholic family of hotshot cops. Before she could walk, her father was killed in the line of duty. Since then, her brothers have all earned high ranks in the same city department. Kelly has always been the kid sister no one took very seriously.

During the day, Kelly works as a waitress. At night, she goes to school. She has maintained straight-A grades. As soon as she gets her associate degree in criminal justice, she intends to begin training in the police cadet academy. Despite her killer schedule, Kelly has always made time for softball. It was during the first practice of the season that Kelly noticed the new shortstop. A week later, they were in bed; in a month, they were an item. Kelly has told herself she can handle it all—work, school, sports, plus all-nighters with her hot new girlfriend. But she can't. Her grades are slipping and her manager at work has started getting customer complaints. In the last few weeks, she has even lost interest in sex. She is sure her new girlfriend won't stick around. Her anxiety has spilled over to other areas. She has started avoiding freeway driving. She can't concentrate in class. She has even begun to think the unthinkable: that she isn't cut out to be a cop. On the verge of dropping out of the program, she has made an appointment with a school counselor.

Many blues-sufferers are not always aware of the duty-bound messages they have absorbed since toddlerhood. Such programming is pervasive—an unconscious part of everyday life in overachieving families. Later on, when the children from such families willingly bury themselves under mountains of obligation, the black dog may be the only available rescue animal. That is true in Kelly's case. Her depression forced her to press the alarm button. She got help. She began to understand the origins of her superhuman expectations of herself. She eventually learned to tolerate her own vulnerability, and most importantly, to set reasonable goals.

The black dog can be a rescuer, a messenger, or the guide who leads us back to our long-buried pasts. But there are other holistic ways to think about this black dog. One such alternative perspective comes from traditional Eastern healing practices.

Western medicine, and the healing methods that spring from it, including psychotherapy, separate the problems of mind from the afflictions of the body. To healers with a holistic orientation, such a division seems artificial, wrong-headed, *and* wrong-bodied. Humans are unified creatures. Consequently, our mental, emotional, physical, and spiritual dimensions are—according to acupuncturists, masseuses, herbalists, and other naturopathic practioners—integrated and indivisible. In fact, if we think about the many physical manifestations of depression, the classification of depression as a purely mental disorder doesn't really make much sense.

There is another significant difference between the practices of Eastern and Western healers. Westerners tend to see the source of illness as invasion. In order to restore health, this invading hostile entity, whether it is microbes or negative thinking, must be quashed or driven away. Eastern practitioners frame the problem of illness quite differently. Illness, according to these practitioners, results from an imbalance or blockage of naturally occurring energies. Therefore the restoration of health depends on renewing the harmony and flow of these life forces. In addition, healing is accomplished by natural methods: by means of touch or sunshine or herbs or—in the case of homeopathy—a hair of the black dog that bit you.

Because such practitioners see illness so differently, they also approach diagnoses very differently. In addition to a painstaking physical examination, most alternative practitioners ask patients scores of questions about what most of us might consider mundane details: Our habits, our preferences, our moods are all grist for the holisitc healer's mill. The information gathered by such practitioners is in stark contrast to the blood pressure, height, and weight data tallied by Western physicians. From the details the holistic practitioner gathers, energy blockages can be pinpointed and remedies prescribed.

For most of us, used to fifteen minutes spent sitting half-naked waiting for the obviously harried doctor to rush in, give the perfunctory once-over and rush out, this kind of meticulous evaluation may seem both exotic and nurturing. The results of such painstaking attention cannot be attributed simply to a feel-good placebo effect. Jackie Wilson, a lesbian physician who practices in San Diego, is so convinced of the efficacy of such an approach that she switched her practice to naturopathic methods. "Western medicine started with the Greeks," Jackie explains in a recent conversation. "Compared with Asian systems of thought that stretch back thousands of years, it is very recent. In fact, it is in its youth.

"Think about it a minute," Jackie adds. "Youth is characterized by a lot of activity, movement, by mechanical solutions. A child is delighted to walk. A teenager is obsessed with movement. In contrast, maturity is characterized by contemplation and stillness. Eastern healing methods are much subtler. Holistic practitioners consider people in more complex ways. Consequently, their remedies will act in subtler, more complicated ways. They will maximize the patient's own internal healing potential."

Jackie describes a patient of hers: a woman whose partner has died and, although depressed, has not responded to conventional antidepressants. Jackie stressed that she had not simply concentrated on the woman's depression. When she examined the patient, she also considered her other complaints—the arthritis in her feet, for example, and her hyperthyroidism for which she took synthetic thyroxin. All these elements added up to a composite picture. The homeopathic remedy Jackie prescribed treated the whole person and relieved all the woman's symptoms—including the depression.

When depression is only one microdot in a much larger pointillist portrait, the black dog doesn't loom so large. It simply becomes part of a whole constellation of unique, identifying features. Other healers use different treatment approaches to heal the black dog.

Fixing up the Dog House

If there were such a title, Amanda Kovattana would be called a habitation psychologist. Instead, she refers to herself as a queer professional organizer. Amanda can size up the mood and temperament of her clients from a quick inspection of their living spaces. Undecorated walls, empty refrigerators, the absence of color, for example, often reflect an inner emptiness, a feeling of bleakness or desolation. Piles of unsorted papers and overflowing drawers also suggest a different variety of the blues. Whoever has adjusted to such intrusiveness is probably feeling hopeless. She no longer believes that she has any control over her life.

Like other holistic healers, Amanda looks for ways to restore harmony and health. Piles of clutter, for example, represent energy obstructions that are getting in the way of health and happiness. Amanda helps blues-sufferers sort through piles and develop filing systems that will prevent further blockages. Because Amanda is also keenly aware that the larger environment also needs healing, all her home problem–solutions are earth-friendly. She fixes what is broken, builds new storage areas from preexisting materials, and recycles whatever is discarded. Amanda reports that such a reordering of personal environments acts as a powerful mood-elevator.

According to Denise Linn, author of *Sacred Space: Clearing and Enhancing the Energy in Your Home* (1996), a one-to-one relationship between your inside and outside space is inevitable. "Our houses," she writes, "are mirrors of ourselves. They reflect our interests, our beliefs, our hestitations, our spirit and our passion. They tell a story about the way we feel about ourselves and the world around us."

In her book, Linn suggests many ways to make room (literally and figuratively) for happier times. She suggests dozens of easy do-it-yourself rituals for purification and protection. One of the antidepressants she recommends acts primarily on the sense of smell. In the winter months, she says, she usually keeps a big pot of water simmering on her wood stove. She adds some pine or fir oil to the water. As well as lifting spirits, the brew also humidifies the room. She has plenty of other very concrete spirit-boosting suggestions: what colors are most soothing; where to place lighting and mirrors; how to arrange furniture and art.

The methods of these healers may be different, but their goal is the same. Rather than banishing the black dog, they attempt to make peace with him—to make him more comfortable. Naturopaths soothe the black dog with herbs and acupuncture; environmental healers do it with color and light and aroma. Yet another class of holistic practitioners has decided that the best way to befriend the dog is to sit perfectly still and let it sniff to its heart's content.

The Black Dog Bites the Buddha

Most of the founding prophets of the world's major religions bear the teeth marks of the black dog. Buddha was no exception. After the black dog starting nipping at his heels, he tried to escape. If he were to become destitute, he was certain, the black dog would lose interest and wander off in search of more interesting prey. But even after he divested himself of everything he owned and practiced extreme forms of asceticism, the dog still hounded him. Eventually he gave up, sat perfectly still, and let the dog sniff wherever it wanted. It was at this moment that Buddha began to distinguish between pain and suffering. The pain of existence—awareness of loss and death—was inevitable and unavoidable. But suffering, he realized, was an entirely different matter. It came from longing, from the desire to avoid pain, from fruitless attempts to distract oneself with pleasure or status.

In the cosmos posited by Buddhists, people with the blues are reluctant prophets. They have been blessed or cursed with a special sensitivity to the pain of existence. But they do not relish the role of witness and, in their efforts to escape, they cause themselves more suffering. The solution? To sit still just as Buddha did. To let the black dog sniff where it wants. To watch the black dog get closer, close enough to count his whiskers, to see his yellow fangs and smell his hot breath.

In his book *The Zen Path Through Depression* (1999), Philip Martin describes the way that this observant stance can help with the blues. Instead of rushing around in search of a cure, Martin suggests that we become intimately familiar with our pain. "When one needs to listen to a strange sound," he writes, "doesn't one naturally stop making noise? One cannot listen carefully as long as one is talking, thinking, or moving about inattentively."

Sitting still and being mindful of what we usually ignore—our breathing, for example—is the first step:

> In. Out. In. Out. Noticing the air filling your chest. Notice your chest. Your shoulders. Then the other parts of your body. After this inventory, you might let your consciousness alight on your pain. Is the depression a physical sensation? Is it mental anguish? Does it have a location or is it free-floating? Is it layered or dense? Does it change shape? Does it wax or wane? Can you accept its existence, and even relax into it? Does your breathing change when you surrender to it? What else do you notice?

An analogy may be helpful to explain why just sitting quietly, noticing the thoughts and sensations as they come and go, reduces suffering. Say you are suffering from insomnia. You know you are supposed to sleep at night. Everyone else, you are certain, is getting the requisite eight hours of zzzzs. Only you are awake. You toss and turn, more and more anxious that you won't be able to function the next day. But say you start to pay attention to the night noises, the lights outside, the traffic, the hum and throb going on all around you. Perhaps, if you are still, you will also notice the myriad changes in your own state. Perhaps you are wide awake, then thoughtful, then drowsy, then vigilant. Perhaps you turn on some music, or prepare some tea. The imperial nocturnal edict to sleep dissolves in this kind of mindfulness. Instead there is change, flux, sensation alternating with perception, light alternating with dark. You may still feel fatigue, but you experience it differently from moment to moment. You are liberated from the suffering that came from rigid attachment to night-sleep.

Focusing on our depression in this slow, painstaking way has a similar liberating effect. At last, we can accept ourselves in a loving, compassionate way. We can stop reproaching ourselves for not being upbeat. As soon as the suffering that comes from wanting to be someone, somewhere else stops, we may even feel a sense of exhilaration. Perhaps we feel tolerance, a moment-to-moment serenity. Perhaps we feel connected with all the sadness in the world. If we remember all those lean and hungry black dogs prowling the earth, we may feel more sympathetic toward our own canine companion. Or perhaps we will remember that dogs are pack animals, and help our lonely pup noir find some companions of his own.

Tribal Magic

Belonging—finding the black dog a pack of his own—is another holistic remedy for the blues. Such group support can come from networks of friends or cadres of task-oriented activists. It can come from psychotherapy marathons or self-help organizations. Group support is also available in cyberspace. Queer blues survivors can use chat rooms, listservs, and bulletin boards to stay in touch and catch up on the latest information about mood disorders.

There was a time when the queer nation was itself a global/local tribe. Simply joining the tribe provided a holistic remedy for the blues. Adrienne Rich writes: " I have an indestructible memory of walking along a particular block in New York City, the hour after I acknowledged to myself that I loved a woman, feeling invincible. For the first time in my life I experienced sexuality as clarifying my mind instead of hazing it over" (Penelope, 1989).

As well as uniting with long-buried parts of ourselves, such declarations made us whole in another sense. They provide entrée to a close-knit tribe.

Research on the importance of group membership is unequivocal. Study after study shows a direct link between social support and general feelings of well-being. The more companions we have, the more likely we are to score highly on psychological mood measures. In addition, research studies also show that dense networks—in which there are a lot of overlapping connections among members—are far more supportive than diffuse networks (Fischer, 1982). It makes sense if you think about it: If your friends all know each other, they are much more likely to get together and act collectively if they know you need help. Such group action is extremely powerful.

As the queer tribe has lost some of its cohesion, however, it has also lost its healing power. Despite the hopeful umbrella designations "LGBT" and "Queer," plenty of once-friendly tribal intersections have turned into faultlines. With the differences between bi's and gays, between trans and womyn-born, and between different generations and ethnicities often too inflamed to ignore, how can we even locate our former tribe?

(Re)joining the Pack

Paradoxically enough, the scores of clans that divide the queer nation also provide oases of unity for some gays and lesbians. Queer twelve-steppers—AA and Al-Anon members, for example—have a strong pack identity. If you happen to identify as a member of a twelve-step group, chances are you're plugged in to a national support network. Even if you leave home, you will be able to find safe harbor in never-before-visited places. There are also networks for queers of color, for sadomasochists, for HIV-positive men. These are just a few of the clans that make up queer nation. There are scores of others. Every year, for example, there is a conference for lesbians over sixty. As well as organizing this conference, the OLOC (Old Lesbian Organizing Committee) links members to each other informally—through electronic and old-fashioned word-of-mouth grapevines.

But despite the fact that there are thousands of queer blues-sufferers—certainly enough to support a pack identity—for the most part, they remain separated from one another. Even though occasionally there are therapy-oriented, time-limited groups for depressed gays or lesbians in some major cities, there are no easily identifiable clans available, no ready-made self-help groups, no local or national organizations for queer blues survivors.

Why? One answer might be that depression is almost too ubiquitous to provide a pack identity. Everyone is depressed in his or her own idiosyncratic way. We don't agree. There is just as much diversity among queer alcoholics or over-sixty lesbians, and they have managed to find a common bond.

We have another theory. We think that—just as homosexuality once was—depression has now become the province of experts: a certifiable medical condition that belongs to the doctors and therapists who treat it. This cultural jurisdiction is reinforced by the effectiveness, for many queers, of pharmaceutical interventions. To many blues-sufferers, the high medical profile of mood disorders is a blessing. It means that depressive symptoms, easily recognized by physicians and therapists, will be treated quickly. But there is also a downside. Our already fragmented communities may be further fragmented by a one-person one-problem approach. Queer blues-sufferers, already feeling isolated, become even more insular. An individually focused treatment approach also means that, because gays and lesbians aren't talking to each other, they may overlook the connection between depression and homophobia. How then to connect the dots—among queer blues-sufferers, and between depression and homophobia?

Visionary Remedies: Developing a Politics of Identity

Some of the depression remedies we've suggested are past-oriented: for example, getting rid of the childhood ghosts who still haunt us. Other remedies have focused on the present, on getting here-and-now relief. But relief from the blues can also emanate from somewhere in the future. The formation of a new pack identity is just such a future-oriented remedy.

We want to propose such a pack, a place where the black dogs can safely congregate, sniff and nuzzle. We know a collective queer blues identity won't happen overnight. Packs develop slowly. But without even being aware of it, most blues-sufferers have already begun the process.

The first step, ironically enough, is the negative self-talk, the pain-laced stories we tell ourselves. Eventually the stories become too unbearable to contain. They spill out. Perhaps blues-sufferers confide in one other person, a friend or a lover. This is the nucleus of the new pack.

At one level, gays and lesbians are getting help, support. But they are also coming out. They are revealing previously hidden parts of themselves. And something else is happening. They are developing their stories. In the process of telling these tales and getting feedback, feelings acquire a sharper focus. Sufferers become survivors. They look back over the ups and downs, and discern patterns and probable causes. Insights, refined even further, lead to new perspectives. Recovery plans are hatched, new remedies tried. At some point, gays and lesbians may feel relieved enough to declare themselves "cured." But what if blues survivors took this process another step?

According to queer theorist Ken Plummer, packs form in stages. One of the turning points is when individual pain, shared with enough people, becomes a "story of identity—of who one is, of a sense of unity, yet difference." (Plummer, 1995)

Stories, told enough times, to enough people, will spark echoing stories about queer blues. In addition to their own uniqueness, the storytellers will begin to detect a resonance with others, a commonality that they never suspected. This sense of unique yet shared identity, spoken and written about enough times, will be the basis of a new pack.

One of those critical take-off points—a moment in time when individual experiences coalesce into a group identity—was captured when Fairy Butch (a.k.a. Karlyn Lotney) convened a group of blues-sufferers and turned on her tape recorder. The result, an article entitled "On Our Prozac: Dykes Talk About Sex, Drugs, and Depression," was published in the journal *On Our Backs* in the spring of 1995.

The lesbians participating in the roundtable were Lisa Johnson, twenty-five, a San Francisco graduate film student who has experienced lifelong depression; Dorian Moore, twenty-nine, a San Diego writer who suffers from chronic fatigue syndrome; and Gail Sweeney, thirty-five, a San Francisco physician who has had bouts of depression for the last five years. Karlyn, also a blues survivor, opened the discussion by observing that depression has its own stigma and its own closet. Dorian agreed. "One of the most common things I hear within the dyke community," she remarked, "is from the new-age lesbians who give me a lot of shit for being on any kind of medication. They say, 'You chose this illness, you're not trying hard enough, you need to try herbs, a juice fast.'"

"It's kind of a new-age version of the 'buck-up ethic,'" Karlyn added.

Each of the women went on to describe the ways Prozac had changed their sex lives and their relationships. The discussion was lively, amusing, and at times poignant. At the end Karlyn wrapped up the encounter with an observation: "In making these connections with one another, we enhance our ability to manage our illnesses, and to enjoy our lives, our sex, and our relationships." In her summary, we can detect the beginnings of a new pack. (To read the whole transcript and find out more about the author, log on to www.FairyButch.com.)

Such public occasions become rallying points for other queer blues-sufferers who, in turn, feel encouraged to share their stories. When enough gays and lesbians meet and talk, when enough queer blues stories are publicly aired, the new pack is born.

Such a process doesn't happen quickly. It doesn't happen in a linear fashion. And, most importantly, it doesn't happen in a vacuum. One of the factors that has an enormous impact on pack identity is the visibility of other blues survivors—queers whose lives are memorable, and whose stories are galvanizing. The list of gay and lesbian celebs—writers and artists—who suffered from depression is voluminous. We included excerpts from some of their poems, diaries, and letters at the end of chapter 4. But what is missing from these lists are the names and deeds of the everyday heros, those queer activists who, though suffering from depression, have tackled the homophobia and racism and genderism that are the roots of the blues. We want to showcase a trio of such activists. We hope that the stories of these depression survivors show that the queer blues pack may indeed be a club we all might be honored to join.

Profiles in Courage: Three Blues Survivors Who Have Made a Difference

Dr. Dee Mosbacher, physician and award-winning documentary filmmaker, has been a frontline activist for thirty years. She worked on anti-war and pro-choice political campaigns as an undergrad. Later, in medical school, her focus shifted to gay rights. Elected as an out lesbian to the board of directors of the American Medical Student Association, she put together a audiovisual presentation called "Closets are Health Hazards." The presentation, radical at the time, evolved into her first video, *Closets Are Health Hazards: Gay and Lesbian Physicians Come Out*. In 1993, Dee formed WomanVision. The nonprofit organization is dedicated to producing videos that combat homophobia.

Dee experienced her first serious bout of the blues when she was in her early forties. She remembers it as a particularly bleak time. Despite the fact that she was doing work that she felt was meaningful, and had a fulfilling partnership, she was unable to convince herself that her life was worthwhile. Despondent, she withdrew from friends and her usual round of activities.

Dee still muses about the sources of her depression, and about queer depression in general. On one hand, she says that homophobia seems to be a cause, or at least a major contributor, to depression. So major, in fact, that her career has been dedicated to its eradication. On the other hand, trained as a physician, she is also a firm a believer in biochemical causes. She speculates that there may be an invisible link between the biochemical and the environmental triggers for depression—perhaps a biochemical predisposition may make certain queers more sensitive to homophobia, or perhaps homophobia affects brain chemistry. Whatever the intersection between the two, Dee credits the antidepressants that were prescribed during her first depression for making it possible for her to resume her work.

Though she has continued to take antidepressants intermittently, she still struggles with the blues. Among the biggest challenges, she says, are the occasions she must solicit funds for a new film project. "In the best of times, approaching groups or individuals, hat in hand, isn't my forte," she says, "but when I'm feeling depressed, I just have to focus on putting one foot ahead of another. There are times," she says, "when the one-step-at-a-time approach doesn't even work. I can't do it at all."

At other times, the wave of enthusiasm that almost always greets her at fund-raising events buoys her up. The hardest part, she says, is the isolation. "I have wonderful consultants, but no full-time staff. It's up to me to provide the momentum."

And she has. Among the films that WomanVision has produced are *Out for a Change: Addressing Homophobia in Women's Sports* and *All God's Children*, a film that deals with sexual orientation within the context of the traditional African-American values of freedom, inclusion, and the Christian love ethic. Films in progress are *Radical Harmonies: The Story of the Women's Music Cultural Movement* and *No Secret Anymore: The Times of Del and Phyllis Lyon.*

Straight from the Heart, a video that features a diverse set of parents talking about their gay and lesbian children, was the first pro-gay film ever to be shown to a bipartisan gathering of members of the U.S. Congress. In 1995, the film was nominated for a short-documentary Oscar. (For more information about Dee's films, e-mail info@Woman-Vision.Org.)

Karlyn Lotney, known as Fairy Butch, is not your usual in-the-trenches activist. She does her anti-homophobia work and queer community organizing on stage, in workshops, in advice columns published online and in various magazines. A single night in the company of Fairy Butch probably banishes as much sexual self-doubt and shame as years spent in a therapy office. Fairy Butch peppers her standing-room-only audiences with morale-boosting quips, provocative loving-ourselves demos, and down-home remedies for queer angst.

Most people witnessing galvanizing performances would be dumbfounded to find out that Karlyn has struggled with the blues as far back as she can remember. As a child, she was so depressed that only the luminous moments of relief stand out. One such moment occurred when, as a nine-year-old, she was playing baseball. As she hit the ball and started rounding the bases, she remembers thinking how rare it was to feel this way—a brief interlude when she wasn't feeling sad.

Since then, Karlyn's chronic low-grade melancholy has been punctuated, intermittently, by serious bouts of depression. Sometimes, she says, the big troughs seem justified—triggered by something as specific as a breakup. At other times, she is at a loss to explain her slides into despair.

As a young teen, one of her coping strategies was escape. Long before she had a license, she would hijack the family car and head for a friend's house. All through college, her sanity depended upon having an escape route and a set of wheels. Seven years ago, she added antidepressants to her time-tested drive-away remedy. She says that the medication has allowed her the luxury of feeling sad. Before, she simply couldn't risk it. Sorrow—she knew from long experience—might deepen into uncontrollable despair. She credits antidepressants with keeping her depression at manageable levels. But Karlyn also struggles with the idea of taking them, and from time to time, has gone off them. At those times, her depression has returned.

As a veteran of depression, Karlyn has learned a variety of coping mechanisms. She still has periods when she feels the end of the world is at hand, but now she knows that they will pass. And she knows what the early warning signs are. If she feels herself slipping, she spends more time at the gym and gets more support from friends. If she feels blue before a show, she takes herself for a walk around the block and gives herself a pep talk. "If I'm not really having fun," she says, "my audience won't either. For the time being, I find somewhere else to put my depression."

Karlyn has also stopped going off her antidepressants. "Depression," she says, "is like a virus—a herpes virus. If you don't take care of yourself, it returns."

Bayard Rustin has been portrayed as the "Socrates of the Civil Rights Movement" (Anderson, 1998, 17). A brilliant analyst and political strategist, he was the chief architect of Martin Luther King's nonviolence campaign. In the '50s and '60s, he put together the broadest civil rights coalition ever assembled. The result was the 1963 March on Washington, at which King delivered the world-changing "I have a Dream" speech. Vernon Jordan gave one of the eulogies at Bayard's memorial service in 1987. "Bayard," he said, "was chairman of the ideas committee for us all" (357) Rachelle Horowitz, another fellow activist, said, "I don't think he had a racist bone in him. This isn't to say he didn't know he was black; for he had a strong black identity. But he simply viewed all people as human, as soul mates" (5).

Bayard was also brilliant. "I don't know what Rustin's IQ was," one of his associates commented, "but it was certainly near the top of the mountain. I never heard him stopped in a debate, discussion, or question period." (5)

Charismatic and gifted, Bayard was also unabashedly gay. When, as a teen, he first discovered his homosexuality, he confided to a friend that he went into the woods and beat his legs with sticks. "And then," his confidante added, "in defiance, he went out and became a great football player and track star in his high school. He was going to show 'em" (155).

Rustin showed them in many ways: by becoming a first-rate athlete and musician, orator and organizer. He also paid a high price for his gayness. In 1953, police caught him having sex with two men. He was sentenced to sixty days in jail on a morals charge.

The publicity surrounding the charge caused Rustin to lose what he cherished most: his high profile position in a left-wing pacifist organization, and the protection of a longtime father figure. After his incarceration, Rustin's mentor, A.J. Muste, abandoned him.

All Rustin's associates remarked upon his ability to recover from painful episodes and resume his work, but this crisis was the worst of his life. His characteristic resilience failed him. Despondent, he began psychoanalysis. His analyst was concerned enough about him to arrange to see him even when he could no longer afford to pay his fees. "Bayard was a very depressed person when I began treating him," Dr. A. recalls (168).

Eventually, Rustin recovered and went on to work as Martin Luther King's advisor. In 1960, he experienced another major setback. Jealous of Rustin's standing with King, Adam Clayton Powell threatened to spread the false rumor that King and Rustin were sexually involved unless King fired Rustin. King bowed to the pressure. It was another crushing blow for Rustin , and, according to one of his associates, he went through another down time.

As before, he recovered, and worked on other fronts before joining the coalition that organized the 1963 March on Washington.

The depressive episodes in Rustin's life are anomalous. He is remembered for his infectious good humor—Rustin was "everyone 's favorite antidepressant." And yet, for the observant, there was evidence of the blues. After actress Liv Ullman heard Rustin sing, she commented not only on his lovely tenor voice but said, "I also didn't find it like singing. It was more like crying out—'Listen, listen, to my sadness'" (8).

Rustin's activism was prompted by a keen awareness of injustice and a dedication to humanistic ideals. But he also used activism to banish the blues. Summing up this strategy, he wrote, "The major aspect of the struggle within is determined without. If one gets out and begins to defend one's rights and the rights of others, spiritual growth takes place." In short, when we heal others, we heal ourselves.

Dee Mosbacher, Karlyn Lotney, and Bayard Rustin are well-known activists—queers who have made outstanding contributions. Dig a little further and we find out that they are also members of the blues survivors' pack. There are plenty of other high profile queers who struggle with depression. In fact, when the blues pack actually does come into existence, it will be so full of leaders and activists, artists and authors and musicians, that the roster of its members will erase, once and for all, the stigmatizing power of the blues.

Leaving Queer Blues Nation: Summing Up

We've covered a lot of territory. And we've used a variety of maps to explore the range and depth of the blues. Some of our maps have been formal—the official diagnostic guides used by therapists. Others have been more impressionistic—the firsthand accounts of gays and lesbians who have strayed or fallen into the blue zone. Our topographies have included other dimensions of depression as well. We've tried to track the blues back to their biological, psychosocial, and environmental sources. We've explored the ways in which culturally ingrained homophobia contributes to depression, and we've pinpointed the hideouts of additional potential mood assassins—everything from blue genes to alcohol abuse, from neurotransmitter short circuits to self-deprecating interior monologues.

When it comes to remedies, we like to think that our maps have morphed into menus. We've offered a series of self-help exercises to choose from and a pharmacopoeia to browse in. We've specified the kinds of support available from counselors, physicians, and nontraditional healers. And we've outlined some of the ways that gays and lesbians—should they opt for outside help—can make informed and empowered choices.

Despite this seemingly inexhaustible catalog of possible remedies, there are dozens of others that we haven't even mentioned, or even thought of. Being aware of such an array is, itself, a powerful

antidepressant. It saves depressed gays and lesbians the added torment of getting mired in internal pro-and-con debates about any one
particular treatment. Instead of worrying about whether or not to
take meds or see a therapist, we hope blues-sufferers will feel
empowered enough to design their own multi-dimensional recovery
programs.

Being aware of the array of potential remedies can also be useful for blues-sufferers who are quite certain about the best cure for
their depressions. Say, for example, you are sure your depression is
biologically based and, consequently, you have opted to take antidepressants. Even though medication may be one option—perhaps the
best—it need not preclude other, supplementary, remedies. In fact,
we recommend that blues survivors approach the range of choices
just as they might a menu: more specifically a takeout menu from a
Chinese restaurant. Perhaps you choose one remedy from column A
(say, joining a support group), one from column B (taking time to
meditate), and one from column C (joining a gym). We recommend
that blues-sufferers mix and match, and try new remedies when the
old ones seem ineffective.

We hope that as well as broadening your horizon of choices, we
have been able to instill a feeling that you belong to a large and
extraordinary clan—one with remarkable talents and daunting challenges. We also hope that by using the exercises, examples, and
resources we have provided, that one day you will be an ex-member
of the Queer Blues clan.

Resources for Support and Information

Depression

Detailed Online Depression Information and Links
http://depression.com

Mental Health Net: Depression Tops List of Health Concerns for Lesbians and Gays
http://eatingdisorders.mentalhelp.net/articles/prn5.htm

Mood Disorders (Depression and Manic Depression) within the Gay, Lesbian, and Bisexual Community
http://comingouttwice.homepage.com

National Depressive and Manic-Depressive Association
730 N. Franklin Street, Suite 501
Chicago, IL 60610
(800) 826-3632

Mental Health Organizations and Referral Sources

American Association of Sex Educators, Counselors, and Therapists
P.O. Box 238
Mt. Vernon, IA 52314
http://www.aasect.org

American Counseling Association
5999 Stevenson Avenue
Alexandria, VA 22304-3300
(800) 347-6647

American Psychiatric Association
1400 K Street NW
Washington, DC 20005
http://www.psych.org

American Psychological Association Division 44 Website (The Society for the Psychological Study of Lesbian, Gay, and Bisexual Issues)
http://www.apa.org/divisions/div44

Association for Gay, Lesbian, and Bisexual Issues in Counseling
P.O. Box 216
Jenkintown, PA 19046
http://www.aglbic.org/

Association of Gay and Lesbian Psychiatrists
4514 Chester Ave.
Philadelphia, PA 19143-3707
http://members.aol.com/aglpnat/homepage.html

Association of Lesbian and Gay Affirmative Psychotherapists
http://www.onisland.com/algap
(212) 807-8402

The Committee on Gay & Lesbian Issues of the American Psychoanalytic Association
http://www.apsa-co.org/ctf/cgli

GLBT Counseling and Psychotherapy Links
http://www.virtualcity.com/youthsuicide/links1.htm

Lesbian and Gay Child & Adolescent Psychiatrists
P.O. Box 570
Glen Oaks, NY 11004

Lesbian and Gay Psychotherapy Association
http://www.lagpa.org

Lesbian, Gay, Bisexual Concerns within the American Psychological Association
http://www.apa.org/pi/lgbc

Mental Health Resources with Leonard Holmes, Ph.D.: G/L/B sites
http://mentalhealth.about.com/health/mentalhealth/msub35.htm

Midwest Association of Lesbian and Gay Psychologists
Box 199
3023 N. Clark
Chicago, IL 60657

National Association of Social Workers
The Committee on Lesbian and Gay Issues
750 First Street, NE, Suite 700
Washington, DC 20002-4241
http://www.naswdc.org
(202) 408-8600

National Self-Help Clearinghouse
City University of New York
33 W. 42nd Street #12222
New York, NY 10036
(212) 840-1259

Pride Institute: L/G/B/T Inpatient and Outpatient Mental Health Treatment Centers (New York, Chicago, Minneapolis, Dallas/Fort Worth, and Fort Lauderdale)
http://www.pride-institute.com
(800) 54-PRIDE

Psychotherapy for Gay and Lesbian Clients
http://www.mhsource.com/pt/p980142.html

San Francisco Bay Area Gay/Lesbian Psychotherapist Association
http://www.gaylesta.org

Self-Help and Psychology Magazine: L/G/B/T Articles
http://www.shpm.com/articles/glb/index.shtml

Chemical Dependency Resources

National Association of Alcoholism and Drug Abuse Counselors
1991 N. Fort Nyer Drive, Suite 900
Arlington, VA 22209
http://www.naadac.org
(800) 548-0497

National Association of Lesbian & Gay Alcoholism Professionals
1147 S. Alvarado Street
Los Angeles, CA 90006

National Clearinghouse for Drug and Alcohol Information: Celebrating the Pride and Diversity Among and Within the Lesbian, Gay, Bisexual, and Transgender Populations
http://www.health.org/features/lgbt/

**Pride Institute: L/G/B/T Inpatient and Outpatient Chemical
Dependency Treatment Centers** (New York, Chicago,
Minneapolis, Dallas/Fort Worth, and Fort Lauderdale)
http://www.pride-institute.com
(800) 54-PRIDE

Queer Health Resources

Gay and Lesbian Medical Association
http://www.glma.org

Gay and Lesbian Resource Network of the American Red Cross
9706 Dilston Rd.
Silver Spring, MD 20903

L/G/B/T health issues
http://gayhealth.com

**National Gay/Lesbian Health Directory-Sourcebook on
Lesbian/Gay Healthcare**
National Lesbian and Gay Health Foundation
1638 R. Street Suite 2
Washington, DC 20009
(202) 797-3708

Queer Youth Resources

Gay Lesbian Straight Education Network
http://www.glsen.org

Gay and Lesbian Youth Talkline
c/o Gay & Lesbian Community Services Center
1625 N. Hudson Ave.
Los Angeles, CA 90028-9998
(213) 462-8130

Gay-Straight Alliance Network
http://www.gsanetwork.org

Lavender Youth Recreation & Information Center
http://thecity.sfsu.edu/~lyric/

Out Proud:
**The National Coalition for Gay, Lesbian, Bisexual, and
Transgender Youth**
http://www.outproud.org

Queer Youth Links
www.youthresource.com

Toronto Coalition for Lesbian, Gay, and Bisexual Youth
65 Wellesley Street East, #300
Toronto, Ontario M4Y 1G7
(416) 924-4126 ext. 456
http://www.tclgbty.com/

National G/L/B/T Youth Resources by State
http://www.yale.edu/lgbt/youth.htm

Aging and Queer

Gay Lesbian Association of Retiring Persons
http://gaylesbianretiring.org

Old Lesbians Organizing Committee
P.O. Box 980422
Houston, TX 77098
http://www.oloc.org
chardenea@worldnet.att.net

Queer Spirituality

Nonviolent Protest of Spiritual Violence Against Queers
http://Soulforce.org

Qspirit
http://www.qspirit.org

Family Issues Support and Information

Parents and Friends of Lesbians and Gays (PFLAG)
http://www.pflag.org

Online Queer Programming and Information

http://GAYBC.com

http://PlanetOut.com

Inspirational Books and Tapes

The Language of Letting Go, by Melody Beattie. 1990. New York: HarperCollins.

8 Meditations for Optimum Health, by Andrew Weil. 1997. New York: Upoya Publishers.

References

Introduction

Goldstone, Stephen, and Susan Ball. 2000. Depression tops HIV on list of health concerns for lesbians and gay men. *Gay Health Magazine (GayHealth.COM)*. April.

New York City Gay and Lesbian Anti-Violence Project. 2000. *Anti-Lesbian, Gay, Transgender and Bisexual Violence in 1999: A Report of the National Coalition of Anti-Violence Programs.* New York: New York City Gay and lesbian Anti-violence Project.

Chapter One

Diagnostic and Statistical Manual of Mental Disorders, Fourth Edition. Text Revised (DSM-IV-TR). 2000. Washington, D.C.: American Psychiatric Association.

Preston, John. 2000. *You Can Beat Depression, Second Edition.* Atascadero, Calif.: Impact Publishers, Inc.

Yapko, Michael. 1997. *Breaking the Patterns of Depression.* New York: Doubleday.

Chapter Two

Blumstein, Philip, and Pepper Schwartz. 1983. *American Couples.* New York: William Morrow.

Boschert, Sherry. 1998. *Directory of Domestic Partner Benefits.* Washington, D.C.: National Lesbian and Gay Journalist Association.

Bradford, Judith, and Caitlin Ryan. 1991. Who we are: Health concerns of middle aged lesbians. In *Lesbians at Midlife*, edited by Barbara Sang, Joyce Warshow, and Adrienne Smith. San Francisco: Spinster Books.

Brownworth, Victoria. 2000. Age: The last closet. *Curve*, October, 48–49.

Cochran, Susan, and V. Mays. 1994. Depressive distress among homosexually active African American men and women. *American Journal of Psychiatry* 151:524–529.

Due, Linnea. 1995. *Joining the Tribe: Growing Up Gay and Lesbian in the 90s*. New York: Doubleday.

Erikson, Eric. 1950. *Childhood and Society*. New York: W. W. Norton.

Faderman, Lillian. 1991. *Odd Girls and Twilight Lovers*. New York: Columbia University Press.

Franklin, Karen. 1998. Unassuming motivations: Contextualizing the narratives of antigay assailants. In *Stigma and Sexual Orientation*, edited by Greg Herek. Thousand Oaks, Calif.: Sage Publications.

Hammelman, T. L. 1993. Gay and lesbian youth: Contributing factors to serious attempts or consideration of suicide. *Journal of Gay and Lesbian Psychotherapy* 2: 77–89.

Hardin, Kimeron N. 1999. *The Gay and Lesbian Self-Esteem Book: A Guide to Loving Ourselves*. Oakland, Calif.: New Harbinger Publications.

Hooker, Evelyn. 1958. Male homosexuality in the Rorschach. *Journal of Projective Techniques* 22:33–35.

Johnson, Susan. 1995. *For Love and for Life*. Tallahassee, Fla.: Naiad Press.

KPMG Peat Marwick Survey of U.S. Business Health Plans. 1997. In *The Augusta Chronicle Online*. Augusta, GA: *Augusta Chronicle*.

Laird, Joan, and Robert Green, eds. 1996. *Lesbians and gays in couples and families*. San Francisco: Jossey-Bass.

Lewin, Ellen. 1993. *Lesbian Mothers: Accounts of Gender in American Culture*. Ithaca, N.Y.: Cornell University Press.

Morgan, Kris. 1992. Caucasian lesbians' use of psychotherapy. *Psychology of Women Quarterly* 16:127–130.

Mullins, Hillary. 1995. Evolution of a tomboy. In *Tomboys*, edited by Lynn Yamaguchi & Karen Barber. Los Angeles: Alyson Publications.

Oetjen, Helen, and Esther Rothblum. 1999. Then lesbians aren't gay: Factors affecting depression among lesbians. *Journal of Homosexuality* 39:49–72.

Pilkington, N. W., and D'Augelli. 1995. Victimization of lesbian, gay and bisexual youth in community settings. *Journal of Community Psychology* 23:33–56.

Ramafedi, G., J. A. Farrow, and R. W. Deisher. 1991. Risk factors for attempted suicide in gay and bisexual youth. *Pediatrics* 87: 869–975.

Sheehy, Gail. 1974. *Passages*. New York: E. P. Dutton.

Shernoff, Michael. 1998. Gay widowers: Grieving in relation to trauma and social supports. *Journal of Gay & Lesbian Medical Association* 2:1–13.

Syzmanski, Dawn, Barry Chung, and Kimberly Balsam. 2000. Correlates of lesbian internalized homophobia. *APA Division 44 Newsletter*. Spring.

Chapter Three

Bailey, J., M. Dunne, and N. G. Martin. 2000. Genetic and environmental influences on sexual orientation and its correlates in an australian twin study. *Journal of Personality and Social Psychology*. 78:524–536.

LeVay, Simon. 1994. *Sexual Brain*. New York: Cit Press.

Meyer, Jeffrey, et al. 1999. Prefrontal cortex 5-HT$_2$ receptors in depression: An ^{18}F setoperone PET imaging study. *American Journal of Psychiatry* 156:1029-1034.

Nemeroff, Charles B. 1998. The neurobiology of depression. *Scientific American* 278:42–49.

Peplau, Letitia, and Linda Garnets. 2000. A new paradigm for understanding women's sexuality and sexual orientation. *Journal of Social Issues* 56:329–350.

Pool, Robert. 1997. Portrait of a gene guy [Dr. Dean Hamer]. *Discover Magazine*, October.

Sapolsky, Robert M. 1998. *Why Zebras Don't Get Ulcers: An Updated Guide to Stress, Stress-Related Diseases, and Coping*. New York: W. H. Freeman and Company.

Somer, Elizabeth. 1995. *Food & Mood: The Complete Guide to Eating Well and Feeling Your Best*. New York: Henry Holt and Company.

Wu, Joseph, et al. 1999. Prediction of antidepressant effects of sleep deprivation by metabolic rates in the ventral anterior cingulated and medial prefrontal cortex. *American Journal of Psychiatry* 156:1149-1158.

Wurtman, Richard, D. O'Rourke, and Judith Wurtman. 1989. Nutrient imbalances in depressive disorders: Possible brain mechanisms. *Annals New York Academy* 575:75–82.

Chapter Four

Barthes, Roland. 1978. *A Lover's Discourse*. New York: Hill and Wang Publishers.

Colgrove, Melba, Harold Bloomfield, and Peter McWilliams. 1976. *How to Survive the Loss of a Love.* New York: Bantam.

Delynn, Jane, and Joan Larkin, ed. 1999. *A Woman Like That.* New York: Avon.

Dickinson, Emily, and Thomas Johnson, ed. 1960. *The Complete Poems of Emily Dickinson.* Boston: Little Brown.

Egan, Jennifer. 2000. Lonely gay teen seeking same. *New York Times Magazine,* December 12, 1–18.

Hall, Marny. 1998. *The Lesbian Love Companion: How to Survive Everything from Heartthrob to Heartbreak.* San Francisco: Harper San Francisco.

Isay, Richard. 1996. *Becoming Gay.* New York: Pantheon Books.

Lister, Anne, and Helena Whitbread, (ed). 1992. *I Know My Own Heart: The Diaries of Anne Lister, 1791–1840.* New York: New York University Press.

Norton, Rictor. 1991. The passions of Michelangelo. In *Gay Roots: 20 Years of Gay Sunshine: An Anthology of Gay History, Sex, Politics, and Culture* edited by Leyland Winston. San Francisco: Sunshine Press.

Millay, Edna St. Vincent, and Mary Jane Moffat, ed. 1982. *Middle of Winter.* New York: Random House.

Mixner, David. 1999. Personal essay. In *Hostile Climate: Report on Antigay Activity.* Washington, D.C.: People for the American Way.

Sarton, May. 1973. *Journal of a Solitude.* New York: W. W. Norton.

Williams, Tennessee, and Donald Windham, ed. 1976. *Tennessee Williams' Letters to Donald Windham 1940–1965.* New York: Holt, Rinehart and Winston.

Chapter Five

Breggin, Peter. 1995. *Talking Back to Prozac: What Doctors Won't Tell You about Today's Most Controversial Drug.* New York: St. Martin's Press.

Chambless, D., et al. 1998. Update on empirically validated therapies II. *The Clinical Psychologist* 31:3–16.

Glenmullen, Joseph. 2000. *Prozac Backlash: Overcoming the Dangers of Prozac, Zoloft, Paxil, and Other Antidepressants with Safe, Effective Alternatives.* New York: Simon & Schuster.

Golant, Mitch, and Susan Golant. 1996. *What to Do When Someone You Love Is Depressed: A Practical, Compassionate, and Helpful Guide.* New York: Henry Holt.

Kramer, Peter. 1997. *Listening to Prozac.* New York: Penguin.

Persons, Jacqueline. 1998. Indications for psychotherapy in the treatment of depression. *Psychiatric Annals* 28.2 80–83.

Peters, Margot. 1997. *May Sarton, A Biography*. New York: Alfred A. Knopf.

Reany, Patricia. 2000. *Couple Curing*. Reuters/ABC News.com.

Sprinkle, Annie. 1996. 101 uses for sex—Or why sex is so important. In *Sexualities*, edited by Marny Hall. New York: Harrington Park Press.

Stubbs, Kenneth. 1999. *The Essential Tantra*. New York: Putnam.

Chapter Six

Beck, Judith. 1995. *Cognitive Therapy: Basics and Beyond*. New York: Guilford.

Hardin, Kimeron N. 1999. *The Gay and Lesbian Self-Esteem Book: A Guide to Loving Ourselves*. Oakland, Calif.: New Harbinger Publications.

Held, Barbara. 1999. *Stop Smiling, Start Kvetching: A 5-Step Guide to Creative Complaining*. Brunswick, Me.: Audenreed Press.

Wann, Marilyn. 1999. *FAT!SO?: Because You Don't Have to Apologize for Your Size*. Berkeley, Calif.: Ten Speed Press.

Chapter Seven

De la Huerta, Christian. 1999. *Coming Out Spiritually: The Next Step*. New York: Jeremy Tarcher Publications.

Diagnostic and Statistical Manual of Mental Disorders, Fourth Edition. Text Revised (DSM-IV-TR). 2000. Washington, D.C.: American Psychiatric Association.

Greene, Beverly. 1997. Ethnic minority lesbians and gay men: Mental health and treatment issues. In *Ethnic and Cultural Diversity Among Lesbians and Gay Men: Psychological Perspectives on Lesbian and Gay Issues, Vol. 3*, edited by Beverly Greene. London: Sage Publications.

Hall, Marny. 1985. *The Lavender Couch: A Consumer's Guide to Psychotherapy for Lesbians and Gay Men*. Los Angeles: Alyson Publications.

Hardin, Kimeron N. 1999. *The Gay and Lesbian Self-Esteem Book: A Guide to Loving Ourselves*. Oakland, Calif.: New Harbinger Publications.

Herink, Richie, ed. 1980. *The Psychotherapy Handbook*. New York: Meridien.

Sullivan, Andrew. 1998. *Love Undetectable: Notes on Friendship, Sex and Survival*. New York: Alfred A. Knopf.

Truax, Charles, and Kevin Mitchell. 1971. Research on certain therapist interpersonal skills in relation to process and outcome. In *Handbook of Psychotherapy and Behavior Change,* edited by A. Bergin and S. Garfield. New York: John Wiley Publications.

Xavier, Cassendre. 2000. Techniques for testing your therapist. In *Dykes with Baggage,* edited by Riggin Waugh. Los Angeles: Alyson Publications.

Chapter Eight

Appleton, William S. 2000. *Prozac and the New Antidepressants: What You Need to Know About Prozac, Zoloft, Paxil, Luvox, Wellbutrin, Effexor, Serzone, Vestra, Celexa, St. John's Wort, and Others,* Revised Edition. New York: Plume.

Granet, Roger, and Robin Levinson. 1998. Other Therapies. In *If You Think You Have Depression.* New York: Doubleday Dell Publishing.

Preston, John. 2000. *You Can Beat Depression, Second Edition.* Atascadero, Calif.: Impact Publishers, Inc.

Preston, John, John O'Neal, and Mary Talago. 2000. *Consumer's Guide to Psychiatric Drugs.* Oakland, Calif.: New Harbinger Publications.

The Physician's Desk Reference for Nutritional Supplements, First Edition. 2001. Montvale, N.J.: Medical Economics Company, Inc.

The Physician's Desk Reference for Herbal Medicines, Second Edition. 2000. Montvale, N.J.: Medical Economics Company, Inc.

Chapter Nine

Anderson, Jervis. 1998. *Bayard Rustin: Troubles I've Seen.* Berkeley, Calif.: University of California Press.

Fischer, Claude. 1982. *To Dwell Among Friends.* Chicago: The University of Chicago Press.

Linn, Denise. 1996. *Sacred Space: Clearing and Enhancing the Energy in Your Home.* New York: Ballantine Books.

Lotney, Karlyn. 1995. On our prozac: Dykes talk about sex, drugs, and depression. *On Our Backs,* Spring.

Martin, Philip. 1999. *The Zen Path Through Depression.* San Francisco: Harper.

Penelope, Julia, and Susan Wolfe, eds. 1989. *The Original Coming Out Stories.* Watertown, Mass.: Persephone Press.

Plummer, Ken. 1995. *Telling Sexual Stories.* New York: Routledge.

Kimeron Hardin, Ph.D., is a licensed clinical psychologist with the SpineCare Medical Group at Seton Medical Center in Daly City, California; and he also has a private practice in San Francisco. In addition, he also holds joint appointments as an assistant clinical professor with the Departments of Psychiatry and Anesthesia at the University of California at San Francisco. He is the author of several books including *The Gay and Lesbian Self-Esteem Book: A Guide to Loving Ourselves.* Kimeron has conducted workshops on both developing healthy self-esteem and strong relationships for GLBT people.

Marny Hall, Ph.D., has been a lesbian therapist, researcher, and writer for the last 25 years. She is the author of several books including *The Lavender Couch: A Consumer's Guide to Psychotherapy for Lesbians and Gay Men, Sexualities,* and *The Lesbian Love Companion: How to Survive Everything from Heartthrob to Heartbreak.* She has also produced a video documentary, and has contributed articles to *Out, Girlfriends, Lambda Book Report,* and a number of academic journals. Marny frequently presents aspects of her work to diverse audiences, leads workshops, and participates in seminars worldwide. In 1998, she was designated a "Fellow" of the gay and lesbian division of the American Psychological Association "in recognition of outstanding and unusual contributions to psychology."

Betty Berzon, Ph.D., is a psychotherapist in private practice in Los Angeles. She is the author of several best-selling books including *The Intimacy Dance: A Guide to Long-Term Success in Gay and Lesbian Relationships, Permanent Partners Building Gay and Lesbian Partnerships That Last, Positively Gay: New Approaches to Gay and Lesbian Life,* and *Setting Them Straight: You Can Do Something about Bigotry and Homophobia in Your Life.* Her autobiography, *Surviving Madness: A Therapist's Own Story,* will be published in the spring of 2002.

Some Other
New Harbinger Titles